Making Human Rights News

Making Human Rights News: Balancing Participation and Professionalism explores the impact of new digital technology and activism on the production of human rights messages. It is the first collection of studies to combine multidisciplinary approaches, "citizen witness" challenges to journalism ethics, and expert assessments of the "liberating role" of the Internet, addressing the following questions:

1. What can scholars from a wide range of disciplines—including communication studies, journalism, sociology, political science, and international relations/studies—add to traditional legal and political human rights discussions, exploring the impact of innovative digital information technologies on the gathering and dissemination of human rights news?
2. What questions about journalism ethics and professionalism arise as growing numbers of untrained "citizen witnesses" use modern mobile technology to document claims of human rights abuses?
3. What are the limits of the "liberating role" of the Internet in challenging traditional sources of authority and credibility, such as professional journalists and human rights professionals?
4. How do greater Internet access and human rights activism interact with variations in press freedom and government censorship worldwide to promote respect for different categories of human rights, such as women's rights and rights to health?

This book was originally published as a special issue of the *Journal of Human Rights*.

John C. Pollock, PhD, Stanford, is Professor of Communication Studies and Affiliate in Public Health at The College of New Jersey, USA. His most recent books include *Tilted Mirrors: Media Alignment with Political and Social Change—A Community Structure Approach* (2007), *Media and Social Inequality: Innovations in Community Structure Research* (2013), and *Journalism and Human Rights: How Demographics Drive Media Coverage* (2015). With special interests in media sociology and political communication, he conducts research on health communication and human rights.

Morton E. Winston, PhD, Illinois, was Professor of Philosophy at the College of New Jersey, USA. His areas of specialization include human rights theory and practice, global ethics, and the philosophy of technology. His most recent books are *On Chomsky* (2001) and *Society, Ethics, and Technology* (2013). He served as Chairman of Amnesty International USA's National Board of Directors and was the Distinguished Chair of Human Rights and International Relations at the Danish Institute of Human Rights.

Making Human Rights News

Balancing participation and professionalism

Edited by
John C. Pollock and Morton E. Winston

Routledge
Taylor & Francis Group

LONDON AND NEW YORK

First published 2018
by Routledge

2 Park Square, Milton Park, Abingdon, Oxfordshire OX14 4RN

711 Third Avenue, New York, NY 10017

Routledge is an imprint of the Taylor & Francis Group, an informa business

First issued in paperback 2018

British Library Cataloguing in Publication Data
A catalogue record for this book is available from the British Library

ISBN 13: 978-1-138-03774-8 (hbk)
ISBN 13: 978-1-138-32926-3 (pbk)

Typeset in Minion Pro
by diacriTech, Chennai

Publisher's Note
The publisher accepts responsibility for any inconsistencies that may have arisen during the conversion of this book from journal articles to book chapters, namely the possible inclusion of journal terminology.

Disclaimer
Every effort has been made to contact copyright holders for their permission to reprint material in this book. The publishers would be grateful to hear from any copyright holder who is not here acknowledged and will undertake to rectify any errors or omissions in future editions of this book.

In Memory of Morton E. Winston
1949–2017
Distinguished human rights scholar, acclaimed activist, educational
leader, and beloved friend

Contents

CONTENTS

Citation Information

The following chapters were originally published in the *Journal of Human Rights*, volume 15, issue 3 (September 2016). When citing this material, please use the original page numbering for each article, as follows:

Introduction
Human rights in the news: Balancing new media participation with the authority of journalists and human rights professionals
Morton E. Winston and John C. Pollock
Journal of Human Rights, volume 15, issue 3 (September 2016) pp. 307–313

Chapter 1
A new era of human rights news? Contrasting two paradigms of human rights news-making
Matthew Powers
Journal of Human Rights, volume 15, issue 3 (September 2016) pp. 314–329

Chapter 2
Source credibility as "information subsidy": Strategies for successful NGO journalism at Mexican human rights NGOs
Ella McPherson
Journal of Human Rights, volume 15, issue 3 (September 2016) pp. 330–346

Chapter 3
The rise of eyewitness video and its implications for human rights: Conceptual and methodological approaches
Sandra Ristovska
Journal of Human Rights, volume 15, issue 3 (September 2016) pp. 347–360

Chapter 5
Promoting the people's surrogate: The case for press freedom as a distinct human right
Wiebke Lamer
Journal of Human Rights, volume 15, issue 3 (September 2016) pp. 361–382

CITATION INFORMATION

Chapter 6

News about her: The effects of media freedom and internet access on women's rights
Jenifer Whitten-Woodring
Journal of Human Rights, volume 15, issue 3 (September 2016) pp. 383–407

Chapter 7

Beyond naming and shaming: New modalities of information politics in human rights
Joel R. Pruce and Alexandra Cosima Budabin
Journal of Human Rights, volume 15, issue 3 (September 2016) pp. 408–425

The following chapter was originally published in the *Atlantic Journal of Communication*, volume 25, issue 1 (January 2017). When citing this material, please use the original page numbering as follows:

Chapter 4

Nonprofit Product Placement: Human Rights Advocacy in Film and Television
Carla Winston
Atlantic Journal of Communication, volume 25, issue 1 (January 2017) pp. 17–32

For any permission-related enquiries please visit:
http://www.tandfonline.com/page/help/permissions

Notes on Contributors

Alexandra Cosima Budabin is a research fellow in the Human Rights Center at the University of Dayton, Ohio, USA. Her research interests include human rights advocacy and transnational politics; conflict resolution, genocide, and humanitarian intervention; development, humanitarianism, and the media; and the role of nonstate actors. Her work has appeared in journals including *Third World Quarterly*, *Celebrity Studies*, and the *Journal of Human Rights*.

Wiebke Lamer is a teaching and research fellow at the European Inter-University Centre for Human Rights and Democratisation in Venice, Italy, where she specializes in International Relations. Her current research interests include communication rights, international organizations, and the global politics of press freedom, with emphasis on the role of the media and NGOs in promoting freedom of the press as a human right.

Ella McPherson is Lecturer in the Sociology of New Media and Digital Technology at the University of Cambridge, UK, where she is a fellow in Sociology at Queens College and a research associate of the Centre of Governance and Human Rights. Her current research is on the use of social media at human rights NGOs, focusing on the construction of knowledge in the digital age, and her previous research was on human rights reporting at Mexican newspapers, which examined the contest for public credibility among state, media, and NGO actors underpinning human rights coverage.

John C. Pollock, PhD, Stanford, is Professor of Communication Studies and Affiliate in Public Health at The College of New Jersey, USA. His most recent books include *Tilted Mirrors: Media Alignment with Political and Social Change—A Community Structure Approach* (2007), *Media and Social Inequality: Innovations in Community Structure Research* (2013), and *Journalism and Human Rights: How Demographics Drive Media Coverage* (2015). With special interests in media sociology and political communication, he conducts research on health communication and human rights.

Matthew Powers is an assistant professor in the Department of Communication at the University of Washington, Seattle, USA. His academic writings have been published in the *Journal of Communication*, *International Journal of Press/Politics*, and *Media, Culture & Society*, among others. At present, he is working on a book manuscript that explores the role of NGOs as information providers in the changing news landscape.

NOTES ON CONTRIBUTORS

Joel R. Pruce is Assistant Professor of Human Rights Studies at the University of Dayton, Ohio, USA. His research interests include human rights, NGOs and advocacy, foreign policy, international organizations, mass media and visual culture, and critical theory. He is the editor of *The Social Practice of Human Rights* (2015).

Sandra Ristovska is a postdoctoral fellow in the Annenberg School for Communication at the University of Pennsylvania, USA. She received the 2013 Top Paper Award from the Philosophy, Theory and Critique Division at the International Communication Association and the 2013 Herbert Schiller Prize from the International Association for Media and Communication Research. She has been published in *The Communication Review*; *Media, Culture & Society*; *Journalism: Theory, Practice & Criticism*; the *American Journal of Sociology*; the *World Policy Institute Blog*; and *Public Books*.

Jenifer Whitten-Woodring is an associate professor of Political Science at the University of Massachusetts–Lowell, USA. Her research focuses on the causes and effects of media freedom and the role of media in repression and dissent. Her book, *Historical Guide to World Media Freedom: A Country-by-Country Analysis* (2014, with Douglas A. Van Belle), is a Choice Outstanding Academic Title. Her articles have been published in *The Journal of Conflict Resolution, International Studies Quarterly, Political Communication*, and *Political Science Research and Methods*.

Carla Winston is an assistant teaching professor at the University of Victoria, Canada, where she specializes in International Relations. She studies contemporary international norms, such as transitional justice, human rights, democracy, and the laws of armed conflict, and their diffusion around the world. She is also keenly interested in the use of technology and culture to transmit norms, particularly to ordinary citizens rather than to policymakers.

Morton E. Winston, PhD, Illinois, was Professor of Philosophy at the College of New Jersey, USA. His areas of specialization included human rights theory and practice, global ethics, and the philosophy of technology. His most recent books were *On Chomsky* (2001) and *Society, Ethics, and Technology* (2013). He served as Chairman of Amnesty International USA's National Board of Directors and was the Distinguished Chair of Human Rights and International Relations at the Danish Institute of Human Rights.

Human rights in the news: Balancing new media participation with the authority of journalists and human rights professionals

Morton E. Winston and John C. Pollock

The College of New Jersey

From the outset the modern human rights movement has relied on the press and media as an essential partner in its work to hold governments accountable for human rights violations. When Peter Benenson sought to draw attention to the plight of "forgotten prisoners," he wrote an article in the London *Observer* published on May 28, 1961, launching an "Appeal for Amnesty." Amnesty International was born from the union of human rights activists and the press. Similarly, Human Rights Watch began in 1978 with the formation of the Helsinki Watch Committee that sought to enforce compliance with the 1975 Helsinki Accords by publicly "naming and shaming" the Soviet Union through media coverage. But at the time these organizations were formed, newspapers were published exclusively on paper printed with ink, television news was broadcast over the airwaves and received by antennas, and letters from human rights activists to government officials were written on typewriters and sent by the post office. The digital information revolution that has radically altered our means of communicating has also dramatically changed the terms of the partnership between human rights campaigners and the media. The articles curated for this special issue of the *Journal of Human Rights*, "Human Rights in the News," explore this altered media landscape and analyze its significance for the global human rights movement.

In "A New Era of Human Rights News? Contrasting Two Paradigms of Human Rights News-Making," Matthew Powers sets the stage by contrasting two "paradigms" of human rights news making. He points out that the concept of "human rights news" can no longer be defined narrowly as information produced by media organizations, but must now be understood as also coming from "NGOs, civic groups, or indeed even individuals" (315). In the older media paradigm, the one that reigned before August 6, 1991, the day the World Wide Web went live, human rights campaigners mainly relied on newspapers, journalists, and editors as the gate-keepers of access to mass audiences. Even well-respected and recognized international human rights nongovernmental organizations (NGOs), such as Amnesty International and Human Rights Watch needed to strategically deploy "facts and narratives in order to capture the attention of journalists" and to "appease dominant news norms that favor conflict and spectacle" (316). The need to satisfy the tastes of news organizations in order to pass through the media gateway often made it difficult for campaigners to get their issues before the public, particularly if the country or region in which the human rights abuses were occurring was obscure and the issues involved complex. This limitation often led to human rights news becoming highly simplified and misleading, as well as to a preference for focusing on abuses of personal liberty and security rights at the expense of the less sensational but more widespread abuses of economic, social, and cultural rights. In the older paradigm, there was always a tension between making the story "timely and newsworthy" and "making sure it was right." Ensuring accuracy often made it difficult for human rights NGOs to make their information timely and "newsworthy."

Paradoxically, the advent of "free news" on the Internet, as well as the shift of advertising revenue to online outlets, has led to a decline in the capacity and commitment of many news organizations to cover international news. At the same time, there has been a shift in the discourse of the major human rights NGOs towards giving more attention to human rights issues in the Western countries in which they are still largely based and towards attention to a wider set of human rights concerns. Moreover, now individuals armed with a mobile phone can record human rights violations, such as police shooting at unarmed demonstrators, and can distribute their videos around the globe online in a matter of minutes. Human rights NGOs have also become savvier about using the new media, social media, and viral video to get their messages out to wider audiences. Powers analyzes several features of the current media human rights landscape that raise important analytical and empirical questions about the ways in which the older and the new paradigms interact and whether these changes will in the end be beneficial or harmful to the human rights movement. Many of these questions are addressed in the other articles selected for this issue.

In her article, Ella McPherson argues that the relationship between news and media organizations and human rights NGOs is a two-way street. Source credibility is central to the logic of professional journalism, and the best NGOs can provide credible and authoritative source material, thus moving beyond a simple "information subsidy" to providing a "verification subsidy" that decreases the cost of fact-finding and checking by news organizations. This kind of verification subsidy is increasingly valuable to news organizations because the advent of digital Internet advertising has disrupted the business models of many traditional news organizations and has forced them to make cuts in their foreign news bureaus resulting in a decline of international reporting. This gap has created an opportunity for the major human rights NGOs to take over part of the job of reporting international human rights news, and the major human rights nongovernmental organizations (HRNGOs) are now working to fill this need. Human Rights Watch, while still headquartered in New York City, now also maintains offices in places such as Beirut, Nairobi, and Tokyo. For the past several years, London-based Amnesty International has been moving "closer to the ground" by decentralizing its research and campaigning units to places like India, Brazil, Kenya, Mexico, and Thailand. Both organizations now routinely deploy their researchers and campaigners as expert interview guests on broadcast news programs, and they are often quoted as key sources by newspapers and other printed media. HRNGOs are also now routinely employing photojournalists to accompany their researchers on investigative missions and are tailoring their messaging to the demands of the cable news networks.

The new digital capabilities for using visuals to convey human rights news is rightly identified by Sandra Ristovska as a change from the older paradigm. In "The Rise of Eyewitness Video and its Implications for Human Rights: Conceptual and Methodological Approaches," she explores the conceptual and methodological issues associated with the increasing use of "eyewitness video" to document human rights violations and to arouse public responses. Despite historical uses of imagery in relation to human rights (ranging from Goya's

"Disasters of War" print series, to photographs depicting the atrocities in the Armenian genocide, to films taken of the liberation of concentration camps at the end of the Second World War), the ubiquity of modern mobile phones with the capability to photograph and videograph events as well as access to immediate Internet connectivity have altered the way in which human rights NGOs as well as the media and private citizens document and communicate visual information about human rights violations. Human rights activists who are not associated with the brand name NGOs can document many more kinds of human rights violations with pictures and videos and can reach mass audiences directly. The organization WITNESS was founded in order to train amateur activists on how to use these capabilities to correctly document human rights concerns. The increasing use of videography and photography in human rights reporting and documentation also fits well with the logic of news organizations, particularly, broadcast news organizations. The major HRNGOs are now also using satellite imagery, remote imaging, and crowd-sourcing to produce human rights news and information for public consumption. While this is certainly valuable from the point of view of raising public awareness, it does not really substitute for the carefully written and edited reports prepared by professionals at major HRNGOs for elite audiences. The press releases that accompany the launches of these reports rarely explain in great detail what the evidence is for the claims and recommendations contained in these reports.

The major professional HRNGOs are staffed by experts who are steeped in international human rights law, and who take great pains to ensure that their claims can be validated both in terms of their factual accuracy and with respect to the relevant norms of international law. Their public documents go through an editorial review process that is more rigorous than that used by most professional news organizations. This institutional rigor is the reason they can provide information subsidies to news organizations seeking to source credibly. But the more colloquial understanding of human rights employed by amateur human rights activists threatens to confuse as much as enlighten public opinion as to what things constitute human rights violations and what should be done to redress them. As always, the information consumer needs to be alert to the differences in credibility of human rights news reported in the press and the many kinds of public relations propaganda that can also be found on the Internet.

The idea that there should still be a special role for professional journalism and the press in the current media environment is strongly defended by Wiebke Lamer in her article "Promoting the People's Surrogate: The Case for Press Freedom as a Distinct Human Right." She points out that, although the U.S. Bill of Rights specifically mentions freedom of the press as a distinct right, it has largely disappeared from contemporary human rights discourse, having been subsumed under the more general right of freedom of expression. Traditional journalism and press freedom have been under attack in many countries, even in the United States. Yet, it is noteworthy that, when Edward Snowden wished to make public his information about National Security Agency (NSA) surveillance programs, he relied on professional press outlets, such as the *Guardian* and *The New York Times*, and professional journalists, such as Glenn Greenwald and Laura Poitras, to ensure that his message reached a mass audience responsibly. The professional press at its best provides important editorial and watchdog roles that remain essential in the digital media age for holding powerful governments to account. It also remains the best way to reach a mass audience in the highly fragmented and siloed environment of digital media. The professional press is thus an essential partner to the people in safeguarding their fundamental rights and freedoms, including their own freedom of expression. These core functions of the press cannot be replaced by social media and blogs, even though these outlets are also increasingly under attack by some governments. While the rise of "citizen journalism" powered by the Internet and mobile phones is an important phenomenon, it should not lead one to dismiss the essential role that professional journalism should continue to play in safeguarding human rights.

To advance human rights agendas, it is important to seek a balance between the excitement of enlarged opportunities for participation in human rights reporting, on the one hand, and the need for continued professional gatekeeping on the other. Whatever the balance a particular community strikes (whether city, state, or nation-state) in bringing attention to human rights issues must contend with enormous variation in political, social, and cultural contexts. Jenifer Whitten-Woodring's contribution, "News about Her: The Effects of Media Freedom and Internet Access on Women's Rights," draws needed attention to those contexts and how they can constrain human rights trajectories, especially of women. Her article explores how a free press can make a difference for women's rights, what surrounding conditions affect a free press's effectiveness, and, especially, how Internet access (in particular, access to social media) might improve women's rights.

Drawing centrally on her ambitious and original 143 country dataset, Whitten-Woodring distinguishes the effects of media freedom on a range of rights (e.g., political, physical security, economic) while controlling for key intervening variables including the level of "executive constraints" on decision making, ratification of international law, the presence or intensity of civil conflict and/or international conflict and war, economic development, population size, cultural attitudes toward gender equality, and previous levels of human rights protection. The author's research design alone is inherently noteworthy.

Whitten-Woodring's findings are uplifting yet sobering. While the "interaction" of media freedom and Internet access has had significant and positive effects on women's rights, those effects were more substantial for women's political rights and physical security than for women's economic rights. In addition, the author's scholarship is consistent with a media version of the "boomerang effect" posited by leading human rights scholars Margaret Keck and Kathryn Sikkink (1998), arguing that marginalized women are capable of harnessing the power of transnational activities through the use of social media and international media to pressure their own governments to improve their situations, promoting awareness and activity at the international level to encourage a "boomerang" of human rights pressure back on domestic governments. Overall, the author's findings suggest the importance of state power as a constraint, in particular, on level of state control of the press. Despite the excitement associated with the use of mobile phones and social media during the "Arab Spring," political forces of repression reasserted themselves dramatically afterward. Whitten-Woodring's findings are consistent with that historical circumstance: The Internet alone cannot promote human rights (in this case, women's rights) robustly unless certain contextual preconditions are present, in particular a high level of freedom of the press from government control.

The final contribution to this special issue is Joel R. Pruce and Alexandra Cosima Budabin's article "Beyond Naming and Shaming: New Modalities of Information Politics in Human Rights." Expanding upon the 1998 pioneering "information politics" work of Keck and Sikkink (1998), Pruce and Budabin develop a theoretical framework for three "modalities" of "media advocacy": juridical, revelatory, and activating. While appreciating the early activities of human rights giants such as Amnesty International and Human Rights Watch, Pruce and Budabin call on readers to reach beyond traditional conceptions of media use to consider multiple methods and technologies and targets for ambitious human rights campaigns. Moving from the relatively bounded "juridical" efforts of the International Red Cross, through the more ambitious "revelatory" endeavors of Doctors Without Borders, Pruce and Budabin encourage scholars and activists alike to pursue ambitious projects, mobilizing mass audiences and deploying a multitude of what some might consider "corporate" strategies to market their messages. One noteworthy case they analyze is the 2012 "Invisible Children" campaign (KONY2012) designed to make the Lord's Resistance Army commander Joseph Kony a (negative) household name by employing films, merchandise, action kits, and donations to target celebrities, politicians, and cultural figures. But this example also raises the issue of credibility and expertise. While the new media provide opportunities for lesser known human rights organizations and activists to produce and disseminate human rights news and information, their analyses, recommendations, and suggested actions are not always in line with what the professional human rights NGOs would endorse. A similar mix of public exposure and elite lobbying campaigns was encountered in the efforts of the 2004 Save Darfur Coalition, which spread a powerful public message through a million-dollar advertising campaign leveraged through newspapers, television, billboards, lawn signs, and green wristbands.

Pruce and Budabin are especially interested in "investigating how and why HROs [Human Rights Organizations] represent stakeholders and frame human rights claims to facilitate mass mobilization campaigns and the grassroots diffusion of human rights norms through media" (413). Curiously, the very "professionalism" in journalism that Lamer and others admire, and that is essential for a gatekeeping process that retains the credibility and authority of critical messages, is also apparent in the implications of Pruce and Budabin's work. If human rights campaigns are to attain reach and prominence then it is reasonable to expect that the most creative minds in advertising should be brought into the mix. And indeed, that very connection has been made and is used effectively today, in particular within the subfield of health rights. The Gates Foundation employs some of the most experienced advertising and public relations firms in the United States to promote health abroad, as do health-related government agencies such as United States Agency for International Development (USAID). Although "stakeholders" often may be bypassed in the way Pruce and Budabin describe, there is little doubt that modern foundations and agencies wish to take advantage of the very latest targeted marketing and creative mobilization techniques previously available to corporations in order to develop and execute successful human rights campaigns, in particular regarding health issues.

Emerging themes

Although each of the contributors to this special issue on "Human Rights in the News" approaches the topic from a particular perspective, emphasizing some concepts, theories, or methodologies more than others, across all of the contributions several major themes emerge.

New media facilitate the universalization of human rights participation and agency

Mobile phones and social media and the Internet generally have clearly transformed access to human rights reporting, multiplying the number of actors participating in reporting on human rights issues and potential violations. Powers and Whitten-Woodring have placed special emphasis on new technologies, as has Ristovska in her articulation of the expanding possibilities for innovative visual communication, whether from individuals or satellites.

In her classic "Justice Cascade" (2011), Kathryn Sikkink articulates the gradual emergence of a social norm of individual criminal accountability for human rights violations from the mid-1980s onward, spreading outward from selected countries in Latin America. The contributions on human rights news in this collection may represent the documentation of an emerging "witness" cascade for potential human rights violations: an expansion of witnessing enabled by explosive access to digital communication throughout the world.

Production of human rights news has diversified in terms of sources, frames, issues, and channels of persuasion and dissemination

While "universalization" refers to growing "numbers" of actors, human rights news has also witnessed a cornucopia of variations as well. Mass media have become supplemented by mobile, personalized technology, opening up a variety of human rights sources (not just traditional NGOs but also advocates of various types) as well as a variety of human rights frames, moving from traditional legal and political rights to economic, social, and cultural rights. These differences are discussed in particular by Powers, who illuminates perpetual framing struggles and training local activists in legal documentation practices, and Whitten-Woodring, who emphasizes critical distinctions among political, physical security, and economic rights for women. Ristovska has emphasized the innovative use of eyewitness videos, and Pruce and Budabin have illuminated the wide range of persuasion and dissemination techniques employed by modern human rights campaigns. A new orchestra of innovative sources, frames, and channels has emerged, and human rights activists today have more choices and opportunities for communication than ever before.

Historical, political, social, and economic contexts of message creation, dissemination, and exchange matter

Messages are not created, disseminated, and received or exchanged in a vacuum, and this collection of human rights contributions demonstrates awareness of ways political, economic, and social contexts can affect message diffusion. Whitten-Woodring explicitly studies the ways multiple contextual variables affect communication about women's rights throughout the world, ranging from different levels of freedom of the press and Internet access to "executive constraints" (how much a nation-state executive is checked or balanced by legislatures, judicial institutions, or even the military), levels of civil conflict, and even specific religious groups. Level of press freedom or state control of the press does indeed make a difference for women's rights.

Further, McPherson's work on NGO "information subsidies" for the press in Mexico is telling, illuminating a possibility that has emerged only recently in Mexican history. Traditionally, at least since the 1940s, although elections have been held, Mexico has been essentially a one-party nation, with the press "subsidized" by the ruling party in its role as institutionalized governor. With the dramatic victory of an opposition coalition in the presidential election of 2000, the concept of a press more independent of the traditional one-party state began to emerge. From that moment on, "subsidies" could be considered not simply as linked to a particular party or state institution but also to other entities as well, a major shift from previous practice. Level of press freedom does make a difference for human rights NGOs and activists, as well as for the press itself.

Debates remain over the balance between citizen participation in news and professional journalism

The excitement associated with increased participation and access for a wide range of human rights issues is apparent in the contributions to this collection. At the same time, despite enormous enthusiasm for the opening up human rights activities to more participants and technologies and channels of communication, a caution is also apparent. Lamer warns that it is not enough to have "freedom of expression"; for human rights to flourish, "freedom of the press," with its capacity for reaching mass audiences, is also essential. The wisdom, experience, and authority of media professionals is also underscored by several authors, in particular Powers, McPherson, and Ristovska, who pose critical questions about seeking a balance between participation and professional journalism judgment. These questions and debates deserve continuing scrutiny as new technologies and new human rights frames emerge. Although newspaper circulations have declined in recent years, the role of journalists and human rights professionals remains important and vibrant.

Carla Winston's contribution on "Non-Profit Product Placement: Rights Advocacy in Film and Television" addresses an aging membership participation challenge for Amnesty International by asserting three product placement goals for work with the artistic community: to educate and spur action on human rights issues, to increase youth membership, and to contribute to building a "culture of human rights". Using discursive and visual analysis to elaborate two basic forms of product placement—simple visual & auditory placements (referred to as product placement or prop placement) and featuring products heavily within a plot (product integration), the author identifies an intersection of fiction, entertainment, outreach, and very serious real world issues that enables nonprofit product placement to create "brand and issue recognition for Amnesty International and, perhaps, norms of political engagement with global human rights issues." The overall impact is to encourage a human rights culture that "normalizes" human rights activism as a facet of everyday life. Ideally, human rights "products" may help human rights activity become "normalized' in a "norm cascade", mainstreamed as standards of appropriate behavior are adopted because key influential actors have already done so.

References

BENENSON, Peter. (1969, December 31) *Amnesty International: Appeal for Amnesty 1961*. Council on Foreign Relations. [Online]. Available: http://www.cfr.org/human-rights/amnesty-international-appeal-amnesty-1961/p25932 [15 March 2016].

KECK, Margaret, and SIKKINK, Kathryn. (1998) *Activists Beyond Borders: Advocacy Networks in International Politics* (Ithaca, NY: Cornell University Press).

SIKKINK, Kathryn. (2011) *The Justice Cascade: How Human Rights Prosecutions Are Changing World Politics* (New York: W. W. Norton & Company).

A new era of human rights news? Contrasting two paradigms of human rights news-making

Matthew Powers

University of Washington

ABSTRACT
Past research suggests that news coverage of human rights is shaped primarily by interactions between journalists, political elites, and leading NGOs. To what degree do contemporary transformations in media, politics, and civil society alter this established wisdom? In this article, I sketch out the possibility that we are witnessing a new era of human rights news, characterized by the expansion of information producers and social contexts to which human rights frames are ascribed. In this era, leading NGOs and news organizations must increasingly interact with individual activists and others on the selection, framing, and dissemination of human rights news. These developments may remedy some of the weaknesses identified in previous research on human rights news, even as they create new concerns about the veracity and pluralistic nature of human rights news content. I suggest ways to study this new era so as to integrate findings with past research.

Introduction

In 2004, a group of Inuit leaders circulated a petition detailing the ways in which climate change had wrought havoc on their daily lives.[1] Rising temperatures, they said, threatened their food supply, endangered their health and imperiled their capacity to live in the Arctic. Seeking redress, they filed a formal complaint to the Inter-American Commission on Human Rights, naming the United States—at the time the world's largest emitter of greenhouse gases—a violator of the 1948 Declaration of the Rights and Duties of Man. To boost awareness of their concerns, they participated in the production of a documentary video and circulated information about the issue online. Attention grew steadily. While the Inuit leaders did not initially pursue coverage in the mainstream media, they received it in late 2004, when a number of news outlets, including the *New York Times* (Revkin 2004), spotlighted the effort to highlight the ways in which communities were increasingly talking about climate change in human rights terms.

The efforts by Inuit leaders to frame climate change in human rights terms differ substantially from the established paradigm of human rights news. For starters, the usual producers and distributors of human rights discourses—nongovernmental organizations (NGOs) and news organizations, respectively—were not integral to the original efforts to publicize the issue. Instead, local activists used low-cost digital technologies to raise awareness and to target international governing bodies. Moreover, the discourse of human rights itself departed from human rights stories that emphasize political violations (e.g., torture, abuse, etc.) that occur in the Global South. By reframing climate change as a human rights issue, the Inuit activists sought to alter public perception of the nature of human rights violations and to implicate culprits in the Global North. Together, these developments suggest the possible dawn of a "new era" of human rights news, one that may be less dependent on the mass media and may involve the use of digital technologies to fashion new forms of human rights reporting.

In this article, I explore some of the ways in which a new era of human rights news may be taking shape. To do so, I (a) identify the extant paradigm and highlight its various strengths and weaknesses, (b) discuss how a set of institutional, discursive, and technological changes may usher in a new paradigm, (c) delineate a set of features that characterizes various cases of human rights news-making today and that seem to depart from the established paradigm of human rights news, and (d) suggest some implications of these developments for future research. The argument put forward raises the question of a new era of human rights; it does not aim to settle it. Instead, it draws out some of the contrasts and orients some key questions for scholars interested in the production and circulation of human rights news. To do so, it draws on recently published research, as well as examples from my own work on the changes in the world of human rights reporting.[2]

Writing about a potential new era of human rights news raises questions about what exactly is meant by the terms "human rights" and "news," respectively. Drawing on Foucault (1977), I will define human rights as a "discursive formation," that is, as a way of speaking that exceeds the boundaries of any single usage. Human rights discourses embody multiple ideals (e.g., legal conventions, political rhetoric, social movement activism), which are sometimes in tension. These various ideals generate debates about the "true" meaning of human rights, which differ from legal interpretations that use international laws to define human rights norms. Yet, news coverage of human rights is more flexible than legal prescriptions; the definition used here reflects that need for a capacious approach. Relatedly, I will define "news" as information and/or commentary on contemporary affairs in which one or more actors identify an issue related to human rights (Schudson 2011). In this definition, news may come from news organizations, but it may also come from NGOs, civic groups, or indeed even individuals. Like human rights, news is defined loosely so as to reflect the shifting information environment in which news is produced and circulated today.

The extant paradigm of human rights news

To date, scholarship examining the relationship between media and human rights suggests a news paradigm that is characterized by (a) news organizations serving as the primary vehicle for reaching large audiences (Keck and Sikkink 1998), (b) NGOs that are heavily reliant on those news organizations to raise awareness of human rights issues (Bob 2005; Hopgood 2006), and (c) human rights issues that pertain primarily to violations of political rights (e.g., torture, illegal detention, etc.) that are committed beyond the United States and Western Europe (Clark 2001; Winston 2001). In this paradigm, news media act as key "gatekeepers" that decide—based on established news norms (Gans 1979)—which of the seemingly infinite number of human rights issues can occupy a portion of the news agenda. This paradigm has its strengths and weaknesses. On the one hand, human rights news can under certain conditions motivate government officials to participate in actions that improve human rights conditions (Clark 2001). On the other hand, media reporting and NGO publicity strategies exhibit biases that limit what types of issues get covered and how (Bob 2005). In this section, I provide an overview of the key features of this paradigm and discuss its relative strengths and weaknesses with respect to the news coverage it produces.

Because of the news media's central role in circulating human rights news, much scholarship has investigated the techniques NGOs and civic groups use to capture public attention. In their pathbreaking work, Keck and Sikkink (1998) discussed the emergence of an "information politics" (18) that saw advocacy groups strategically deploying facts and narratives in order to capture the attention of journalists—and, by extension, larger publics. In their account, NGOs provide news organizations with credible information that also adheres to established news norms of drama and timeliness. As they note: "[B]oth credibility and drama seem to be essential components of a strategy aimed at persuading publics and policymakers to changes their minds" (Keck and Sikkink 1998: 19). More recent accounts have further developed analyses of the methods such groups use to gather credible information (Clark 2001; Hopgood 2006), how NGOs translate their issues to appease dominant news norms that favor conflict and spectacle (Cottle and Nolan 2007; Waisbord 2011), and what conditions lead news organizations to pick up the information messages that NGOs send to them (Powers 2015a). Together, they point to the central role played by NGOs and the news media in shaping human rights news.

These efforts by NGOs to capture media attention have led to a number of success stories. Numerous case studies attest to instances where NGOs have broken into the news and secured substantial amounts of sympathetic coverage. For example, early efforts by Amnesty International to raise awareness of human rights violations under the Greek military junta in the 1960s successfully captured media attention in part due to the group's framing of political torture occurring in the "cradle of democracy" (Clark 2001). These efforts isolated the junta from the Council of Europe, which Greece was forced to leave — under threat of expulsion—in 1968 (Clark 2001: 41). Human Rights Watch enjoyed similar early successes by attacking the complicity of the Reagan administration in human rights violations throughout Latin America. By challenging the administration's claims with on-the-ground research, the group was able in some instances to get the administration to change policy (Neier 2003). More recent cases have identified similar instances where NGOs successfully work within the extant paradigm of human rights news to capture media attention and to force governments to alter their behavior on specific issues (Becker 2013).

Despite evidence of these successes, research has also identified a number of ways in which this paradigm limits what issues get covered and how. For starters, the total number of actors involved in producing most human rights news tends to be limited to a few elite NGOs (Thrall et al. 2014). Smaller groups are typically excluded from coverage, unless they can convince leading NGOs to partner with them. According to Bob (2005), such partnering efforts are often unsuccessful, as leading NGOs typically privilege causes and issues that conform to their own cultural, linguistic, and organizational preferences (as opposed to the nature of the human rights violation per se). Moreover, the relationship between NGOs and news outlets is itself not marked by parity. As Waisbord (2011) notes, the journalistic "beat" system favors governments, not NGOs. Groups like Amnesty International and Human

Rights Watch may succeed in capturing media attention, yet many of their efforts to generate coverage fall flat (Ron et al. 2005). In particular, their efforts to capture media attention on issues far outside the media spotlight are often futile. As one Amnesty International executive has put it: "You can work all you like on Mauritania, but the press couldn't give a rat's ass about Mauritania" (as quoted in Ron et al. 2005: 576).

This comment links up with a more general limitation of the human rights news paradigm: namely, its tendency to focus on a few topics and places that align with a narrow vision of human rights. Systematic content analyses conducted by Ramos and his collaborators (Ramos et al. 2007), for example, find that human rights news tends to be negatively associated with poverty. Other analyses argue that human rights tends to focus primarily on "political" violations like torture and detention, while sidelining human economic, social, and cultural rights (e.g., right not to live in poverty or, as indicated in the introductory example, "the right to be cold"; see, e.g., Williams 2010; Winston 2001). Still others find that attention cycles in the news media tend to be limited to a few cases (Thrall et al. 2014). Together, this means that many countries and issues fail to ever capture any level of news attention that would match objective measures of human rights conditions (e.g., levels of violence, poverty, etc.) in their country.

A final limitation of the extant human rights news paradigm is its tendency towards simplified, and sometimes highly misleading, narratives. This stems from the need for timeliness and drama required by news organizations to cover human rights issues (Cottle and Nolan 2007). Because news organizations provide news access to topics and issues that are newsworthy (rather than important per se), scholars have identified multiple instances where NGOs oversell or distort their claims to satisfy the news media's demands. In a particularly egregious example, Cohen and Green (2012) find that news reports systematically overstated the relative rate of sexual violence during the Liberian civil war. In that case, both NGOs and journalists claimed that 75% or more of women had been raped, even though detailed surveys and interviews placed that number at somewhere between 10% and 20%. Such instances raise questions about whether the desire (and need) for media coverage may in fact reduce the long-term credibility of human rights news providers.

Taken together, the available research points to a paradigm of human rights news that is premised on the central role of the news media as gatekeepers, the important role played by leading NGOs as information providers, and a tendency to focus on human rights violations that emerge in the realm of politics more than economics, society, or culture. This paradigm has helped to make human rights news a regular topic in the news and, in some cases, it has also helped to spur government action on human rights problems. At the same time, though, the paradigm of human rights news tends to exclude a great number of human rights actors and issues; furthermore, its coverage of human rights issues often simplifies and distorts complex situations. This is a paradigm that came of age during the dominance of print and television news. As I discuss below, a number of changing contexts raise questions about the degree to which such a paradigm remains in operation today.

Changing institutional, discursive, and technological contexts

The paradigm of human rights news described above is based on a set of institutional, discursive, and technological contexts that are themselves being transformed. This raises interesting questions about whether the paradigm for human rights news will change alongside them, or if it will endure despite these changes. Below, I highlight three sets of changes that set the stage for thinking about a possible "new era" of human rights that may depart in some ways from this established paradigm of human rights news.

In the extant model of human rights news, the news media function as the primary gatekeepers, and NGOs are essentially reliant on them for publicity. Yet, remarkable changes in both sectors suggest that this relationship may be in the process of being reconfigured. Consider journalism first. Since the end of the Cold War, US news outlets have slashed their foreign news budgets: Fewer correspondents now staff fewer news bureaus in fewer parts of the world (Hannerz 2004). The amount of news space dedicated to international news has similarly decreased: from an average of nearly 40% of all news content in the 1980s to about 17% today (Powers 2013).Whatever the quality of their earlier "gatekeeping" efforts, today there exist real questions about the media's role in human rights news (both in terms of whether they will report on an issue and in terms of how they will be able to separate out competing claims with little on-the-ground expertise; see Otto and Meyer 2012).

At the same time as the news media have cut back on human rights coverage, NGOs have assumed increasingly prominent roles in the provision of human rights news as a result of growing professionalization (as well as the institutionalization of human rights norms internationally). In addition to conducting original research, advocating with public officials, and waging public awareness campaigns, these groups take on a number of seemingly "journalistic" functions. To take just the two leading human rights NGOs as examples: Human Rights Watch now assigns photographers and videographers to produce multimedia packages that can accompany research reports (Bogert 2010). It draws from a staff of more than 400, a workforce that rivals the entire foreign news bureaus of leading US news providers like the *New York Times* or *Washington Post*. Similarly, Amnesty International staffs a "new unit" charged with being an online portal for human rights news (Bartlett 2011). It employs more than 125 research staff to gather information about human rights issues worldwide (Powers 2015b). Together, these changes in the journalism and NGO sectors raise the possibility of NGOs playing a more direct role in shaping news coverage of human rights, both in the news media and beyond for a variety of purposes, including but not limited to mobilizing supporters, to raising funds, and to providing the legal basis for criminal prosecution.

Beyond these institutional changes, the past decade has witnessed a transformation in the discursive meaning of human rights itself. If human rights news consistently focused on political abuses, this stemmed in part from the focus that the human rights community paid to these issues (Clark 2001). Over the past decade, though, the human rights community has developed a greater interest in social and economic rights (Robinson 2003). Moreover, human rights discourses are increasingly used to frame not only international affairs but domestic ones. In the United States and Europe, same-sex unions, reparations, and prison abuses are increasingly framed as human rights issues (see, e.g., Becker 2013). Analysts have evaluated these developments in negative or positive terms; my point here is simply to note the evolution of human rights discourses to accommodate a growing number of issues under its umbrella. This raises the possibility of human rights news focusing on a growing number of issues, perhaps on a growing number of places, including not just underdeveloped countries in the Global South but issues in the developed Global North that garner little media traction.

Finally, the development of new information technologies creates new possibilities for the production and distribution of human rights news. In terms of production, the costs of documenting human rights abuses have fallen precipitously (Beutz Land 2009). With little more than a mobile phone, individual activists can—and do—capture human rights abuses. In terms of distribution, new information technologies also provide activists with ways to bypass the traditional journalistic and NGO gatekeepers (Bennett and Segerberg 2013; Chadwick 2013). Case studies, for example, have shown activists make creative use of social media, gaming technologies, and more as a way to raise public awareness of human rights issues (Becker 2013). This raises questions about how and in what ways the elite NGOs and news organizations do or do not incorporate these novel technological possibilities into their news-making practices.

Taken together, these institutional, discursive and technological changes amount to a possible departure from the status quo. They create the possibility of more information producers inserting human rights frames with more news stories in a range of different contexts. This may correct for some of the weaknesses of the extant paradigm of human rights news, or it may reinforce those same tendencies. In the next section, I describe some of the features of the new era of human rights news, noting the strengths and weaknesses of these developments vis-à-vis their predecessors.

Features of a new era of human rights news

Here I want to highlight five features of human rights today that result from the shifting institutional, discursive, and technological contexts discussed above. In discussing them, my aim is to highlight ways in which these features contrast with the established paradigm of human rights news. From the outset, I want to stress that this potentially new mode does not wholly displace its predecessor. Rather, I identify these features so that they can be explored subsequently in terms of how and in what ways they interact with the extant paradigm of human rights.

With these preliminaries in mind, I want to suggest that the following features point to a possible new era of human rights news that can be characterized as follows: Human rights news involves a growing number of newsmakers and a proliferating number of contexts in which issues become human rights topics. These developments have the potential to add a greater number of human rights frames onto news stories. At the same time, uncertainty about the veracity of human rights reporting, as well as a tendency towards simplified and misleading coverage, is likely to co-occur as a result of an intense battle for limited public attention.

Human rights news is increasingly produced by a mix of amateurs and professionals

The first feature of human rights news today is that a growing mix of amateurs and professionals produce it. By amateurs, I refer to persons without training or membership in a field of human rights information production. By professionals, I refer to persons that have experience working in and producing human rights news, usually as a journalist or NGO professional. While human rights news was never solely the production of elite NGOs and news organizations, these groups did set the agenda and produced much of the information. Today, it is increasingly common for individuals, acting alone or in small groups, to document human rights issues with digital devices, oftentimes from places where media coverage or NGO presence is quite limited. Moreover, in many cases, leading NGOs are responding to these developments by dedicating growing resources to monitoring and evaluating the social media feeds of amateur producers. These trends have the potential to loosen the editorial grip of information elites even as it raises questions about the veracity of the information being provided.

Several recent examples are illustrative of this trend. Papo Reto (Straight Talk) is a Brazilian collective that uses mobile technologies to document political violence in favelas on the outskirts of Rio de Janeiro (Shaer 2015). It is comprised mostly of activists who live in the favelas and have little to no experience in either journalism or human rights reporting. After they receive word of a violent event (many of which involve police officers), members of the collective go to the scene, record what is happening and then disseminate the information through text messages, group chats, and social media channels. Initially, Papo Reto members gathered this information to ensure the safety of the favela's residents. At some point, larger NGOs, like the New York-based Witness, became interested in partnering with the group to document human rights violations in places with little media or NGO presence. These larger organizations held trainings to teach Papo Reto members about the types of information needed to hold human rights violators to account. These techniques include capturing the time and location, as well as details about who committed the violation (e.g., a police officer's badge number). Through this collaboration between amateurs and professionals, a growing number of human rights violations are documented and circulated.

A similarly illustrative, if less rosy, example further highlights the growing interactions between amateurs and professionals. Since the start of the Syrian civil war, amateur reportage has served as a primary source of information for both journalists and leading NGOs, whose access to the country remains heavily restricted (Lynch et al. 2014). Both Amnesty International and Human Rights Watch dedicate growing resources to monitor the information feeds produced by amateurs purporting to be on the ground (McPherson 2015). Moreover, in some cases, these groups are teaming up with bloggers like UK-based Brown Moses in an effort to verify information about human rights abuses (Radden Keefe 2013). In addition to successful collaborations, both Amnesty International and Human Rights Watch have also helped to circulate bogus information. In 2011, for example, both groups drew attention to the case of an 18-year-old woman who, they claimed, had been beheaded by the Syrian government. This was information they gathered from a video uploaded to YouTube. The findings were reported in several prominent news outlets (CNN, Associated Press). Weeks later, the young woman appeared on Syrian television, claiming she had fled her home to escape domestic abuse. Both Amnesty International and Human Rights Watch issued retractions (Mawad 2012).

The key takeaway here is that the growing prominence of amateurs may loosen the grip of NGOs and news organizations in producing human rights news. The effect of these developments on the quality of human rights news remains to be seen. On the one hand, growing collaborations between professionals and amateurs raise the potential for a greater number of human rights issues to circulate publicly. The shadow of publicity this creates may incentivize governments to minimize violations, and the collaborations themselves may loosen the grip of leading NGOs and news outlets on deciding which human rights issues become news. On the other hand, these developments raise questions about the veracity of the underlying materials and suggest that incentives for overhyped and misleading narratives continue to persist in the new media environment. In fact, a member of a leading human rights news provider from Syria—the Syrian Observatory of Human Rights—remarked to me in an interview that journalists often seem most interested in reports about "clashes" rather than death tolls per se (the former being seen as more newsworthy) (Interview with Syrian Observatory for Human Rights official, May 2, 2012). Thus, the mixture of amateurs and professionals may challenge some aspects of the human rights news paradigm, even as it reinforces old tendencies towards sensationalism and dramatization.

Efforts to publicize human rights news are not solely dependent on the mass media

A second distinguishing feature of human rights news today is that the path to publicity has diversified. Under the old paradigm, the news media functioned as the primary gatekeeper for human rights news. Without media coverage, issues failed to gain public traction. Today's media space contains a mixture of mainstream media, niche sites, and social media (Chadwick 2013). This creates opportunities for human rights advocates to diversify their publicity strategies, using direct targeting when it makes sense and seeking mass media publicity at other points. Together, these different publicity options suggest an information environment that fosters different levels and types of public engagement, from communicating with political elites to raising citizen awareness of human rights issues.

Today's publicity options seem to diverge from the past reliance on mass media in at least two ways. First, advocacy groups can now act as their own "newsmakers" outside of the mainstream media. The largest NGOs, like Amnesty International and Human Rights Watch, have websites that serve as de facto news destinations. These sites provide access to reports and news releases, as well as a growing number of videos, slideshows, and interactive maps (Powers 2015b). These groups also publish social media feeds that push information out to journalists, government officials, other activists, and the public. There is evidence that leading NGOs see opportunities in these new technologies to reach new types of audiences. For example, on a recent reporting trip to the Central African Republic, Human Rights Watch paid a professional photojournalist to supplement a researcher's account with visual imagery (Interview with Human Rights Watch staff member, March 4, 2015). These efforts helped the group to reach policymakers and human rights advocates sympathetic to the issue.

A second way that publicity differs today is that human rights advocates can pursue "hybrid" (Chadwick 2013) strategies in their efforts to raise broad public awareness of key issues. The highly controversial campaign by Invisible Children to make Ugandan warlord Joseph Kony "famous" is a case in point. Rather than target the news media with information about human rights abuses in Uganda, the organization asked celebrities to recirculate the information to their social media followers (Zuckerman 2012). Following the precepts of what Andrew Cooper (2007) calls "celebrity diplomacy," the group enlisted celebrities to help put the issue on the agenda with the hope of generating mass media coverage (it also led to coverage questioning both the ethics and efficacy of Invisible Children's larger strategy for achieving social change). In this case, publicity was "hybrid" in that it integrated the novel features of digital media (e.g., viral sharing outside the realm of traditional news providers) in order to ultimately garner the attention of leading news outlets.

The diversification of publicity options raises a broader question about what types of public pressure are most effective for human rights news to spur social change. In the past, news coverage by leading newspapers was often seen as a proxy for access to government officials (Clark 2001). Of course, many nongovernment officials also read these newspapers, yet this readership was often seen as almost incidental to the desired audience of political elites. Today, the diverse paths to publicity raise questions about how best to reach any of these publics. Is the *New York Times* still the most effective way to reach policymakers in the US State Department? Or would human rights newsmakers be better served by targeting blogs or niche websites that staffers might be more likely to read? Relatedly, is presence in the mainstream media still the most effective way to generate widespread public support of human rights causes? Or might advocacy groups find alternate routes that more successfully achieve this goal, perhaps while also maintaining a greater degree of editorial control over their information materials?

Almost all news has the potential for a human rights news frame

The third feature of human rights news today is what might be called perpetual framing struggles. As advocacy groups, including NGOs, commit greater resources to information production, they have advocacy reporting and action recommendations at the ready. Their staffers look to find ways to insert these materials into the flow of daily news. As a result, human rights is not framed once and for all (by the publication of a single news story generated from a press release); rather, the effort to make a story a human rights issue is a continual effort, labored over by constantly monitoring the news agenda. As the discursive meaning of human rights expands and the digital environment enables real-time monitoring, this suggests that nearly *any* news story has the potential for a human rights frame.

An example from my own research helps to illustrate the point. In 2011, Amnesty International was reporting on human rights violations in Libya in the context of the "Arab Spring." Every day, the press officers would meet to discuss ways to get a human rights angle into this broader story. In June 2011, the UK press was debating what should happen to then-president-in-hiding Muammar al-Gaddafi. To Amnesty staffers, this was a debate with a clear human rights dimension: Gaddafi had committed numerous war crimes and should be prosecuted as such. To insert this frame into the debate, they sent press releases, monitored social media feeds and contacted reporters with the message that Gaddafi needed to be seen as a human rights violator. They tailored their language to suit the needs of the press, invoking Britishisms for greater journalistic and public appeal. In doing this, Amnesty was able to get the human rights dimension into news coverage about Libya.

Framing struggles also complicate the idea of what constitutes a human rights violation. As Moyn (2010) has argued, the relatively recent triumph of human rights discourses vis-à-vis alternative political ideologies has led to a cascading effect where various political goals (e.g., climate change, torture, poverty, etc.) are discussed under the banner of human rights. This creates a situation wherein a seemingly endless number of topics are framed as human rights issues. The anecdote at the introduction of this article suggests, for example, how climate change activists use human rights discourses to reframe the issue as one of personal and cultural autonomy. In the United States, human rights groups—in the context of documented police violence (Rios 2006)—have with increasing regularity addressed racial disparities as human rights problems (as opposed to civil rights). In 2014, for example, Amnesty International dispatched a research team to gather facts in the aftermath of the shooting of a 19-year-old black man by a white police officer. While there, the leader of the organization's US section, Steven W. Hawkins, took to the airwaves to call the situation a human rights crisis.

In each of these cases, the point is that what constitutes human rights news is always potentially under negotiation. News articles without a human rights angle may become the object of advocacy reporting and action recommendations. And issues that otherwise find little traction in the press might be framed in human rights terms. The key issue here is that an expanded meaning of human rights as a discourse couples with technological capacities for monitoring that make it possible to insert advocacy reporting and action recommendations into the flow of daily news content.

Human rights news not only informs and persuades but it produces legal documentation of violations

A fourth feature of human rights today is that it aims not only to inform and persuade but also to document actual human rights violations. This development may help to reshape both the content and form of human rights news by mixing emotive appeals and calls for action with empirical evidence of a human rights violation. In the extant paradigm of human rights news, media coverage is useful for its capacity to shame violators, to raise public awareness, and to boost organizational branding. None of this has disappeared. However, it has been supplemented by a type of human rights news that functions simultaneously as information, provocation, and *documentation* of the human rights abuses. This latter function is key. In the past, clippings from the *New York Times* were rarely used in legal proceedings. In part, this was because there was no legal proceeding—no International Criminal Court—to which they could be submitted; thus, the institutional development of human rights bodies helps to fashion new types of human rights news. At the same time, this was also the case because coverage in the news media was seen as an intermediary point, between research and action. The former—that is, the research—was understood to be the evidentiary basis for the latter.

Today, there are growing efforts to ensure that human rights coverage can be used not simply for dramatic and attention-grabbing purposes but also as legal evidence. Human rights NGOs dedicate substantial resources to training local activists around the world in documentation practices. Activists are instructed to include geographic landmarks (e.g., mountains, historic buildings, etc.) in their visual efforts, which specify where the actions occurred. They are trained in best practices for capturing metadata (e.g., automated recording of the date and time of the filming; see, e.g., McPherson 2015). And they are informed to capture information that not only maximizes emotional impact but provides information that can be used in the human rights methodology. As one NGO professional puts it: "It's instinctual to shoot that puddle of blood or the body lying on the ground. It's not instinctual to turn around and get a badge number or the location of a communications tower. If you're strictly a media activist, you're not going to show the world a communications tower. It's not going to make the news…But from a legal sense, you need those details" (as quoted in Shaer 2015: para. 25).

Efforts to document violations through public channels also blur the lines between research and publicity itself. The legal evidence discussed in the preceding paragraph was always captured by NGOs; however, it was typically tucked into a research report whose circulation was limited largely to policymakers. As evidence is documented publicly, the line between research and publicity changes. This blurring can be seen in the ongoing battle over fake images and videos that are repurposed in the immediate aftermath of a human rights violation (Mawad 2012). The value of these images lies in their appearance as truthful statements about current realities—that is, as a form of documentation. The threat is that false images cast doubt on all other documents too. This has practical implications for how NGOs cultivate social media materials. McPherson (2015), for example, has described the ways in which Amnesty International's efforts to evaluate social media information has led the group to favor accounts with more resources (suitable for providing metadata and the like). Thus, the blurring of research and publicity presents itself as an opportunity to reinscribe the lines of professionalism in the production of human rights news.

The methods for producing human rights news have diversified

A fifth feature of human rights news today has to do with the diversification of the methods of its production. Human rights news became an object for analysis in large part through the "boots on the ground" efforts of human rights activists and sympathetic journalists (Powers 2015b). Its credibility was boosted by the development of a methodology that could take the observations of witnesses—who were sympathetic but not inherently trustworthy—and find ways to generate veridical accounts of what happened. On-the-ground interviews have not gone away. But they, too, are being supplanted in the changing landscape of human rights news. These developments create the possibility for new types of human rights storytelling (not all of which are inherently positive, as discussed below).

In the past decade, leading NGOs have invested resources in the use of satellite-imaging devices (Herscher 2011). Unlike eyewitness reports, these images provide a bird's eye view of events on the ground, which allows researchers to view the overall amount of destruction wrought upon a specific locale. In cases where access is difficult and reports are conflicting, such imagery is used as a monitoring device. This creates not only an additional sort of witness but an altogether different type of witnessing. If human rights news was initially premised on the statements of individuals whose rights had been violated, technologies like satellite imaging are premised on the capacity for mechanical witnessing — a power premised on having the resources to be able to see in this way. This development creates the opportunity to shed light on human rights issues to a degree and scale previously unimaginable.

At the same time, the diversification of the method for human rights storytelling may also create doubt about the individuals who once formed the core of human rights reporting. In 2009, for example, human rights reporters in Sri Lanka declared that it was impossible to adjudicate competing claims between government officials (who said civilian deaths resulted from their conscription by rebels as human shields) and rebel groups (who said that the government directly targeted civilians; see, e.g., Herscher 2011). After looking into the events, the UN Under-Secretary for Humanitarian Affairs claimed that it was impossible to know the truth because "no-one was there" (Herscher 2011: 143). Of course, that statement was hardly true: Many civilians *were* there. It was just that newer methods like satellite imagery were not available and thus definitive evidence seemed mixed. Thus, on the whole, it is difficult to generalize about the effects of the diversification of human rights reporting techniques.

Together, the five features discussed here suggest some ways in which the new mode of human rights news may improve upon its predecessor. It may cover more issues and include a greater number of voices. At the same time, questions arise about the veracity of the informa-tion provided as well as the degree to which more complexity is incorporated into the news coverage (because the same developments that allow activists to bypass the media also encour-age the simplification of information). In the next section, I consider the implications of these developments for future research examining the intersection of media and human rights.

Implications for research

The features identified above suggest the outlines of a new era of human rights news, one marked by the growing interdependence of amateurs and professionals, of multiple routes for achieving publicity and of perpetual framing struggles. The available scholar-ship on human rights news has not yet systematically examined these developments. Too often, the available research tends to assume the staying power of a paradigm marked by the dominance of news organizations and elite NGOs. It tests what factors drive the deci-sion making of these two entities but pays far less attention to the role of amateurs, the information-generating practices of variously sized advocacy groups, or to the changing discursive meanings of human rights. As a result, scholarship generally retains a theoreti-cal assumption in favor of the extent paradigm, with relatively little scholarship asking how and in what ways new developments may either alter that paradigm, or perhaps even usher in a new one (see the overview in Powers 2015c).

Here I want to highlight two questions that deserve further analysis and suggest some of the ways in which they might be studied so as to bring some of the theoretical issues raised by the potential emergence of a new human rights news paradigm to the fore. One question is empirical. In effect, it asks how and in what ways the new features identified here interact with the established paradigm of human rights news. This can be studied both with respect to the mainstream media and in emergent online news spaces. For mainstream media (which still constitute the lion's share of news production and consumption), there are ques-tions about whether a new era of human rights news-making—characterized by the five fea-tures listed above—will open the news gates to a wider variety of topics and actors. For example, it is possible that the *prevalence* of human rights sources (e.g., NGOs, advocates, etc.) and frames (e.g., issues for which human rights angles are developed) is expanding as a result of the shifting institutional, discursive, and technological contexts. Related questions concern whether human rights advocates are able to widen the news agenda by introducing topics and issues otherwise excluded or marginalized in the news.

With respect to digital media, there are important empirical questions about how and in what ways human rights is produced and circulated in online spaces. While scholarship has begun to document some of the ways that human rights news is being produced through digi-tal channels (described above), much less research has examined the degree to which new developments alter old paradigms. For example, social media use by advocates and NGOs may challenge extant patterns of news-making (bypassing the news media and targeting large audiences directly) or it may reinforce those same norms (by using social media primarily as a digital echo chamber). Relatedly, when and how human rights issues spill over from the digital sphere and break into the news more broadly remains scarcely understood. Finally, research-ers know little about how advocates select publicity strategies, now that they have so many dif-ferent options available to them. Each of these is an important empirical concern that requires further attention.

A second set of issues is analytical. In effect, it asks the following: To the extent that a new era does or does not supplant the characteristics of an earlier era, what explains it? The present status of human rights news offers an interesting test case for institutional theories of change. According to a dominant strand of institutional theory (see, e.g., Starr 2004), organizations and institutions tend to endure over time according to the principles and norms upon which they are founded. Journalism in the United States, for example, is premised on ideals of objectivity and news worth that can be traced back to struggles in the nineteenth and early twentieth century to differentiate news from public relations. For institutional and organizational theorists, the possibility of change typically arises during a period of churn or systemic shocks. The various institutional, discursive, and technological transformations make it plausible to imagine change (and to note key features of what this change may produce). Whether or not this change actually transpires will therefore be an empirical question with important analytical takeaways. In particular, continuity or change will require an account of the various mechanisms that help to ensure either a continuation of or departure from the status quo.

Such an analysis will help to inform key debates in human rights, communications, and journalism. Researchers have done much to identify the macrolevel conditions shaping human rights news coverage (e.g., the degree to which coverage corresponds to factors such as political violence, military aid, foreign assistance, the size of a country's civil society sector). Largely absent from these discussions are the meso-level conditions within the fields of journalism and advocacy that help to shape human rights coverage (for an exception, see Pollock 2014). Long-standing interests, for example, in the role played by funding, organizational dynamics, and professional norms are all likely to matter in shaping the degree to which a new era of technical affordances ends up creating a new paradigm of human rights news (Powers 2014).

Conclusion

Over the past half century, human rights news has formed a key part of the human rights advocacy paradigm. Reliance on the mainstream news media has led to occasional policy successes but frequent failures. Today, institutional, discursive, and technological changes raise the possibility of a new paradigm of human rights news-making: one that is more open to a wider range of actors and topics yet is also confronted with challenges about the veracity of on-the-ground reporting. To what degree such a new paradigm takes hold remains an open question. Here, my effort has been to contrast it with the extant paradigm of human rights news.

Whether a new era of human rights news marks an improvement over its predecessor also remains an open question. If newer forms of human rights news-making are indeed able to pioneer new information formats and broaden the number and types of issues with a human rights frame, then there will be room for cautious optimism. Yet if newer forms of human rights news correspond with growing levels of doubt or new forms of informational elitism, then the new paradigm may — somewhat paradoxically — reinforce the tendencies of the paradigm it displaces. In short, whether and how a new paradigm of human rights replaces its predecessor remains an important question for observation, analysis, and evaluation.

Notes

1. This example is taken from Callison (2014).
2. Since 2011, I have been engaged in interviews and observations with NGOs and journalists about how these actors produce human rights news. To date, I have conducted more than 70 interviews with human rights professionals in the United States and Europe. As a doctoral student at New York University, this research — covered under Institutional Review Board (IRB) protocol HS#11-8339, "Making Foreign News: Journalism, Civil Society and the Public Sphere" — was determined exempt from requirements to obtain signed consent. As an assistant professor at the University of Washington, this research — IRB protocol #49863, "The New Boots on the Ground: NGOs in the Changing News Landscape" —was also determined to have exempt status. Interviews were conducted with journalists and NGO professionals (researchers, advocacy officers, and public relations professionals) with the aim of understanding how human rights news is produced in the twenty-first century. Interview questions examined the professional trajectories, daily practices, and respondents' perceptions of changes in the production of human rights news over time. For details, see Powers (2013) and Powers (2015b).

References

BARTLETT, Rachel. (2010) Amnesty International launches news service. *Journalism*. [Online]. Available: www.journalism.co.uk/news/-media140–amnesty-international-launchesnews-service/s2/a543699/ [7 May 2015].

BECKER, Jo. (2013) *Campaigning for Justice: Human Rights Advocacy in Practice* (Stanford, CA: Stanford University Press).

BENNETT, W. Lance, and SEGERBERG, Alexandra. (2013) *The Logic of Connective Action: Digital Media and the Personalization of Contentious Politics* (Cambridge, UK: Cambridge University Press).

BEUTZ LAND, Molly. (2009) Peer producing human rights. *Alberta Law Review*, 46(4), 1115–1140.

BOB, Clifford. (2005) *The Marketing of Rebellion: Insurgents, Media and International Activism* (New York: Cambridge University Press).

BOGERT, Carroll. (2010) Similar paths, different missions. *Nieman Reports*, 64(2), 59–61.

CALLISON, Candis. (2014) *How Climate Change Comes to Matter* (Durham, NC: Duke University Press).

CHADWICK, Andrew. (2013) *The Hybrid Media System: Politics and Power* (New York: Oxford University Press).

CLARK, Ann Marie. (2001) *Diplomacy of Conscience: Amnesty International and Changing Human Rights Norms* (Princeton, NJ: Princeton University Press).

COHEN, Dara Kay, and GREEN, Amelia Hoover. (2012) Dueling incentives: Sexual violence in Liberia and the politics of human rights advocacy. *Journal of Peace Research*, 49(3), 445–458.

COOPER, Andrew Fenton. (2008) *Celebrity Diplomacy* (Boulder, CO: Paradigm Publishers).

COTTLE, Simon, and NOLAN, David. (2007) Global humanitarianism and the changing aid-media field. *Journalism Studies*, 8(6), 862–878.

FOUCAULT, Michel. (1977) *Power/Knowledge* (New York: Pantheon).

GANS, Herbert. (1979) *Deciding What's News* (New York: Random House).

HANNERZ, Ulf. (2004) *Foreign News: Exploring the World of Foreign Correspondents* (Chicago: University of Chicago Press).

HERSCHER, Andrew. (2011) From target to witness: Architecture, satellite surveillance, human rights. In *Architecture and Violence*, Bechir Kenzari (ed.) (Barcelona: Actar).

HOPGOOD, Stephen. (2006) *Keepers of the Flame: Understanding Amnesty International* (Ithaca, NY: Cornell University Press).

KECK, Margaret, and SIKKINK, Katherine. (1998) *Activists Beyond Borders* (Ithaca, NY: Cornell University Press).

LYNCH, Marc, FREELON, Deen, and Aday, Sean. (2014) Syria's socially mediated civil war. [Online]. Available: http://www.usip.org/publications/syria-s-socially-mediated-civil-war [6 May 2015].

MAWAD, Dalal. (2012) Syria: Too much information? [Online]. Available: http://www.cjr.org/behind_the_news/syria_too_much_information.php [6 May 2015].

MCPHERSON, Ella. (2015) Advocacy organizations' evaluations of social media information for NGO journalism: The evidence and engagement models. *American Behavioral Scientist*, 59(1), 124–148.

MOYN, Samuel. (2010) *The Last Utopia: Human Rights in History* (Cambridge, MA: Harvard University Press).

NEIER, Aryeh. (2003) *Taking Liberties: Four Decades in the Struggle for Rights* (New York: Public Affairs).

OTTO, Florian, and MEYER, Christoph O. (2012) Missing the story?: Changes in foreign news reporting and their implications for conflict prevention. *Media, War & Conflict*, 5(3), 205–221.

POLLOCK, John C. (2014) Illustrating human rights: How demographics drive media coverage. *Atlantic Journal of Communication*, 22(3/4), 141–159.

POWERS, Matthew. (2013) Humanity's Publics: NGO, Journalism and the International Pubic Sphere. Doctoral Dissertation, New York University.

POWERS, Matthew. (2014) The structural organization of NGO publicity: Explaining divergent publicity strategies at humanitarian and human rights organizations. *International Journal of Communication*, 8, 90–107.

POWERS, Matthew. (2015a) Opening the news gates? Humanitarian and human rights NGOs in the US news media, 1990–2010. *Media, Culture & Society*. Advance online publication. doi:10.1177/0163443715594868.

POWERS, Matthew. (2015b) The new boots on the ground: NGOs in the changing landscape of international news. *Journalism: Theory, Practice & Criticism*. Advance online publication. doi:10.1177/1464884914568077.

POWERS, Matthew. (2015c) Contemporary NGO-journalist relations: Reviewing and evaluating an emergent area of research. *Sociology Compass*, 9(6), 427–437.

RADDEN KEEFE, Patrick. (2013, November 25) Rocket man. [Online]. Available: http://www.newyorker.com/magazine/2013/11/25/rocket-man-2 [6 May 2015].

RAMOS, Howard, RON, James, and THOMS, Oskar. (2007) Shaping the northern media's human rights coverage, 1986–2000. *Journal of Peace Research*, 44(4), 385–406.

REVKIN, Andrew. (2014) Eskimos seek to recast global warming as a rights issue. [Online]. Available: http://www.nytimes.com/2004/12/15/world/americas/eskimos-seek-to-recast-global-warming-as-a-rights-issue.html [4 January 2016].

RIOS, Victor. (2006) The hyper-criminalization of Black and Latino male youth in the era of mass incarceration. *Souls*, 8(2), 40–54.

ROBINSON, Fiona. (2003) NGOs and the advancement of economic and social rights: Philosophical and practical controversies. *International Relations*, 17(1), 79–96.

RON, James, RAMOS, Howard, and RODGERS, Kathleen. (2005) Transnational information politics: NGO human rights reporting, 1986–2000. *International Studies Quarterly*, 49(3), 557–588.

SCHUDSON, Michael. (2011) *The Sociology of News* (New York: Norton).

SHAER, Matthew. (2015, February 18) The media doesn't care what happens here. [Online]. Available: http://www.nytimes.com/2015/02/22/magazine/the-media-doesnt-care-what-happens-here.html [6 May 2015].

STARR, Paul. (2004) *The Creation of the Media* (New York: Basic Books).

THRALL, A. Trevor, STECULA, Dominik, and SWEET, Diana. (2014) May we have your attention please?: Human rights NGOs and the problem of global communication. *International Journal of Press/Politics*, 19(2), 135–159.

WAISBORD, Silvio. (2011) Can NGOs change the news? *International Journal of Communication*, 5, 142–165.

WILLIAMS, Randall. (2010) *The Divided World: Human Rights and its Violence* (Minneapolis, MN: University of Minnesota Press).

WINSTON, Morton. (2001) Assessing the effectiveness of human rights NGOs: Amnesty International. In *NGOs and Human Rights: Promise and Performance*, Claude E. Welch, Jr. (ed.) (Philadelphia, PA: University of Pennsylvania Press).

ZUCKERMAN, Ethan. (2012) Unpacking Kony 2012. [Online]. Available: http://www.ethanzuckerman.com/blog/2012/03/08/unpacking-kony-2012/ [6 May 2015].

Source credibility as "information subsidy": Strategies for successful NGO journalism at Mexican human rights NGOs

Ella McPherson

University of Cambridge

ABSTRACT

This article draws on Gandy's (1982) influential concept of "information subsidies" to examine strategies Mexican human rights NGOs employ to get their information into the news. By building their credibility as sources — through interpersonal relationships with journalists, through authority with human rights leaders, and through associations with NGO networks — NGOs provide a verification subsidy that shortens the time journalists need to evaluate the sources of their information. By playing to NGOs' strengths, namely their symbolic and social capital, this type of information subsidy holds promise for pluralism and accountability in the public sphere. This promise varies, however, according to what kind of pluralism we mean: namely, pluralism vis-à-vis the field of power, pluralism within the field of human rights NGOs, and pluralism of access to human rights accountability. It also varies according to the resources of the NGO in question, which affect the NGO's ability to demonstrate credibility and thus to provide information subsidies. The article's focus on the information subsidies provided by subordinate journalistic sources, particularly those that address information values about sources rather than about content, as well as on the centrality of credibility in communication across fields, further develops these concepts in media sociology.

Introduction

In theory, human rights nongovernmental organizations (NGOs) and news outlets interested in journalism that supports democracy should be efficient collaborators. After all, both are interested in pluralism, namely increasing the variety of voices in the public sphere. Both are also interested in holding power to account — news outlets in their watchdog role and human rights organizations in their drive to hold governments and other bodies to account for human rights violations. In practice, however, this collaboration is fraught. One way of understanding these tensions is as arising from the meeting of distinct logics (e.g., Cottle and Nolan 2007; Fenton 2010; Waisbord 2011; Powers 2014). After Thompson (e.g., 2010) and Bourdieu (e.g., 1983), we can think of a particular logic as the rules, explicit and implicit, that govern success in a particular field and thus the practices in that field. Rules about the value and use of information are central to the logics of both the journalistic field and the human rights NGO field, though these rules differ across the two fields. Gandy's (1982: 8) influential concept of *information subsidies* — namely, "efforts to reduce the prices faced by others for certain information, in order to increase its consumption" — is useful for understanding practices that aim to communicate across fields and therefore to bridge information logics.

A significant theme in the literature on the NGO–media relationship is the critique of the information subsidies NGOs must provide to attract attention in the context of commercializing journalistic logics. This critique is important and troubling, but it is not one that human rights NGOs can do much about except lament. As the largely dependent partner in the NGO–media relationship, it is unavoidable that NGOs are sensitive and responsive to the information-related needs and wants of news outlets, including their increasingly commercial imperatives. In contrast to the above critique, which focuses on discord between the information logics at NGOs and at news outlets, this article, by drawing on my media ethnography of human rights reporting in Mexico, turns to areas of accord.[1] My argument is that information subsidies that play to the strengths of NGOs' logics while also following the rules of news outlets' information logics create a win-win scenario for these two fields as well as for the broader goals of pluralism and accountability they share. These information subsidies form part of the trend towards NGO journalism, or the adoption of journalistic values and practices by the NGOs who increasingly supply our news (Powers 2015a; Wright 2015).

Rules about the value of information identify characteristics that make the information valuable for activity in the field in question; hence, news values are part of journalistic logics (Waisbord 2011). These information values are divisible into those related to the information's content and those related to the information's source (McPherson 2015a). Information subsidies can thus subsidize practices related to the information's content, such as locating, evaluating, and shaping it. The can also subsidize practices related to the information's source, namely evaluating the source according to valued characteristics. The existing literature on information subsidies predominantly addresses the former and, concerning NGO journalism specifically, raises the aforementioned critique of the provision of commercialized content. In contrast, in this article, I largely address the latter — and particularly strategies that facilitate the evaluation of the source in question's credibility, which we can think of as a type of *verification subsidy*.[2]

As I explain in a subsequent section of this article, the symbolic capital (Bourdieu 1993) of credibility is central to the logics of human rights NGOs and of news outlets; NGOs' demonstration of their credibility as sources can therefore be an effective subsidy for information evaluation across these fields. I identify three strategies deployed by my informants at human rights NGOs in Mexico for building source credibility with journalists: credibility in interpersonal relationships, credibility via authority, and credibility via networks. These are all underpinned by the demonstration of credibility via performance over time. As credibility, or the ability to be believed, is a relational characteristic built between the seeker and the evaluator of credibility, it also relies on other core characteristics of NGOs' logics: their emphasis on solidarity and their related experience with networking social capital.

One of the most analytically useful aspects of the information-subsidy concept is that, as an economic metaphor, it highlights the connection between the ability to provide information subsidies and the possession of other forms of capital — and thus between pluralism and power. Accordingly, I argue that the information subsidy of source credibility, which draws on NGOs' symbolic and social capital, influences three types of pluralism: the pluralism of human rights NGOs in the public sphere vis-à-vis other sources; the pluralism among human rights NGOs in the public sphere; and the pluralism of access to public accountability, a fundamental aspect of the "naming and shaming" (Human Rights Watch 2013) mechanism of human rights. Though, overall, human rights NGOs' information subsidies derived from demonstrations of source credibility hold promise for pluralism and accountability in the public sphere, NGOs' ability to provide such subsidies is unequal and maps onto the general distribution of power amongst them.

The relationship between human rights NGOs and the media in Mexico

Because many newspapers in Mexico have a dedicated human rights beat, the relationship between the field of newspapers and the field of domestic human rights NGOs in Mexico is one of mutual dependency, though one in which human rights NGOs are subordinate. Journalists could consult other sources for human rights information, namely the governmental human rights commissions or international organizations — or they could decide to divert their reporting resources to other topics. Human rights defenders, on the other hand, have tended to see a presence in the news as absolutely essential to their work. As a result, and as part of an overall process of professionalization (Waisbord 2011), they have been developing and deploying information subsidies to encourage journalists' selection of their information as news.

My interviewees at Mexican human rights NGOs said that media coverage helps them to educate the public, to raise their profiles, and to generate a "bigger discussion."[3] "We don't have the resources," one interviewee said, "So our way of discussion is often through the printed press [and] some radio stations."[4] Crucially, they explained, the media also supports their NGOs in the generation of public moral outrage. A mechanism for stirring this outrage is known in Mexico as the *denuncia*, which translates as "denunciation" — namely, a condemnation or an accusation levied publicly. This public aspect of the *denuncia* is all important, for, as one human rights defender put it, "When human rights problems are not really known, this favors impunity and permits repression."[5] Exposing violations to "public opinion,"[6] however, places a check on human rights violators, as another informant described it, creating a "guarantee of protection"[7] for targets and witnesses of violations. This is because the public moral pressure engendered by human rights reporting ideally will cause "an authority [...] to think twice before a repressive action because he is starting to feel he is under a gaze."[8]

Human rights defenders said, however, that alone, their organizations could not generate the same "level of audience"[9] as they could by working with the media. They therefore traditionally relied on the mainstream media as their "door... so that public opinion realizes what is happening."[10] In a political context where considerable emphasis was put on at least the appearance of democracy, public opinion did matter. The media, as one interviewee put it, is "a space that counts a lot"[11] for politicians, as it is politicians' gateway to publics as well. As one human rights reporter whimsically explained it: "Here we have a phrase: 'Authorities are like dogs. They only understand when they have been slapped by a newspaper.'"[12] It is no surprise, then, that interviewees described their relationships with journalists as an indispensable aspect of their strategies.

Human rights defenders did not speak of these relationships — and the news coverage issuing from them — as a matter of circumstance but rather as the product of strategic action. These strategies involve first understanding the journalistic logic, including news outlets' information values. For example, one NGO's training guide on "Communication and Visibility Strategies for Civil Society Organizations" states, "If we want our organization, our actions, or our words to be news, we have to consider certain basic norms that govern the genre" (Comunicación e Información de la Mujer AC 2004: 43). A second aspect of these strategies entails shaping NGO information — both in terms of content and in terms of source characteristics — to match these information values. By doing this, NGOs take on some of news outlets' costs in identifying, evaluating, and preparing information for publication; in other words, they provide "information subsidies" (Gandy 1982).

Returning to the notion of logics of the field, we can see information subsidies as a communication strategy designed to bridge two logics. Information subsidies convert the type of information valued by the communicator field into the type of information valued by the target audience field. Gandy posits that consumers, in the context of finite resources, are more likely to consume cheaper information (1982). We shall examine, in turn, two categories of information subsidies used by Mexican human rights NGOs: commercialized content and demonstrations of source credibility.

Commercialized content as information subsidy

Studies of the relationships between NGOs and the media have raised the concern that NGOs are subordinating their logics to journalistic logics in order to make the news. Of particular worry has been the nature of information subsidies that NGOs have provided to match the progressively more commercial information values of news outlets. For example, NGOs' information increasingly features celebrities, is timed to coincide with news events and is written with a personalized angle (Cottle and Nolan 2007; Fenton 2010; Waisbord 2011). According to this line of argument, which echoes a concern shared more widely in the literature addressing the commercialization of the media (e.g., Bourdieu 1998), this subordination can detract from NGOs' work. This occurs both through diverting NGO resources to media strategies and through diluting the norms at the heart of their logics, such as their impartiality and their commitment to "universal humanitarianism" (Cottle and Nolan 2007: 864; Fenton 2010).

At the time of my research, newspapers in Mexico were dealing with shrinking profits and growing competition, leading to the rise of a "spot news" model described by one editor as "very graphic; brief, clear, short articles in a simple language; direct; the most information in the least space" (quoted in McPherson 2012: 2305). Newspaper stands were also punctuated with what are known as *nota roja* publications, the term in Mexico for a popular variation on tabloid news about crime and violence that translates literally as "red news." In this context, the human rights defenders I interviewed in Mexico were indeed struggling with a perceived clash of logics between their field and the journalistic field. At times, they described this clash as manifested in fundamentally opposite information values; human rights work values lengthy tomes, while journalistic work values the pared news pyramid. As one human rights defender explained it, "It is not easy to translate your activity into a press article. How do you prioritize, have a title, hook the media? [Avoid] using 20,000 words when you can use one."[13] Human rights work has a long-term optic, while journalistic work is topically volatile, in the view of another interviewee. Human rights rhetoric can be passionate, while journalistic language is usually dispassionate (Powers 2015a). One human rights defender illustrated this by describing a colleague's behavior at a press conference commemorating the Aguas Blancas massacre in Mexico:

> Every time he spoke, the people turned off their tape recorders. "The fascism of the government…." — automatically the four reporters went to get a coffee, and we knew that these positions, they are not disposed to accept them. They need to have a more ordered discourse — less "Grrrrrrrr!" — so that they can describe something about you. You have to tone down certain discourses.[14]

Furthermore, the thematic foci of human rights information may also be at odds with what the media seeks. As one informant described it:

> Human rights is hard to place in papers. It isn't *nota roja*. It isn't [always] accompanied by police brutality. It is more legal, ethical. So it is a little complicated for the media to sell this.[15]

The latter's use of commercial terminology was not isolated. In fact, my NGO informants spoke to me so frequently about their relationship with the media in terms of the *selling* of information, that I stopped one to ask, "Why do you use 'buy' and 'sell' as words [in your description]?" She replied:

> The newspaper is a product… The newspaper is sold — it is supply and demand. The public [reads] the article that captures their attention — and unfortunately, these articles in some cases have to do with accidents, assaults. They are easier for the people to see and to buy. For the press, if the people are not interested, there is no sale, and if there is no sale, they say, "You know what, I won't write about this but instead about something else…." If readers are not interested, what do you do?[16]

Commerciality, then, was an information value perceived in the Mexican media by human rights defenders, and they tailored the content they targeted at journalists accordingly. In addition to seeking news pegs on which to hang their long-term research and shaping their information to fit journalistic expectations, some tended to target reporters with information about only certain types of violations, those that lend themselves to the "scandalous" and to "hard news."[17] As one interviewee explained it:

> At the end of the day, they are selling information, selling to editors and to the public. If the news is not red, yellow, spectacular, it is not news. If there are not deaths, wounded, corruption, information on a politician, it is not very attractive.[18]

These tactics, as well as human rights defenders' spontaneous usage of market terminology when discussing their relationships with the media, may indicate, as Cottle and Nolan (2007: 874) found with respect to international humanitarian aid agencies, the "institutionaliz [ation]" and "normaliz[ation]" of commercial information values into NGO logics. This finding is troubling, particularly if it constricts pluralism by limiting the types of human rights violations for which subjects and witnesses can seek accountability through the media. That said, for those whose stories are covered, being in the news is one of the most effective strategies for pluralism in terms of being heard by wide audiences; furthermore, news coverage is just one of the range of advocacy strategies that NGOs employ and thus just one of a number of strategies for human rights pluralism (Powers 2015b, 2015c).

In any case, it is important to move beyond this finding for a number of reasons. First, this is just one trend at the meeting of two logics that, despite some dominant and shared characteristics, are overall quite diverse. This diversity ranges not only across each field but also within each institution, both at the section level and at the individual level (Orgad 2013;

Waisbord 2011; Powers 2014; Wright 2016). Second, this is a trend about which NGOs, as the subordinate participant in the NGO–journalism relationship, can do little but lament at worst and be "pragmatic" at best (Waisbord 2011: 145). Bringing these two points together, we can move to investigating how alternative aspects of these complex logics might be informing other types of information subsidies — types that do not require NGOs to eclipse their values. The NGO communications strategy manual referenced above is guided by the question: "How can we be in the media without losing ourselves?" (Comunicación e Información de la Mujer AC 2004: 12). One answer is the provision of source credibility as an information subsidy to support journalists in the resource-intensive process of source verification.

Source credibility as information subsidy

Time and again, reporters, editors, and human rights defenders told me of the importance of credibility to their organizations' successes. Credibility, or the ability to be believed, is a reputational resource, namely as a type of symbolic capital that can be mobilized in the pursuit of power (Bourdieu 1993; Thompson 2000). Often, this occurs via the utilization of credibility for communication — an action that, without credibility, is nigh impossible; to communicate, as in to get one's message across, one must be believed. Credibility is also a relational resource created between the entity seeking credibility and the entity evaluating credibility (Hardin 2002). One can build credibility in a number of ways, including, as explored below in the case of Mexican human rights NGOs, via interpersonal relationships, via authority, and via networks. One can also damage one's credibility in these ways, or it can be destroyed through the propagation of *discrediting discourses* by one's opponents. As such, credibility, like other reputational resources, is precarious (Thompson 2000).

Because communication is at the core of both journalistic and human rights work, it is no surprise that actors in both fields value their credibility. Journalists need credibility with publics in order to maintain and build audiences as well as credibility with individuals such as sources (Waisbord 2006; Franklin and Carlson 2011; McPherson 2012). Human rights NGOs rely on credibility with publics to mobilize the moral outrage that underpins their "name and shame" methodology as well as credibility with individuals such as journalists, volunteers, and donors (Gibelman and Gelman 2004; Cottle and Nolan 2007; Brown 2008; Land 2009). This concern with credibility is reflected in the practices of journalists and human rights defenders to build and safeguard it. It is also shared across a variety of news outlets and NGOs studied around the world (see, e.g., Orentlicher 1990; Schlesinger 1990; Manning 2001; Hopgood 2006; Waisbord 2006; Fenton 2010; Franklin and Carlson 2011; Reich 2011). Each organization, however, also operates within particular contexts that have implications for building credibility. In the Mexican context, this includes "authoritarian enclaves" that persist in institutions and cultures, a legacy of the semi-authoritarian regime that governed for much of the twentieth century and whose party has returned to power today (Lawson 2000). In this section, I first outline this context before going on to detail the practices NGOs undertake to demonstrate source credibility as an information subsidy.

The Mexican political context

Human rights NGOs and newspapers were both instrumental to the slow political liberalization in Mexico leading to the 2000 election of the opposition. In the decades preceding this, a handful of journalists decided to break with the tradition of cozy cash-for-coverage relationships with government officials in order to found and revamp print publications dedicated to supporting democratization (Hughes 2006). These publications, and the emulators they sparked, discovered that looking to the market for revenue, rather than the state, was sustainable. This was in part due to audience — and thus advertiser — demand for information that critiqued the government and that included voices from civil society (Lawson 2002). These market-oriented newspapers were trying to recruit and retain audiences and advertisers well aware of their sector's history — and their peers' ongoing practice — of financial-informational contracts with government officials. Their journalists were thus concerned with building credibility with respect to incorruptibility and to independence; human rights coverage, which by its nature is critical of government officials, was one way to do this. Journalists' concern with credibility, however, also made them extremely careful about verifying the credibility of their sources, including those on the human rights beat (McPherson 2012).

The human rights beat consisted of governmental human rights commissions as well as the most "serious"[19] (in interviewee journalists' words) of the human rights NGOs that flourished in Mexico starting in the early 1990s (Sikkink 1993; Acosta 1994; Aguayo Quezada and Parra Rosales 1997). Human rights defenders at these organizations were well versed in the power of credibility for communicating as media sources or otherwise — a kind of power that one interviewee referred to as "moral."[20] They were also repeatedly subject to discrediting discourses propagated by particular government officials who retaliated against accusations of violations by publicly accusing NGOs of financial and political corruption (see, e.g., Amnesty International 2001). I turn next to this contested but core aspect of human rights NGOs' logics and how we might conceptualize the related work that NGOs do to communicate across NGO and journalistic fields.

Strategies for building source credibility

Mexican human rights NGOs had developed practices for building source credibility because, as mentioned above, they knew that journalists valued it. Journalists' concern with their own credibility led them to worry about being tainted by association with discredited sources, particularly in the context of corrupt traditions in the journalistic and other fields. As such, journalists at Mexican newspapers took care to verify their sources' credibility. One editor explained verification to me using the example of a fictional NGO:

> You have to first investigate the organization if it is not well-known and go to see that — if it is an organization that says that it helps drug-addicted children rehabilitate — you have to go see that there is a building with addicted children inside; that there are doctors, specialists, talking to the children; that you go and talk to a child who says, "I am here because I am addicted" — this part is very important to investigate. (quoted in McPherson 2012: 2307)[21]

Obviously source verification makes significant demands on the resource of time, which was in short supply under the spot news model. Furthermore, verification's informational return might be zero should the evaluation yield a noncredible source. It makes sense, then, that human rights NGOs were employing strategies to build source credibility as a way to speed verification and thus to make their information cheaper for journalists.

The strategies NGOs employ for building source credibility are oriented around relationships. These relationships, as explained below, are with journalists themselves or with authoritative individuals and networks that, because journalists already deem them credible, can provide credibility by association. Underpinning these relationships of credibility is credible performance over time. Namely, this includes a public performance in terms of a history of commitment to their causes and a reputation of truth telling as well as private performances within each relationship (Fenton 2010; Hopgood 2006; Orentlicher 1990).

Interpersonal credibility with journalists

The first strategy for boosting source credibility is to initiate personal relationships with sympathetic reporters, "getting them to know us," as one human rights defender put it, "by name and by face."[22] As the NGO communication strategy guide quoted earlier counsels:

> First and foremost, no media is monolithic. All of them are made up of people, and in every human team surely we can find women and men to consider allies for breaking the circle, for [helping us] to enter the media. (Comunicación e Información de la Mujer AC 2004: 39)

Human rights defenders are therefore seeking reporters whose interpretations of the journalistic logic overlaps with their human rights NGO logics with respect to, as one interviewee put it, "journalism that helps the citizenship."[23] These defenders told me they actively invest in and "take advantage" of the "utility"[24] of these "personal relationships."[25] A human rights defender explained it in the following way: "There is a rapprochement much at the level of friendship. We know each other personally, we live here — it is a small town."[26]

The utility of these personal relationships includes being the first port of call for reporters investigating a story, which is the strongest guarantee of getting published, a higher likelihood of attendance at press conferences and of phone calls from reporters catching up on conferences they miss, and insider knowledge of use to the NGOs. As one NGO spokesperson explained it:

> We exchange information. Many times the reporters give you pieces of information on places you can't access, like the government, because the political class is very interested in them. They are also a source of information; we take good care of our relationship with them.[27]

These relationships — friendships, even — are ideally characterized by trust, credibility, and reciprocity. In terms of the latter, "They get elements for their articles," this NGO interviewee said, "And we have the possibility of positioning articles through advance information and their trust."[28] In some cases, a natural affinity exists because human rights reporters have switched professions to become human rights defenders and vice versa. These individuals understand the logics of both fields, but, beyond this, they have social capital — networks — in both fields and can serve as an interpersonal credibility bridge between the two types of institutions. As such, they can be extremely valuable for NGOs, as they become the conduit through which information, and the organizations themselves as sources, can enter the news.

Credibility via authority

A second NGO technique for shoring up source credibility is via institutionalized relationships with individuals who have authority through their positions as public figures in the human rights field, which in turn are based on performance and expertise. Human rights defenders at NGOs with these institutionalized relationships told me that these leaders are a draw for reporters; as one described it: "The media look for concrete people who have a trajectory in the topic and look for their opinion. They don't look for the opinion of the institution, but of a person."[29] As another human rights defender explained, this is not always the best way for media to get information, but they do it nonetheless:

> They like famous names. They will ask for Don Miguel [Concha Malo, a ground breaker for human rights in Mexico] even if [our coordinator of education, promotion, and diffusion] knows more [on the topic in question]. And this is the criticism of the media — they don't give space to the young. Don Miguel is their point of reference.[30]

In other words, human rights NGOs populated by young workers (who, by inference, lack a history of credible performance) can harness the credible reputations of field leaders to get their information into the media — people who, as another human rights defender described them, "have a lot of credibility [and] moral authority."[31]

Credibility via networks

In addition to building relationships with credible individuals, NGOs boost their credibility via association with other NGOs, particularly those with more established reputations. These may be informal, temporary associations or formal, permanent networks. An example of the former are the temporary alliances formed for the duration of a press conference between two or three smaller NGOs and the Human Rights Centre Fray Bartolomé de las Casas. This organization's communications coordinator described this sort of press conference: "The only organization that speaks is Fray Bartolomé, which has a certain respect [and] is recognized.... It is easier to [get the media to] listen to a very well-known voice than to try and position a new organization."[32]

The formalized networks of NGOs are themselves administered by NGOs. For example, the National Network of Human Rights Civil Organisations for All Rights for All serves as an umbrella for dozens of human rights organizations in the majority of Mexico's states, ranging from big groups with paid staff to tiny volunteer groups, and from the "group always connected to the Internet to the one that has neither Internet nor electricity,"[33] according to its executive secretary. Networks like this serve as a "bridge,"[34] as one of their directors explained it, between the media and their member organizations, both in terms of information and in terms of credibility. Network headquarters develop interpersonal relationships of credibility with journalists. They feed these journalists the press releases of member organizations, invite them to large press conferences they organize on behalf of their members and respond to their requests for information on a particular issue by connecting them with experts in their membership. A human rights worker at one of these networks described her role accordingly: "Visibility services is what we do — bringing social movements and the media closer together."[35] As such, networks are valuable to both groups. They allow the smallest NGOs to gain source credibility by association with the more prominent NGOs that already possess it. These networks also mitigate reporters' need to fully engage in the time-consuming process of source verification, since organizations already deemed credible by these reporters are vouching for untested NGOs.

These strategies for building source credibility are not usually an end in themselves but rather a means to building credibility with the publics and policy makers who are often the targets of human rights advocacy. As Gandy (1982) and Carlson and Franklin (2011) point out, appearing in the media implies a sort of credibility endorsement. It is therefore a verification subsidy for target audiences, in that these audiences can assume that the media has undertaken an evaluation of the source's credibility on their behalf; journalists are thus the gatekeepers to public credibility as well as to the public sphere. It is to the implications of NGOs' verification subsidies for pluralism and accountability in the public sphere that I turn to next.

Implications for pluralism and accountability in the public sphere

To understand the implications of information subsidies based on source credibility for pluralism and accountability, we must return to the connection, underscored by the concept of information subsidies, between resources and voice. It is useful to recall Bourdieu's (1986) point that different forms of capital are convertible. The verification subsidies outlined here depend in part on symbolic capital (a reputation of credibility), on cultural capital (knowledge about building credibility and about effective communication strategies), and on social capital (relationships). These in turn depend on other resources; economic capital, for example, can determine the extent of cultural capital an NGO has in terms of media literacy amongst its staff. Human rights NGOs vary among each other and in comparison with other categories of sources in their distribution of these resources. This distribution has an impact on pluralism in the public sphere, but this too varies according to what kind of pluralism we mean: namely, pluralism vis-à-vis the field of power; pluralism within the field of human rights NGOs; and pluralism of access to human rights accountability.

As a field competing with the field of power for column inches, demonstrating credibility plays to human rights NGOs' strengths in terms of the forms of capital that dominate their fields. Building credibility through relationship with journalists, authoritative individuals, and networks of NGOs requires NGOs to deploy social capital, which they are strong on due to the centrality of solidarity and networking in NGO logics (Keck and Sikkink 1998; Atack 1999; McLagan 2006; Dütting and Sogge 2010). Credibility and networks of solidarity allow NGOs to punch above their weight in terms of presence in the public sphere — if that weight is measured purely by the economic and political capital that are the dominant currencies of power in many societies (Lehmann and Bebbington 1998). They also equip NGOs to take on hostile contenders, such as the retaliatory government officials mentioned above (Aguayo Quezada and Parra Rosales 1997). The verification subsidies outlined in this article thus boost pluralism if we define it as the presence of alternative and critical voices in the public sphere — though, granted, NGO voices are not *always* alternative and critical (Powers 2016a).

This does not mean, however, that NGOs are equal contenders with the political-economic elite for journalists' attention, nor does it mean that this visibility is shared equally between all NGOs (Waisbord 2006; Fenton 2010; Thrall, Stecula, and Sweet 2014; Powers 2016b). If we look at pluralism of voice within the human rights NGO field, we see that the uneven distribution of resources allows some NGOs much more voice than their poorer peers. Even if hierarchy is deemphasized within NGO networks (Sikkink 1993), it is a strong organizing principle in journalists' relationship with the constituents of the human rights NGO field. This "hierarchy of credibility" (Becker 1967) is a product of limits on journalists' time to evaluate new sources and NGOs' differential abilities to provide information subsidies. As one human rights reporter explained it to me: "There are a lot of sources, but we don't know them or use them, or they don't approach us — or they don't know how to approach us. [So,] there are reactions of silence to their work."[36] Thus, many human rights NGOs lack the capital — whether cultural, social, symbolic, or economic — to know how to and to be able to build bridges to the journalistic field. As a human rights worker described it:

> It is not just because they [human rights NGOs] are *nice* that their topics come out in the media. It has to do with this — that they understand, that they have a media strategy, that they have invested time and economic resources. There are others for whom this is more difficult, and I see there the problem of economic sustainability. Being in a media is not an accident, not luck — but rather that you construct [a strategy] and maybe hire someone, or give a press conference. It is not easy to finance it.[37]

The ability to demonstrate source credibility, then, like all information subsidies, maps onto the distribution of resources within a field as well as across fields. They thus restrict the pluralism of voice within the NGO field, and there is only so much that the solidarity of networks can do to overcome this. For example, a communications officer at an NGO network for the rights of children told me, "It has happened that we channeled certain organizations to newspapers and they [the journalists] call us [afterwards] and say, 'No more with them! That organization does not have the technical abilities to do the interview.'"[38]

Though important, thinking about pluralism of voice in terms of NGOs' voices, whether vis-à-vis the field of power or within the human rights NGO field, is not the *most* important type of pluralism in human rights communication. Instead, the pluralism that should most concern us is the pluralism of access to the accountability mechanism of human rights for those who have been subjects of human rights violations. This accountability mechanism has several methodologies and several players, but those relevant here are the work of NGOs, via the media, towards "publicly 'naming and shaming' abusive governments," as Human Rights Watch (2013) describes it. Even if the centrality of credibility in media and NGO logics keeps poorer NGOs out of the news as sources, the solidarity and networking aspects of the NGO logic can help the content of their information — and thus the subjects and witnesses of violations they represent — get coverage. So it may be that these smaller NGOs do not themselves get voice, but the subjects and witnesses of violations they have investigated do if the larger NGOs take up smaller NGOs' information about their cases. Whether or not they do this depends on a variety of factors. This includes the cases' alignment with the goals of the larger NGO, as illustrated by one human rights defender's reasons for uploading the press releases of less digitally literate NGOs to her NGO's website: "It is an act of solidarity, to reinforce the work in certain topics that are strategic for us — like economic, social and cultural rights, labour, torture."[39] Another factor is the credibility of the smaller NGO and ultimately the credibility of the subject or witness of the human rights violation; it is a given that credibility evaluations occur at each point along the human rights communication chain — and that resources matter every time.

Conclusion

By shedding light on source strategies — and not just powerful sources, but rather the competitive and collaborative activities of a field that tends to critique the field of power—this article has helped redress the imbalance of the sociology of journalism, which has been weighted towards journalists over their essential collaborators — their sources (Gandy 1982; Schlesinger 1990). Furthermore, a productive by-product of showing how subordinate sources build information subsidies has been rescuing the concept from the pejorative meaning it has come to carry through its association with powerful sources. I have shown it to be an analytically useful tool for understanding and assessing strategies that have the potential to boost pluralism and accountability in the public sphere.

Another critique of information subsidies, present in the literature on NGO journalism, is their association with "selling out" to commercial media. Indeed, as seen in the case of featured Mexican human rights NGOs, journalistic logics can significantly shape the information that human rights defenders proffer to the news cycle. In this case, it is clear that the subjects and witnesses of non-gory, slow-burn human rights violations (like violations of economic, social, and cultural rights) are more likely to be omitted from access to the public sphere — at least via newspapers. Still, this omission should be seen in the whole picture of the advocacy activities that human rights defenders deploy, in which communicating with the mainstream media plays an important but not exclusive role. Furthermore, these other activities and the logics that drive them may be actively distinguished and shielded from the commercial aspects of journalistic logics.

Though information subsidies in the form of commercialized content can be deleterious for certain categories of voice (though beneficial for others), this does not mean that we should tar all information subsidies with the same brush. Information subsidies may very well be an inescapable aspect of successful communication and therefore pluralism. Any time an actor tries to communicate outside of her field, she increases the likelihood she will be heard if she tailors her communication to the information values of her target audience. As we have seen with Mexican human rights NGOs' development of source credibility as information subsidy, deploying information subsidies can be a matter of capitalizing on rather than capitulating one's own information values. The ability to effectively do so, however, depends on one's resources, and so information subsidies cannot escape entirely their stratification effect on pluralism. This was evident in the distribution of credibility among human rights sources as perceived by journalists. Indeed, the symbolic capital of credibility may play a more important role in source selection and in the pluralism of attention and voice as a whole than it has been given credit for in the media sociology literature to date.

In sum, in this article, we have seen how the centrality of credibility for both human rights NGOs and news outlets' logic allows NGOs to use their strengths for creating information subsidies. Through demonstrating their credibility as sources, NGOs speed up journalists' verification practices. This reduces the cost of these NGOs' information to journalists and thus facilitates its entry into the public sphere. These information subsidies, rooted in a performed credibility across time, are transmitted via the social capital in networked relationships of solidarity between NGOs and journalists, between NGOs and human rights figureheads, and among NGOs. Overall, we see that this type of information subsidy holds promise for pluralism in the public sphere for the human rights field vis-à-vis the field of power and for the pluralism of access to the accountability mechanism of human rights — even if the dimensions of credibility that make it a form of capital mean that a "hierarchy of credibility" (Becker 1967) exists within the human rights field with respect to individual NGOs' attempts to build informational bridges to the media field.

This does not mean, however, that recommending that NGOs invest in the verification subsidies outlined in this article is unproblematic. First of all, while credibility is a strength for NGOs, it is also their Achilles' heel. Compared to other sectors of society, NGOs are particularly vulnerable to discrediting discourses (Gibelman and Gelman 2004). This is because their relative dearth of economic resources mean that they trade predominantly on their symbolic and social capital (Brysk 1994). Furthermore, because of the networks of associations that run through civil society, an accusation of corruption against one NGO can taint many more (Global Policy Forum 2012). Repairing a damaged reputation of credibility can divert precious resources from NGOs' core missions (Cottle and Nolan 2007; Brown 2008).

Second of all, recommending that NGOs be strategic about their communication practices is akin to condoning the professionalization of the NGO sector — a trend also critiqued for diverting resources from the operational and ethical cores of NGO logics (Cottle and Nolan 2007). While I agree with this critique, the fact of the matter is that the dynamics of the journalistic field, to which the human rights NGO field is subordinate in the news-making relationship, increasingly require this of sources. The practical implication of this critique for NGOs is that they withdraw from the melee in disdain — which is self-defeating, not only for each NGO's purposes but also for the wider societal goals of pluralism and accountability. Given limited resources, NGOs inevitably will face decisions about which types of information subsidies to prioritize. It may make sense to prioritize investing in source-credibility information subsidies — and not just because, unlike commercialized-content information subsidies, they do not threaten NGOs' logics. This is also because my evidence indicates that source credibility is a journalist's first hurdle for the assessment of newsworthiness (McPherson 2012). Investing in content information subsidies without suitably investing in demonstrations of source credibility may therefore be ineffective.

The case developed in this article is specifically about a number of Mexican human rights NGOs. As mentioned above, human rights and journalistic fields' concerns with credibility have been documented in a variety of cases, and this argument would therefore benefit from being tested in other settings. Still, its theoretical focus on credibility and communication in the public sphere may shed light on the broader context of political transition in Mexico and elsewhere. Transitions from authoritarian rule tend to be characterized by the liberalizing of the state, which widens access to rights and to the public sphere — often conciliatory gestures in a misguided attempt to hold onto power. An explosion of civil society rushes in to fill this space, including human rights organizations and news outlets (O'Donnell and Schmitter 2013). We can also understand this transition of a state that quashes dissenters to one that tolerates them as a transition from a monopoly on public credibility to its decentralization. From this perspective, the keen concern with credibility we saw among Mexican human rights defenders and journalists may reflect not only the general importance of credibility to advocacy and journalism. It may also be part and parcel of a scramble for the previously inaccessible and precious resource of public credibility. Thinking about how public credibility is distributed and denied — via, for example, the discrediting discourses about human rights organizations propagated by some Mexican government officials — highlights another dimension of the dynamics of political transition. The credibility behind the communications of civil society actors may have significant impacts on transitions, such as the spread of the human rights "justice cascade" in Latin America (Lutz and Sikkink 2001).

Furthermore, thinking about the communicators and recipients of information as having information logics — logics whose differences can be addressed via information subsidies that are correlated with resources — also benefits future research about communicating across field boundaries. This framework yields insight on the potential of digital direct-to-citizen communications, a significant trend in today's human rights communication, for pluralism and accountability in the public sphere. Earlier research indicates that resources may matter even more when online communication enters the NGO toolkit (Fenton 2010; Thrall, Stecula, and Sweet 2014). Without the credibility endorsement that comes with being a mainstream media source, we can imagine that human rights NGOs need to build up credibility directly with audiences. This may prove more difficult, as audiences do not all belong to the same field and are, therefore, located and motivated differentially. It may well be that understanding communication as facilitated by the information subsidy of source credibility will reveal yet another way in which digital technologies do not level the communications playing field.

Notes

1. The empirical findings in this article form part of the media ethnography I conducted of human rights reporting in Mexico in 2006. For several months, I shadowed the human rights beat at two of Mexico's highest-circulation newspapers, *La Jornada* and *El Universal*. In addition to this participant observation of newsrooms and of journalist-source interactions, I collected artifacts and conducted 26 in-depth, semi-structured interviews with human rights reporters and 26 further interviews with their editors at national and regional newspapers. I also interviewed 18 human rights defenders assigned communication roles at their organizations, which included local and national NGOs, umbrella NGOs that served to network NGOs across the country, and government human rights commissions. The information in this article is largely based on the latter interviews. In general, my interview guides covered the following: how interviewees saw their workplaces, their collaborators and competitors, and their roles; how they understood human rights and human rights newsworthiness; what influenced the decisions they made about human rights information and what these decisions were; what conflicts they faced and how they faced them; and what had happened in the past and what they expected of the future with respect to this sort of reporting. Interviewees were all offered anonymity, and though most elected nonanonymous interviews, I have chosen in most cases to preserve their anonymity. I transcribed and translated these interviews and conducted thematic analysis on them as well as on my field notes and the artifacts.
2. Verification subsidies exist in a variety of forms; another type highly relevant to the use of digital reports from civilian witnesses in human rights fact finding is the inclusion of metadata with these reports. This refers to data about this information — such as time, place, and source of production — that facilitate the information's corroboration (McPherson 2015b).
3. Interview date: August 2, 2006.
4. Interview date: August 2, 2006.
5. Interview date: July 4, 2006.
6. Interview date: July 5, 2006.
7. Interview date: August 2, 2006.
8. Interview date: July 4, 2006.
9. Interview date: July 5, 2006.
10. Interview date: July 5, 2006.
11. Interview date: July 31, 2006.
12. Interview date: July 12, 2006.
13. Interview date: July 5, 2006.
14. Interview date: July 12, 2006.
15. Interview date: July 31, 2006.
16. Interview date: July 5, 2006.

17. Interview date: July 4, 2006.
18. Interview date: July 31, 2006.
19. Interview date: May 14, 2006.
20. Interview date: July 13, 2006.
21. Interview date: June 26, 2006.
22. Interview date: July 5, 2006.
23. Interview date: July 31, 2006.
24. Interview date: July 4, 2006.
25. Interview date: July 5, 2006.
26. Interview date: July 31, 2006.
27. Interview date: July 31, 2006.
28. Interview date: July 31, 2006.
29. Interview date: July 4, 2006.
30. Interview date: August 2, 2006.
31. Interview date: July 4, 2006.
32. Interview date: July 31, 2006.
33. Interview date: July 4, 2006.
34. Interview date: July 13, 2006.
35. Interview date: July 13, 2006.
36. Interview date: June 22, 2006.
37. Interview date: July 11, 2006.
38. Interview date: July 5, 2006.
39. Interview date: August 2, 2006.

Funding

This work was supported by the Economic and Social Research Council (Grant no. ES/K009850/1), the Isaac Newton Trust, and the Gates Cambridge Trust.

References

ACOSTA, Mariclaire. (1994, July 17) El Sexenio Salinista y los derechos humanos. *Reforma*, Enfoque 14.

AGUAYO QUEZADA, Sergio, and PARRA ROSALES, Luz Paula. (1997) *Las Organizaciones No Gubernamentales de Derechos Humanos en México: Entre La Democracia Participativa y La Electoral* (Mexico City, DF: Academia Mexicana de Derechos Humanos).

AMNESTY INTERNATIONAL. (2001, December 10) *Mexico: Daring to raise their voices*. [Online]. Available: https://www.amnesty.org/en/documents/amr41/040/2001/en/ [2 May 2016].

ATACK, Iain. (1999) Four criteria of development NGO legitimacy. *World Development*, 27(5), 855–864.

BECKER, Howard S. (1967) Whose side are we on? *Social Problems*, 14(3), 239–247.

BOURDIEU, Pierre. (1983) The field of cultural production, or: The economic world reversed. *Poetics*, 12(4–5): 311–356.

BOURDIEU, Pierre. (1986) The forms of capital. In *Handbook of Theory and Research for the Sociology of Education*, John E. Richardson (ed.) (New York: Greenwood Press).

BOURDIEU, Pierre. (1993) *The Field of Cultural Production: Essays on Art and Literature* (New York: Columbia University Press).

BOURDIEU, Pierre. (1998) *On Television* (New York: The New Press).

BROWN, L. David. (2008) *Creating Credibility* (Sterling, VA: Kumarian Press, Inc.).

BRYSK, Alison. (1994) *The Politics of Human Rights in Argentina: Protest, Change, and Democratization* (Stanford, CA: Stanford University Press).

CARLSON, Matt, and FRANKLIN, Bob. (2011) Introduction. In *Journalists, Sources, and Credibility*, Bob Franklin, and Matt Carlson (eds.) (New York: Routledge).

COMUNICACIÓN E INFORMACIÓN DE LA MUJER AC. (2004) *Estrategias de Comunicación Y Visibilidad Para Las Organizaciones de La Sociedad Civil* (Mexico City, DF: Comunicación e Información de la Mujer AC).

COTTLE, Simon, and NOLAN, David. (2007) Global humanitarianism and the changing aid-media field: Everyone was dying for footage. *Journalism Studies*, 8(6), 862–878.

DÜTTING, Gisela, and SOGGE, David. (2010) Building safety nets in the global politic: NGO collaboration for solidarity and sustainability. *Development*, 53(3), 350–355.

FENTON, Natalie. (2010) NGOs, new media and the mainstream news: News from everywhere. In *New Media, Old News: Journalism & Democracy in the Digital Age*, Natalie Fenton (ed.) (London: Sage Publications Ltd.).

FRANKLIN, Bob, and CARLSON, Matt. (eds.). (2011) *Journalists, Sources, and Credibility: New Perspectives* (New York: Routledge).

GANDY, Oscar H. (1982) *Beyond Agenda Setting: Information Subsidies and Public Policy* (Norwood, NJ: Ablex).

GIBELMAN, Margaret, and GELMAN, Sheldon R. (2004) A loss of credibility: Patterns of wrongdoing among nongovernmental organizations. *Voluntas: International Journal of Voluntary and Nonprofit Organizations*, 15(4), 355–381.

GLOBAL POLICY FORUM. (2012) Credibility and legitimacy of NGOs. *Global Policy Forum*. [Online]. Available: https://www.globalpolicy.org/ngos/introduction/credibility-and-legitimacy.html [2 May 2016].

HARDIN, Russell. (2002) *Trust and Trustworthiness* (New York: Russell Sage Foundation).

HOPGOOD, Stephen. (2006) *Keepers of the Flame: Understanding Amnesty International* (Ithaca, NY: Cornell University Press).

HUGHES, Sallie. (2006) *Newsrooms in Conflict: Journalism and the Democratization of Mexico* (Pittsburgh, PA: University of Pittsburgh Press).

HUMAN RIGHTS WATCH. (2013) *Our History*. [Online]. Available: http://www.hrw.org/node/75134 [2 May 2016].

KECK, Margaret E., and SIKKINK, Kathryn. (1998) *Activists Beyond Borders: Advocacy Networks in International Politics* (Ithaca, NY: Cornell University Press).

LAND, Molly. (2009) Networked activism. *Harvard Human Rights Journal*, 22(2), 205–243.

LAWSON, Chappell. (2000) Mexico's unfinished transition: Democratization and authoritarian enclaves in Mexico. *Mexican Studies / Estudios Mexicanos*, 16(2), 267–287.

LAWSON, Chappell. (2002) *Building the Fourth Estate: Democratization and the Rise of a Free Press in Mexico* (Berkeley, CA: University of California Press).

LEHMANN, David, and BEBBINGTON, Anthony. (1998) NGOs, the state and the development process: The dilemmas of institutionalization. In *The Changing Role of the State in Latin America*, Menno Vellinga (ed.) (Boulder, CO: Westview Press).

LUTZ, Ellen, and SIKKINK, Kathryn. (2001) The justice cascade: The evolution and impact of foreign human rights trials in Latin America. *Chicago Journal of International Law*, 2(1), 1–33.

MANNING, Paul. (2001) *News and News Sources: A Critical Introduction* (London: Sage Publications).

MCLAGAN, Meg. (2006) Introduction: Making human rights claims public. *American Anthropologist*, 108(1), 191–195.

MCPHERSON, Ella. (2012) Spot news versus reportage: Newspaper models, the distribution of newsroom credibility, and implications for democratic journalism in Mexico. *International Journal of Communication*, 6, 2301–2317.

MCPHERSON, Ella. (2015a) Advocacy organizations' evaluation of social media information for NGO journalism: The evidence and engagement models. *American Behavioral Scientist*, 59(1), 124–148.

MCPHERSON, Ella. (2015b) Digital human rights reporting by civilian witnesses: Surmounting the verification barrier. In *Produsing Theory in a Digital World 2.0: The Intersection of Audiences and Production in Contemporary Theory*, Rebecca Ann Lind (ed.) (New York: Peter Lang Publishing).

O'DONNELL, Guillermo, and SCHMITTER, Philippe C. (2013) *Transitions from Authoritarian Rule: Tentative Conclusions about Uncertain Democracies*, new edition (Baltimore, MD: Johns Hopkins University Press).

ORENTLICHER, Diane F. (1990) Bearing witness: The art and science of human rights fact-finding. *Harvard Human Rights Journal*, 3, 83–136.

ORGAD, Shani. (2013) Visualizers of solidarity: Organizational politics in humanitarian and international development NGOs. *Visual Communication*, 12(3), 295–314.

POWERS, Matthew. (2014) The structural organization of NGO publicity work: Explaining divergent publicity strategies at humanitarian and human rights organizations. *International Journal of Communication*, 8, 90–107.

POWERS, Matthew. (2015a) Contemporary NGO-journalist relations: Reviewing and evaluating an emergent area of research. *Sociology Compass*, 9(6), 427–437.

POWERS, Matthew. (2015b) NGOs as journalistic entities: The possibilities, promises and limits of boundary crossing. In *Boundaries of Journalism: Professionalism, Practices and Participation*, Matt Carlson, and Seth C. Lewis (eds.) (Abingdon, UK: Routledge).

POWERS, Matthew. (2015c) The new boots on the ground: NGOs in the changing landscape of international news. *Journalism*. Advance online publication. doi:10.1177/1464884914568077.

POWERS, Matthew. (2016a) Beyond boon or bane: Using normative theories to evaluate the newsmaking efforts of NGOs. *Journalism Studies*. Advance online publication. doi:10.1080/1461670X.2015.1124733.

POWERS, Matthew. (2016b) Opening the news gates? Humanitarian and human rights NGOs in the US news media, 1990–2010. *Media, Culture & Society*, 38(3), 315–331.

REICH, Zvi. (2011) Source credibility and journalism: Between visceral and discretional judgment. *Journalism Practice*, 5(1), 51–67.

SCHLESINGER, Philip. (1990) Rethinking the sociology of journalism: Source strategies and the limits of media-centrism. In *Public Communication: The New Imperatives*, Marjorie Ferguson (ed.) (London: Sage Publications).

SIKKINK, Kathryn. (1993) Human rights, principled issue-networks, and sovereignty in Latin America. *International Organization*, 47(3), 411–441.

THOMPSON, John B. (2000) *Political Scandal: Power and Visibility in the Media Age* (Cambridge, UK: Polity Press).

THOMPSON, John B. (2010) *Merchants of Culture* (Cambridge, UK: Polity).

THRALL, A. Trevor, STECULA, Dominik, and SWEET, Diana. (2014) May we have your attention please? Human-rights NGOs and the problem of global communication. *The International Journal of Press/Politics*, 19(2), 135–159.

WAISBORD, Silvio. (2006) In journalism we trust? Credibility and fragmented journalism in Latin America. In *Mass Media and Political Communication in New Democracies*, Katrin Voltmer (ed.) (London: Routledge).

WAISBORD, Silvio. (2011) Can NGOs change the news? *International Journal of Communication*, 5, 142–165.

WRIGHT, Kate. (2015) "These grey areas," How and why freelance work blurs INGOs and news organizations. *Journalism Studies*. Advance online publication. doi:10.1080/1461670X.2015.1036904.

WRIGHT, Kate. (2016) Moral economies: Interrogating the interactions of nongovernmental organizations, journalists, and freelancers. *International Journal of Communication*, 10, 1510–1529.

The rise of eyewitness video and its implications for human rights: Conceptual and methodological approaches

Sandra Ristovska

University of Pennsylvania

ABSTRACT
The advent of visual technologies and digital media has elevated the status of images as an important platform for studying human rights. Focusing on eyewitness video as an increasingly central vehicle through which human rights claims are made public, this article maps out (1) how human rights organizations utilize eyewitness video as an investigative tool in their advocacy work, (2) how eyewitness video configures within global news crises coverage, and (3) how eyewitness footage operates as a form of legal evidence in courtrooms. In doing so, the article proposes a conceptual framework that accommodates the unfolding role of eyewitness video at the crossroad of the cultural, political, and legal mechanisms that together ferret out human rights violations. The article also suggests that new developments in ethnography provide fruitful methodological grounds for studying the relationship between visual media and human rights from within the institutional networks that render images meaningful.

The international human rights movement developed during the 1970s not only as a result of Cold War politics, various civil rights movements, and the boom of nongovernmental organizations but also because of the information revolution happening at that time (Neire 2013). Information is the oxygen of the human rights movement; thus, it is not surprising that human rights advocates have been early adopters of new technologies. As technologies shape the material relay of knowledge, they are intimately connected to the ways in which the public learns about and remembers atrocities. Visual technologies, in particular, have facilitated the production of wide-ranging imagery, generating public discussions about the notion of human rights itself. According to Sharon Sliwinski:

> [T]he very recognition of what we call human rights is inextricably bound to an aesthetic experience. The conception of rights did not emerge from the abstract articulation of an inalienable human dignity but rather from a particular visual encounter with atrocity. (2011: 58)

Surveying different visual images of the earthquake in Lisbon in 1755 and the genocides in Congo, Bosnia, Rwanda, and the Holocaust centuries later, Sliwinski argues that it was the *sight* of suffering that shaped an active international debate about what it meant to be human and the nature of global empathy, even before the concept of human rights emerged in global politics. Indeed, the United Nations General Assembly adopted the Universal Declaration of Human Rights in 1948 in the echo of the mass circulation of photographs depicting the horrors of the Holocaust.

The assumption that we need complete visual records of atrocities lingers in longstanding and diverse human rights practices. Despite the premise that "seeing is believing" (and, in turn, ends wrongdoings), the production and circulation of such visual evidence has simply left us with more crimes to witness. Human rights claims continue to be represented and articulated through various visual media, each burdened with the hope of providing more compelling evidence, more reasons to demand action and policy change, and less ground to forget. From engravings, photographs, film, and video to satellite and other aerial images, the visual in its multiple manifestations remains a critical tool and platform through which human rights witnessing takes place.

There is indeed an established scholarly tradition that examines images in the context of humanitarian communication: how visuals mobilize publics on human rights issues (e.g., Torchin 2012), and how they position the viewer—often situated in the West—in moral engagement with a victim of human rights abuse—often in the Global South—generating (or not) cosmopolitan solidarity (e.g., Boltanski 1999; Chouliaraki 2006, 2013). In the current media moment, however, the rise of digital video has brought human rights activists, human rights abuse victims, journalists, and legal professionals into greater proximity, extending the spaces and practices within which we usually associate images. As a result, the current entanglement between visual media and human rights provides new possibilities and challenges for further engagement with human rights issues. At the core of this article, then, is a call to consider visuals a platform that cuts across various mechanisms that investigate, document and present human rights claims in order to bring relief to the victims of violations and abuses.

Alongside the advent of social media, recent technological advances enhancing mobile phones with cameras and easy Bluetooth and Internet connectivity have democratized image-making processes, propelling video to the forefront of public culture. These changes have incited scholars, journalists, and technology experts to proclaim "the second Gutenberg shift" (Kelly 2008: para. 3), the visual as "the king in the digital era" (Schiappa 2015), and "the video revolution" (Sasseen 2012). The unfolding of the Arab Spring uprisings in the Middle East, the Black Lives Matter movement in the United States, and the Syrian refugee crisis in Europe are recent reminders of the prevalence of digital video in uncovering human rights violations and humanitarian crises around the world. Human rights advocates believe that "video provides so much detail that is very powerful in many cases" (C. Koettl 2015, pers. comm., July 22). Indeed, video has been considered a powerful tool for social change in dominant human rights discourses ever since George Holiday documented the police brutality against Rodney King in Los Angeles in 1991. WITNESS, a New York-based human rights organization that specializes in video advocacy, considers the idea of the "accidental witness," epitomized by the amateur recording of the beating of Rodney King, as its founding story. Ryan Kautz, Senior Video Producer and Editor at WITNESS, explains that in the contemporary moment:

> People are gravitating towards video. Everyone uploads clips on YouTube, and I think people get the idea that, you know "bad stuff is happening, I have a camera, I should film that and put that out to the world." So, I think that almost everyone working in human rights now sees the effectiveness of video and probably had for a long time but the technology hasn't been as accessible. (2015, pers. comm., July 2)

As news media have long been an important vehicle for broader public engagement with human rights issues, activists' abilities to visualize injustice have been central to successful news access. With the proliferation of visual technologies, however, the concern that media underreport human rights stories due to a lack of accompanying audio-visual materials (International Council on Human Rights Policy 2002) has evolved into a concern about the ability of news media to properly assess and use the abundance of online video with a human rights focus (Sasseen 2012). This blending of the visual with global human rights claims means that images often dictate "which violences are redeemed and which get recognized" (McLagan 2006: 191). In particular, videos captured by bystanders, accidental witnesses, and activists perform the eyewitness function in human rights advocacy, news reporting, and trial proceedings. Therefore, this article argues that video is rising in importance as a platform worth studying when tackling contemporary human rights issues. In choosing to refer to these materials as "eyewitness videos" as opposed to other terms (e.g., citizen videos, user-generated content, or amateur images), I follow a line of scholarship that theorizes the interplay between technology and the professional, political, and institutional ambiguity associated with these visuals (Al-Ghazzi 2014; Mortensen 2014).

By highlighting how the unfolding shape of video is at the crossroads of witnessing in advocacy, journalism, and law, this article shows how visual meaning-making permeates what we recognize as a human rights violation in the current media moment. The article maps out (1) how human rights organizations utilize eyewitness video as an investigative tool in their advocacy work, (2) how eyewitness video becomes embroiled within global news crises coverage, and (3) how eyewitness footage operates as a form of legal evidence in courtrooms. In doing so, it demonstrates how eyewitness video is becoming an investigative tool, a mode of information relay, and a form of evidence on its own terms. Arguing that attentiveness to images and the networks that set them in motion is valuable to the study of human rights, the article proposes a conceptual framework that looks across the technological, cultural, political, and legal frames that delineate, support or challenge the potential of visuals in achieving human rights. Methodologically, it shows that new developments in ethnography provide fruitful grounds for engaging with the interpretative forces and institutional spaces that define the role of eyewitness video in human rights work. Specifically, it discusses how the concept of *thin description* (Jackson 2013) offers a possibility to study human rights from within the very information networks that render eyewitness videos meaningful.

Eyewitness video in advocacy

There is a long history of the uses of images in humanitarian advocacy to raise public awareness of human rights offenses around the world in order to stop them. The current media moment, however, has turned images into an important tool for gathering evidence. Human rights advocacy organizations, such as Amnesty International (hereafter Amnesty) and Human Rights Watch (HRW), increasingly utilize eyewitness video in their research and advocacy efforts. Eyewitness footage has become a valuable investigative tool that can trigger a human rights inquiry, can serve as a piece of evidence or can corroborate other evidentiary materials. Christoph Koettl (2013), Emergency Response Manager at Amnesty, believes that eyewitness video can be an important tool for gathering evidence in war crime investigations, particularly around the treatment of and direct attacks against civilians. Moreover, in his view, "video can be especially powerful in connection with digital social networks [because] that's the way to raise awareness in an environment where others don't have access to" media (2015, pers. comm., July 22). In Syria, for example, where an international presence is highly limited, the methodology of several reports by Amnesty, HRW, and the United Nations Commission of Inquiry includes eyewitness video obtained through social media as an evidentiary tool to establish the government's use of barrel bombs and chemical weapons against civilians (Amnesty International 2015; Human Rights Watch 2014; Independent International Commission of Inquiry on the Syrian Arab Republic 2015).

The advent of eyewitness video is thus shaping the workflow of human rights organizations. Both HRW and Amnesty have image analysts on staff. Josh Lyons, Satellite Imagery Analyst at HRW, explains why his organization is expanding its technical capacity in response to the recent avalanche of eyewitness videos:

> It is not as if video was never considered to be a source of potential evidentiary material, or that it wouldn't be relevant to a human rights investigation. It was just [that previously it was] a very exotic and hard to come by source of information. The fact that it's now a ubiquitous form of data, that in most cases we would need to work with, changes the approach from an ad hoc best effort basis towards an obligation to have a professional methodology and workflow that can be scaled across the organization. (2015, pers. comm., August 19)

Similarly, Amnesty started training its field researchers in video-assessment techniques, which are becoming "a standard set of skills" (C. Koettl, 2015, pers. comm., July 22). Best practices for eyewitness video include authenticating the location, time, and source and cross-referencing the content of the video with on-the-ground investigation, personal testimonies, and satellite images. In this sense, video forensics is becoming an essential skill to master in order to facilitate the rigorous accounting of human rights violations.

Although WITNESS is a small organization that does not engage in research and advocacy on the scale of Amnesty and HRW, it is also a prominent player in the visual human rights landscape. Sameer Padania, former technology expert at WITNESS, remembers how within the organization, "there was an understanding from the beginning that eyewitness footage is important" (2015, pers. comm., July 28). The organization has featured eyewitness video on multiple platforms, seeking to establish verification and ethical standards in this field since 2007 when it launched its first online curatorial space, *The Hub*. Although the potential of eyewitness video was not widely recognized at the time, its status has changed. Video's ability to harness the voices of marginalized communities and victims of human rights abuses is gradually accepted by journalists and political actors. Raja Althaibani, Middle East and North Africa Program Coordinator at WITNESS, states the following:

> Citizen video is most useful when it's coming from communities that are marginalized, isolated, from areas that are hard to reach, areas too dangerous to really enter as a foreigner. Citizen videos are [thus] an extremely important tool and type of media that carries information that can be extremely critical for journalists and human rights stakeholders. (2015, pers. comm., August 8)

As a result, WITNESS works on platforms, tools, and strategies for effective and safe use of eyewitness video in human rights advocacy. On-the-ground and online trainings, video guides, and tools are intended to assist activists around the world in capturing more easily verifiable videos that can be of use to human rights investigators, journalists, and lawyers. There has even been an investment in developing custom technology to streamline these processes further: CameraV, a smart-phone-based verification app developed by WITNESS and The Guardian Project, for example, is the latest in a series of human rights apps that captures encrypted metadata—such as time, GPS coordinates, light, and temperature—to facilitate video authentication.

Surveying how eyewitness video figures into the advocacy work of Amnesty, HRW, and WITNESS illuminates why human rights scholars need to account for the role of visuals beyond their simple consideration as a supplement to the written record, used only in campaigns to mobilize public support on a human rights issue. The work of these organizations shows how video has become an important tool and platform for human rights advocacy on its own terms. By incorporating eyewitness video as a standard feature of their investigative toolkit and by developing and promoting verification and ethical measures for these videos, human rights advocacy groups are emerging as prominent stakeholders who assert interpretative expertise over unfolding forms of traumatic imagery. Mastering eyewitness video-assessment techniques to uncover violations, especially from inaccessible conflict areas, helps these organizations legitimize human rights claims in the public realm. Therefore, the purchase of eyewitness video to human rights advocacy merits scholarly engagement.

Eyewitness video in news reporting

Words have long held a privileged place in journalism. Images have been positioned "in a supportive role to words, where the verbal record underpinning journalists' authority as arbiters of the real world takes precedence over its visual counterpart" (Zelizer 2010: 3). The superiority of words has been premised on their ability to provide information and evidence, fostering public deliberations. Yet, in a highly visual information landscape, journalism is gradually—though reluctantly—embracing the potential of eyewitness videos to offer initial coverage of or provide key data for difficult news events otherwise inaccessible to journalists reporting on site.

The growing prevalence of eyewitness video in crises coverage that we have observed over the last few years stems from a longstanding news pattern: a pronounced turn to visuals when written or verbal records are insufficient to capture the complexities of traumatic occurrences (Zelizer 1998, 2010). What is changing is the kind of visual content being used, subsequently producing the need for standards on how to handle it. In a time when "reaching for one's smartphone during an emergency is quickly becoming the norm for those living in the digital age" (Bock 2014: 349), journalists feature videos produced by bystanders, accidental witnesses, and activists (even terrorist groups and perpetrators of violence) when other images are unavailable. For Malachy Browne, former News Editor at Storyful, the first social media news agency:

> [Eyewitness video] is most valuable to journalists in a big breaking news story in those 30-minutes when the professional camera isn't there…where correspondents might not be available…[or in remote areas when] it's telling the story of people who are utterly removed or basically forgotten by mainstream media. (2015, pers. comm., July 21)

Myanmar (Burma), a country characterized by strict censorship regulations and restricted (foreign) news reporting until 2011, epitomizes the potential of eyewitness video to tell stories from the periphery of media attention. Western media covered the country's Saffron Revolution of 2007 using videos shot by activists—who were part of the Democratic Voice of Burma and WITNESS's network—risking their lives to document the uprisings and the military crackdowns on the peaceful demonstrations (Brough and Li 2013).

Eyewitness footage often overlaps with the spaces long associated with human rights activists. Yomna Kamel (2014) argues that global reporting on war and conflict is frequently driven by local activists who use new media platforms to reach international news organizations and to gain visibility for their causes. In her view, activist reporting on social media during the Tunisian and Egyptian revolutions helped put the "revolutions' stories on the news agenda" (Kamel 2014: 232). Journalists use eyewitness video because it fosters instantaneous information gathering (Anden-Papadopoulos and Pantti 2011) and facilitates coverage from areas with limited international news presence. In such instances, these videos perform the eyewitness function of journalism. According to Gavin Sheridan, former Innovation Director at Storyful:

> Editorially, I think, the core principle is that journalists can't be everywhere all the time. There are only so many journalists in the world and that number is actually decreasing. So, what you have is vicarious sensors, humans who carry around cameras in their pockets that are probably connected to the Internet. So, they will just go about their daily lives doing things and then they will witness things and take a video…the editorial value is often in that kind of bearing witness [purpose]. (2015, pers. comm., June 30)

Eyewitness videos, then, allow access to spaces beyond the scope of traditional news and journalistic sources.

Valued for their witnessing potential, eyewitness videos can shape, affirm, complement, challenge or offset mainstream news content. The human rights implications of the rise of eyewitness video in journalism are twofold. On the one hand, eyewitness videos have the ability to influence news agendas; they can propel human rights stories to the forefront of public debate, as we have seen in the case of Syria. Even US Secretary of State, John Kerry, cited eyewitness videos when briefing on the administration's response about the chemical attacks from August 2013 (Fisher 2013). On the other hand, the ability to navigate through the ever-growing repository of eyewitness videos can be either challenged by the sheer abundance of (often difficult to authenticate) content or remain dependent upon journalistic and geopolitical framings. As Omar Al-Ghazzi (2015) argues, the virality of amateur videos coming out of Syria is implicated in global politics and remains closely tied to the gatekeeping role of journalists through their selection of which news stories receive mainstream publicity. Examining a 2015 social media campaign entitled "Planet Syria Sends a Signal to Earth," Al-Ghazzi shows the ways in which Syrian activists produce videos that sarcastically protest how the world has forgotten their plight. This case acutely reminds us of the struggle for visibility in a crowded media landscape: while ISIS videos continue to get ample attention by Western publics and governments, many eyewitness videos that document human rights offenses are only a small part of the ever-proliferating Internet archive.

Activists are not the only ones facing challenges. When using eyewitness videos, journalists struggle how to look for and verify content. For Sheridan, the primary challenge from an editorial standpoint is the following:

> Finding the best content in a swathe of [a] large amount of content and then testing it for its news value and applying manual techniques to verify the material. To be honest, technology helps a lot [with the verification process]…it's essentially leveraging technology to contextualize events. (2015, pers. comm., June 30)

Technological tools help identify the source of the video as well as spatial and temporal markers, but the content is also triangulated with other sources of information and eyewitness testimonies. Browne describes this process as:

good old-fashioned "checking your source," checking that the story fits and all of the facts stand up. It's really a traditional journalism…it's applied to a different age or a different technology. Now, there are some things that you need to learn, but they aren't rocket science…you're asking the same questions just in a different way. (2015, pers. comm., July 21)

Another challenge is how to publish/broadcast eyewitness footage in a way that takes into consideration the personal safety and individual rights of the video-maker, as news organizations have a responsibility to protect and support the producers of eyewitness footage (Wardle et al. 2014).

Despite eyewitness video's potential to serve as an evidence-gathering tool for investigative journalism and a mode of information relay in its own right, visual news standards for these materials are lacking (Wardle et al. 2014). On the one hand, journalists are generally reluctant to embrace new technologies (Singer 2004; Boczkowski 2005). On the other hand, the utilization of eyewitness video in news demands financial and human resources (R. Tsubaki 2015, pers. comm., August 3), which are becoming scarce in rapidly diminishing newsrooms. Different actors have thus emerged, seeking to address the lack of formalized journalistic principles for handling eyewitness footage, such as improper credit, label and fact-checking, as well as the underused potential of these materials for investigative journalism.

Storyful, Bellingcat, Eyewitness Media Hub, Reported.ly, and Verification Junkie are among the pioneers in the field and form part of the newly established Google News Lab's First Draft Coalition, created to facilitate a conversation around the ethics, practice, and legal obligations of using eyewitness media in news reporting. The purpose of this coalition is to provide training, resources, and tools for journalists. What is particularly noteworthy about Google's new venture is how human rights work is intrinsically folded in. The Arab Spring uprisings, for example, were central to much of Storyful's early reporting, and the investigative work of Bellingcat continually involves stories about human rights violations. Browne, now with Reported.ly, nodded to this synthesis, explaining that "there's a lot of overlap in the type of news that I'm interested in and what human rights workers deal with" (2015, pers. comm., July 21). In addition, human rights advocates from WITNESS and Amnesty work alongside entrepreneurial journalists on verification measures. They were featured in a two-part verification handbook by the European Journalism Center together with a few of the First Draft Coalition's eyewitness media experts (see Silverman 2014, 2015).

The rise of eyewitness video in journalism shows how visual meaning-making has also become central to international news reporting. Images, long relegated secondary to words and used predominantly to complement the news story, are now important data or central pieces of evidence. As eyewitness video provides a meeting point for journalism and human rights in the context of global crises, it becomes an important lens through which to illuminate the practices and processes that legitimize and disseminate human rights information in the public realm.

Eyewitness video in the courtroom

Law, like journalism, has built its authority on words, not images. It used to consider film "as an alien, disruptive element in the courtroom" (Schwartz 2009: 15). Yet, the law has also shifted towards visual communication by admitting certain uses of video as evidence, testimony, confession, closing argument, settlement, and even as an audio-visual record of legal proceedings. It is not surprising, then, that the 2000s marked a profound attentiveness to images by legal scholars. As evidenced by literature on modern visual evidence (Joseph 2014), visual legal advocacy (Austin 2006), victim impact videos (Austin 2010), videotaped confessions (Silbey 2006), camera witnessing (Delage 2014), visual jurisprudence (Feigenson and Spiesel 2009; Feigenson 2014; Sherwin 2011), and visual legal pedagogy (Sherwin et al. 2007), "law awakens from its dogmatic slumber upon contact with the flesh of the world, and the skin of the image" (Sherwin 2012: 141). The role of eyewitness images in legal environments is a growing area of research and practice. According to Lawrence Krasner (2014), a civil rights attorney based in Philadelphia, mobile video, for example, has become a central component of criminal law. In his view, cell phones are among the most crucial advances in criminal justice since DNA because they have democratized the gathering of evidence by enabling citizens to easily take pictures. Eyewitness video is "an enormous development in terms of the potential for real justice" (cited in Denvir 2013: para. 6).

Although the belief that video tells the truth is deeply ingrained, the recent proliferation of video documentation does not necessarily result in justice or accountability. Kelly Matheson, Senior Attorney and Program Manager at WITNESS, believes that:

> Video can be an incredibly powerful tool for telling the truth. It hasn't yet become a powerful tool for accountability. We know, as a public, that Eric Garner was held in an illegal chokehold by a police officer…that is absolutely clear from the verified video. We also know from the forensics report that corroborates the video that the impartial cause for his death was that illegal chokehold, but the officer was not indicted…so I see spaces and places where video does an excellent job of truth telling, but the batting average is not as high when it comes to accountability. (2015, pers. comm., July 22)

The distinct rhetorical strategies employed by the prosecution and the defense that framed the meaning of the Rodney King tape in the courtroom was an early lesson about "the struggle for interpretative dominance" (Nichols 1994: 18) over an image's evidentiary quality, raising now familiar questions about the entanglement of racial politics and visuality and its implications for social justice.

The history of eyewitness image use in human rights courts is as old as the legal framing of the concept of human rights itself post-WWII. Images—used with varying degrees—were part of the evidentiary display in the Holocaust trials. Films, for example, played a central role in the Nuremberg Trials. In his opening statement, Justice Robert H. Jackson, the chief US prosecutor, insisted on the unique value of the visual as a legal evidence, referring to the eyewitness footage shot by the Nazis:

> We will not ask you to convict these men on the testimonies of their faults. There's no court in the indictment that cannot be proved by books and other records. We will show you their own films, you will see their own conduct and hear their own voices. (Nuremberg: Its Lessons for Today 2009)

Since Nuremberg, eyewitness videos have become a regular feature of the evidentiary panoply in human rights courtrooms. Despite the linkages made between the rise of eyewitness video and the global upheavals in the 2000s, such as the Green Revolution in Iran and the Arab Spring uprisings, eyewitness footage (shot on VHS tapes) marked earlier conflicts as well. The war in Bosnia two decades earlier, believed to be the most recorded and reported of all conflicts at that time (Gow et al. 1997), was also characterized by a range of eyewitness images, some of which were admitted as evidence at the International Criminal Tribunal for the former

Yugoslavia (ICTY). What is changing is the sheer volume of such materials that contemporary courts need to tackle. Therefore, the International Criminal Court (ICC) established a Scientific Advisory Board in June 2014 to advise the Office of the Prosecutor on new technological developments, of which eyewitness video shot on mobile media and circulated online is a component.

As efficacy in the realm of human rights is often measured by policy change or legal outcomes, the legal arena is important to study as an environment that renders eyewitness video meaningful. Looking at the legal space through a visual lens helps tackle the emerging patterns of visual forensics that solidify the admissibility of eyewitness video as evidence as well as the relationship between law and visuality more broadly.

An image's power, however, rests upon its conceptual and evidentiary features. Thus, any attempt to dissect its meaning inevitably leaves room for interpretation. In this sense, Thomas Keenan and Eyal Weizman write:

> forensics is not only about the science of investigation but rather about its presentation to the forum. Indeed there is an arduous labor of truth-construction embodied in the notion of forensics, one that is conducted with all sorts of scientific, rhetorical, theatrical and visual mechanisms. It is in the gesture, techniques, and truth of demonstration, whether poetic, dramatic, or narrative, that forensic aesthetics can make things appear in the world. (2011: para. 21)

The proliferation of images inside the courtroom, then, necessitates unpacking the assumptions about images working as evidence as well as the narrative strategies and mechanisms for authentication of visual materials that shape evolving forms of human rights practices.

Conceptual and methodological approaches

The rise of eyewitness video in today's digital environment has influenced the work of human rights advocacy organizations, journalists, and legal professionals. Visual forensics is no longer a practice reserved for law-enforcement agencies. Activists, journalists, and civil society are also embracing this approach in order to navigate the profusion of visual information in the current media ecology. Interpreting images is becoming an essential skill within the struggles to unveil human rights offenses, to report on global crises, and to successfully present legal evidence. Therefore, human rights scholarship needs to accommodate the growing prevalence of the visual as a platform that provides intricate access to human rights abuses beyond the traditional views of images in humanitarian communication as a mere campaigning tool or a supplement to news reports. Attention to the role of eyewitness video within the context of human rights advocacy, journalism, and the law opens up fruitful conceptual and methodological possibilities for tracing how, when, and why visuals drive the recognition and restitution of human rights violations. According to McLagan and McKee:

> attention to images, their mode of circulation, and the platforms on which they are made public instantiate a different relationship between the aesthetics and the political in which the two are seen as mutually active on the constitution of political subjects. (2012: 18)

As a result, the conceptual focus on eyewitness videos as they move across social media, human rights reports, advocacy practices, news stories, and courtrooms sheds light on how human rights claims are made, legitimized, challenged, or given restitution.

The rise of images as a platform worth study in a human rights context also illuminates the responsiveness of the visual to different methodological interventions. Research on human rights lends itself easily to interdisciplinarity because it necessitates an examination of the moral, cultural, political, and legal means of achieving human rights globally. As images are at the crossroad where these forces meet, they are uniquely positioned to facilitate a wide range of methodological approaches to their study. Perhaps nowhere is the interpretative labor that goes into any engagement with images more readily available than in the case of eyewitness video, which gets embedded in evidentiary service to further the human rights mission by different stakeholders. Therefore, it is important to tackle eyewitness video from within the institutional networks that define its meaning and veracity. In what follows, the article discusses the affordances of ethnography, particularly the notion of *thin description* (Jackson 2013) as a methodological guide on how to examine the current relationship between visuals and human rights.

As a method that incorporates *experiencing, examining*, and *enquiring*, ethnography is a holistic approach, *a way of looking*, which takes cultural interpretation as its main purpose (Walcott 1999). Comprised mainly of fieldwork, participant observation and a range of interviewing techniques, ethnography is both a process and a product that offers empirically grounded and socially contextualized research. The notion of *thick description* (Geertz 1973), a symbolic interpretative mechanism for studying social phenomena through a cultural prism that details structures and meanings, has been the reign of ethnographic engagement as anthropology's central practice and episteme. However, in a global networked society (Castells 1996), where social phenomena are at once pervasive and dispersed, the partiality of any perspective becomes ever more visible. Anthropologists have responded by revisiting what ethnography can do in the context of the contemporary media landscape.

John Jackson's provocative concept of *thin description* calls for a "flat ethnography, where you slice into a world from different perspectives, scales, registers, and angles—all distinctively useful, valid and worthy of considerations" (2013: 16). Moving away from historic assumptions that ethnography can—or should—provide a complete account embedded in the concept of *thickness*, thin description, for Jackson, privileges dialogue. It engages intellectually with the vernacular of the communities and phenomena it seeks to understand and considers the complexities of current information flows. The advent of digital media, for example, has given ample opportunity for conversations across the academy and various subjects of scholarly pursuits. The ethnographer does not write in isolation, and there is no natural endpoint for fieldwork because the online sphere sheds light on various ongoing modes of self-expression and self-theorizing generated by the communities one studies. *Thin*, then, does not mean less substantial; instead, it usefully and fruitfully acknowledges the relativity and partiality that the notion of thick description elides. This methodological commitment, then, urges the ethnographer to be part of an active conversation with those who have stakes in the topic.

The application of the concept of *thin* to studying the relationship between eyewitness video and human rights is important on three levels: It offers a methodological accommodation for the partiality of the researcher's assessment; it encourages dialogue with various stakeholders who put images into service to human rights; and it recognizes the inevitably thin portrayals that any visual documentation carries. The particular and multiple positionalities of the researcher and image users are methodologically as relevant as the "flatness" of the visual. Despite popular understandings of visual imagery as a transparent medium, visual culture scholars have long shown how the production and reception of images are situated within cultural, social, and political relations. *Thinness* is a testimony to the incompleteness of any visual record despite the urge to operationalize its status as an undeniable portrayal of the real. Studying how eyewitness video shapes the recognition and restitution of human rights claims through the methodological affordances of thin description urges the researcher to look at the various platforms that render images meaningful as a way of epistemologically claiming the partiality of visual documentation without falling into the trap of totalizing discourses. Thin description thus draws attention to the agents, spaces, and processes through which images broadly, and eyewitness videos specifically, are inscribed with truth claims and human rights significance.

The ethos of thin description was in part foreshadowed in the critical interventions in ethnography proposed by Annelise Riles (2006). In her view, globalizing processes generate networks of institutions, knowledge practices, and multiple artifacts; in turn, modern anthropology often shares the interests, passions, and challenges of the subjects it pursues. In this way, scholarly research, although speaking from a different position, is inevitably part of an enduring and direct dialogue with other knowledge producers. Thus, ethnography can only speak from "inside out" the information networks it seeks to understand (Riles 2000). The relevance of eyewitness video to human rights necessitates a scholarly positioning from within the transnational human rights networks or "inside out" the ethnographic material. It demands scrutiny of the processes of circulation of eyewitness video across platforms and institutional spaces, which define its ability to serve human rights by tracing the practices and interpretative labors that deem it relevant. Doing so means an ethnographic commitment to dialogue with human rights advocacy communities, journalists, and legal professionals. It also means engagement with the multiple forms of documentation they produce, particularly content that addresses the institutionalizing of eyewitness videos as reliable sources of information (e.g., blog posts on verification methods and video-assessment skills, judicial records, and legal studies on visual evidence).

This methodological orientation, then, provides a point of access into the complex entanglement between visual media and human rights from within the heart of the institutional networks that propel human rights claims into the public sphere. Hence, the conceptual and methodological approaches proposed in this article respond to the changing status of image uses as a practice central to human rights. At times when visual meaning-making is inevitably implicated in human rights research, reporting, advocacy, and legal work, such scholarly endeavors are necessary.

Conclusion

In emphasizing the salience of eyewitness video to human rights advocacy, journalism, and the law, this article shows how visuals are becoming an important tool for gathering evidence, a mode of information relay, and a form of evidence that is no longer inferior to words. As images are at the heart of how human rights claims are made, legitimized, and publicized, attention to eyewitness videos provides an important lens to study human rights in the contemporary moment. Familiar questions about the role of images in human rights endeavors remain relevant in light of new media circumstances: How, when, and why are the conceptual and evidentiary qualities of eyewitness videos mobilized to unveil, to promote, to protect, or even to undermine human rights in today's rapidly-changing media ecology? Where does the moral and political agency of ever-growing visual records of atrocities rest? What kinds of structures—technological, cultural, political, and legal—support, challenge or undermine the potential of eyewitness video to achieve human rights?

By offering conceptual and methodological signposts to tackle these questions, this article articulates a call to consider the complex interplay between images and human rights beyond merely relegating visuals to the familiar terrains of humanitarian communication or evoking their long-assumed status as adjuncts to words. Instead, the article charts a conceptual framework that responds to the diffusion of visual information across different institutional spaces, inscribing eyewitness videos with human rights meaning. It also proposes that new developments in ethnography provide a productive methodological orientation to study the intersection of eyewitness video and human rights. Thin description in particular enables a dialogical engagement from within the advocacy, journalism, and legal networks through which eyewitness video becomes relevant for human rights. As visuals surface across the moral, cultural, political, and legal resisters that seek to uncover and prevent global injustice, the scrutiny of the role and the shape of images in human rights work is a task worth pursuing.

Acknowledgments

The author would like to thank Barbie Zelizer, Alexandra Sastre, and Debora Lui for their helpful suggestions. She also thanks the human rights advocates and journalists cited in the article, who took the time to share their experiences and opinions with her.

References

AL-GHAZZI, Omar. (2014) "Citizen Journalism" in the Syrian uprising: Problematizing Western narratives in a local context. *Communication Theory*, 24(2), 435–454.

AL-GHAZZI, Omar. (2015, May) *Digital Occidentalism: Imaging the West in War-Torn Syria*. Paper presented at the International Communication Association, San Juan, Puerto Rico.

AMNESTY INTERNATIONAL (2015) *Amnesty International Report 2014/15: Syria*. [Online]. Available: https://www.amnesty.org/en/countries/middle-east-and-north-africa/syria/report-syria/ [23 October 2015].

ANDEN-PAPADOPOLOUS, Kari, and PANTTI, Mervi. (2011) *Amateur Images and Global News* (Bristol, UK: Intellect Ltd.).

AUSTIN, Regina. (2006) The next "new wave": Law-genre documentaries, lawyering in support of the creative process and visual legal advocacy. *Fordham Intellectual Property, Media and Entertainment Law Journal*, 16(3), 809–868.

AUSTIN, Regina. (2010) Documentation, documentary, and the law: What should be made of victim impact videos? *Cardozo Law Review*, 31(4), 979–1017.

BOCK, Mary Angela. (2014) Little brother is watching: Citizen video journalists and witness narratives. In *Citizen Journalism: Global Perspectives*, Volume 2, Stuart Allan and Einar Thorsen (eds.) (New York: Peter Lang Publishing).

BOCZKOWSKI, Pablo. (2005) *Digitizing the News: Innovation in Online Newspapers* (Boston: MIT Press).

BOLTANSKI, Luc. (1999) *Distant Suffering: Morality, Media and Politics* (Cambridge: Cambridge University Press).

BROUGH, Melissa, and LI, Zhan. (2013) Media systems dependency, symbolic power, and human rights online video: Learning from Burma's "saffron revolution" and WITNESS's hub. *International Journal of Communication*, 7, 281–304.

CASTELLS, Manuel. (1996) *The Rise of the Network Society* (Oxford: Blackwell Publishers Ltd.).

CHOULIARAKI, Lilie. (2006) *The Spectatorship of Suffering* (London: Sage Publications).

CHOULIARAKI, Lilie. (2013) *The Ironic Spectator: Solidarity in the Age of Post-Humanitarianism* (Cambridge, UK: Polity Press).

DELAGE, Christian. (2014) *Caught on Camera: Film in the Courtroom from the Nuremberg Trials to the Trials of Khmer Rouge* (Philadelphia: University of Pennsylvania Press).

DENVIR, Daniel. (2013, March 6) Police brutality in the iPhone era. *Philadelphia City Paper*. [Online]. Available: http://citypaper.net/Cover/Police-brutality-in-the-iPhone-era/ [23 October 2015].

FEIGENSON, Neal. (2014) The visual in law: Some problems for legal theory. *Law, Culture and the Humanities*, 10(1), 13–23.

FEIGENSON, Neal, and SPIESEL, Christina. (2011) *Law and Display: the Digital Transformation of Legal Persuasion and Judgment* (New York: New York University Press).

FISHER, Max. (2013, August 26) Read the full transcript: Kerry's speech on Syria, chemical weapons and the need to respond. *The Washington Post*. [Online]. Available: https://www.washingtonpost.com/news/worldviews/wp/2013/08/26/read-the-full-transcript-kerrys-speech-on-syria-chemical-weapons-and-the-need-to-respond/ [23 October 2015].

GEERTZ, Clifford. (1973) *The Interpretation of Culture* (New York: Basic Books).

GOW, James, PETERSON, Richard, and PRESTON, Alison. (1997) *Bosnia by Television* (London: British Film Institute).

HUMAN RIGHTS WATCH. (2014) *Syria: Barrage of Barrel Bombs: Attacks on Civilians Defy UN Resolution*. [Online]. Available: https://www.hrw.org/news/2014/07/30/syria-barrage-barrel-bombs [20 October 2015].

INDEPENDENT INTERNATIONAL COMMISSION OF INQUIRY ON THE SYRIAN ARAB REPUBLIC. (2015) *10th Report of the Commission of Inquiry on Syria (A/HRC/30/48), 13 August 2015*. [Online]. Available: http://www.ohchr.org/EN/HRBodies/HRC/IICISyria/Pages/IndependentInternationalCommission.aspx [20 October 2015].

INTERNATIONAL COUNCIL ON HUMAN RIGHTS POLICY. (2002) *Journalism, Media and the Challenge of Human Rights Reporting* (Vernier, Switzerland: ATAR Roto Press SA).

JACKSON, John. (2013) *Thin Description: Ethnography and the African Hebrew Israelites of Jerusalem* (Cambridge, MA: Harvard University Press).

JOSEPH, Gregory. (2014) *Modern Visual Evidence* (New York: Law Journal Press).

KAMEL, Yomna. (2014) Reporting a revolution and its aftermath: When activists drive the news coverage. In *Citizen Journalism: Global Perspectives*, Volume 2, Stuart Allan and Einar Thorsen (eds.) (New York: Peter Lang Publishing).

KEENAN, Thomas, and WEIZMAN, Eyal. (2011) Mengele's skull. *Cabinet*, 43. [Online]. Available: http://www.cabinetmagazine.org/issues/43/keenan_weizman.php [1 May 2015].

KELLY, Kevin. (2008, November 21) Becoming screen literate. *The New York Times*, p. MM48.

KOETTL, Christoph. (2013) Can video document possible war crimes in Syria? *WITNESS Blog*. [Online]. Available: http://blog.witness.org/2013/01/video-war-crimes-in-syria/ [23 October 2015].

KRASNER, Lawrence. (2014, November 6–7) *Eyes Everywhere: Cellphones and Criminal Justice*. Paper presented to Ubiquity, Mobility, Globality, University of Pennsylvania, Philadelphia.

MCLAGAN, Meg. (2006) Making human rights claims public. *Visual Anthropology*, 108(1), 191–195.

MCLAGAN, Meg, and MCKEE, Yates. (2012) *Sensible Politics: The Visual Culture of Nongovernmental Activism* (New York: Zone Books).

MORTENSEN, Mette. (2014) *Journalism and Eyewitness Images: Digital Media, Participation, and Conflict* (New York: Routledge).

NEIRE, Aryeh. (2013) *The International Human Rights Movement: A History* (Princeton: Princeton University Press).

NICHOLS, Bill. (1994) *Blurred Boundaries: Questions of Meaning in Contemporary Culture* (Bloomington, IN: Indiana University Press).

RILES, Annelise. (2000) *The Network Inside Out* (Ann Arbor, MI: University of Michigan Press).

RILES, Annelise. (2006) *Documents: Artifacts of Modern Knowledge* (Ann Arbor, MI: University of Michigan Press).

SASSEEN, Jane. (2012) *The Video Revolution: A Report to the Center for International Media Assistance*. [Online]. Available: http://www.cima.ned.org/wp-content/uploads/2015/01/Video-revolution-FINAL.pdf [1 May 2015].

SCHIAPPA, Edward. (2015) *Visual Persuasion in the Digital Age: A Webinar with Edward Schiappa*. [Online]. Available: http://cmsw.mit.edu/visual-persuasion-digital-age/ [1 May 2015].

SCHULBERG, Stuart. (2009) *Nuremberg: Its Lessons for Today [The Schulberg/Waletzky Restoration]*. Produced by Sandra Schulberg.

SCHWARTZ, Louis-Georges. (2009) *Mechanical Witness: A History of Motion Picture Evidence in U.S. Courts* (New York: University of Oxford Press).

SHERWIN, Richard. (2011) *Visualizing Law in the Age of the Digital Baroque: Arabesques and Entanglements* (New York: Routledge).

SHERWIN, Richard. (2012) Visual jurisprudence. *New York Law School Review*, 56(1), 138–165.

SHERWIN, Richard, FEIGENSON, Neal, and SPIESEL, Christina. (2007) What is visual knowledge, and what is it good for?: Potential ethnographic lessons from the field of legal practice. *Visual Anthropology*, 20(2–3), 143–178.

SILBEY, Jessica M. (2006) Videotaped confessions and the genre of documentary. *Fordham Intellectual Property, Media and Entertainment Law Journal*, 16(3), 789–807.

SILVERMAN, Craig. (2014) Verification Handbook: An Ultimate Guideline on Digital Age Sourcing for Emergency Coverage. [Online]. Available: http://verificationhandbook.com/book/ [12 February 2016].

SILVERMAN, Craig. (2015) Verification Handbook for Investigative Reporting: A Guide to Online Search and Research Techniques for Using UGC and Open Source Information in Investigations. [Online]. Available: http://verificationhandbook.com/book2/ [12 February 2016].

SINGER, Jane. (2004) Strange bedfellows?: The Diffusion of convergence in four news organizations. *Journalism Studies*, 5(1), 3–18.

SLIWINSKI, Sharon. (2011) *Human Rights in Camera* (Chicago: University of Chicago Press).

TORCHIN, Leshu. (2012) *Creating the Witness: Documenting Genocide on Film, Video, and the Internet* (Minneapolis, MN: University of Minnesota Press).

WALCOTT, Henry. (1999) *Ethnography: A Way of Seeing* (Plymouth, MA: Alta Mira Press).

WARDLE, Claire, DUBBERLEY, Sam, and BROWN, Pete. (2014) *Amateur footage: A global study of user-generated content in TV and online news output*. [Online]. Available: http://usergenerated news.towcenter.org/wp-content/uploads/2014/05/Tow-Center-UGC-Report.pdf [20 October 2015].

ZELIZER, Barbie. (1998) *Remembering to Forget: Holocaust Memory Through the Camera's Eye* (Chicago: University of Chicago Press).

ZELIZER, Barbie. (2010) *About to Die: How News Images Move the Public* (New York: Oxford University Press).

Nonprofit Product Placement: Human Rights Advocacy in Film and Television

Carla Winston

Department of Political Science, University of British Columbia

ABSTRACT

As non-governmental organizations attempt to gain influence, membership, and funds in an increasingly crowded field, they are turning to popular culture as a way to spread both their brand and their message. This article examines Amnesty International USA's use of what has traditionally been a corporate advertising technique: product placement in popular film and television. It argues that NGOs engage in product placement as a form of strategic communication with three interrelated goals: brand management, issue advocacy, and social norms marketing. This overlap creates theoretical outcomes and ethical considerations which, while not unique to second-order forms of communication, have not yet been explored with relation to human rights advocacy. This article first defines and gives examples of such product placement and concludes with a discussion of ethics considerations for advocacy organizations contemplating using this strategy.

Amnesty International (Amnesty) is one of the world's oldest and best-known human rights advocacy organizations. Founded in 1961, it has a history of working toward human rights for all by using both government pressure and grassroots education to get its messages out. It operates via a network of in-country researchers and activists, national sections that pressure their own governments, and international secretariat that coordinates efforts and works with international institutions. It is also a membership-based organization: Amnesty boasts more than 7 million members, supporters, and activists in more than 70 national sections (Amnesty International, 2016). As generations change, however, AI is in danger of losing both its popular appeal and its political power in the face of competition from other organizations and an increasingly graying membership base. As Dennis Palmieri, then-spokesperson for Amnesty's U.S. section (AIUSA), explained in 2002, "We need to get our message out to people who are not doctoral students" (Calvo, 2002). But how to do it?

Although an increasing number of nongovernmental organizations (NGOs) are making forays into cultural marketing, AIUSA stands out as particularly active in the field of human rights and culture. It has sponsored concert series, held film festivals, enlisted celebrity spokespeople, created teaching guides for popular films, sold specially commissioned music albums, and more. Amnesty's overall work with the artistic community suggests three interconnected goals: to educate and spur action on specific human rights issues, to increase youth membership, and to contribute to building a "culture of human rights." The collective desire for entertainment, the power of the arts to teach and influence viewers, and the popularity of the cultural elite offer a different way to make political issues interesting: by making them "cool," "normal," and possibly both.

One of the less well-known aspects of AIUSA's (and other NGOs') cultural marketing efforts is the use of embedded advertising in popular film and television. This article argues that by engaging in product placement, or the placement of Amnesty's logo, image, and issues within popular fictional films and television shows, it is trying to "sell itself" as both an organization and as a cause. Amnesty itself may be thought of as a brand, but its "product," instead of being a consumer item such as shoes or computers, is human rights activism. However, unlike other forms of cultural engagement, product placement uses an inherently fictional creation to advance real-world goals. This intersection of fiction, entertainment, outreach, and very serious real-world issues presents both opportunities and challenges, risking trivialization of the issues and people at hand at the same time as it heralds the possibility of engaging new supporters. It also leads to new ethical dilemmas beyond the concerns related to the increasing corporatization of nonprofit work.

This article analyzes the rationale for such efforts, explains the process and typology of product placement, provides some illustrative examples, and discusses a few of its ethical implications when applied to political or nonprofit activism. Using discursive and visual analysis of films and television shows, I examine how different types of product placement serve to create brand and issue recognition for Amnesty and, perhaps, norms of political engagement with global human rights issues. In doing so, I offer an alternative frame through which to understand the increasingly corporatized nature of modern political advocacy: Rather than harming the activist landscape by deradicalizing political engagement, pushing for a "human rights culture" seeks to do exactly the opposite: to normalize human rights activism as a facet of everyday life.

Politics on screen

The intersection of fiction and real-world politics is not well studied within political science. Whereas studies abound of politics and activism with respect to the news media (Krain, 2012; Ramos, Ron, & Thoms, 2007; Vestergaard, 2008), relatively little has been written about the way in which nondocumentary media affect our perceptions of what politics, political behavior, or political advocacy is or should be. Cinema and media studies have long recognized that the way life, including political life, is presented on screen affects how viewers understand it (van Zoonen, 2007).

A limited number of studies have suggested that television and film about politics can indeed have an effect on how viewers respond to politics in general (Holbert et al., 2003). This is possible because television and film cut across the multiple ways that people process politics: media discourse, experiential knowledge, and popular wisdom. "Media discourse" here means the spread of politics, and political topics, beyond its traditional home of news and documentary media. The "popular wisdom" portion of this equation is the general sense of the world shared by both the fiction and the viewer's sense of the real world. The care taken to make films and television seem like real life—using multiple consultants, language or movement coaches, filming locations, set decoration choices, even employing former speechwriters as screenwriters—enhances our belief that what is on the screen is reflective of the real world, even if the exact circumstances are different (van Zoonen, 2007, p. 58). Last, "experiential knowledge" results from the familiarity with characters and emotional investment that people make in following a story or television show. This connection—the feeling that we "know" a character—makes their experiences and opinions more important to us than persons met only fleetingly.

Given these three forms of gaining and interpreting political knowledge, I suggest that it may be possible for organizations and norm entrepreneurs to make use of both symbolic and information politics (Keck & Sikkink, 1998) by inserting real-world issues and information into fictional constructs (also known as "edutainment"). [1] If a film or TV show incorporates a real-life issue or situation into its storyline, the dramatized version of reality will still be in some way "true to life." Information that the audience may not have known before can be presented, be framed in such a way as to make it emotionally compelling for the

---

[1]The term "edutainment" arose in the 1990s as media, software, and technology developers increasingly tried to integrate educational content into entertainment products and vice versa (Carlson, 2012).

viewer, and potentially offer solutions via individual action. This process, although occurring in a fictional universe, is the same thing that Amnesty has attempted to do for decades by telling the stories of individuals affected by and fighting for human rights and by providing members the opportunity to become human rights defenders themselves.

Product placement: Brand management and normative change

Product placement, or the strategic placement of an organization's name, logo, or products within a fictional world, is a well-known and often very successful form of corporate marketing.[2] Also known as embedded advertising, it has been employed for more than 50 years, with increasing frequency and variety of format: One study calculated that the television audience sees, on average, one product placement every 3 min of programming (La Ferle & Edwards, 2006). It is used by filmmakers to reflect a world in which corporations and products actually exist, but it is also used strategically by corporations to build brand and product knowledge, to enhance image or popularity, or to "normalize" products or the actions that might require them.[3] I argue that in seeking organizational visibility, AIUSA and other NGOs act much like corporations seeking consumers.

"Amnesty International" is a brand. It was one of the first human rights groups to use image branding, through its distinctive candle-in-barbed-wire logo (Cmiel, 1999). Just like Nike or Apple, which each have distinctive identities and logos to match, people associate Amnesty with a certain type of "product"—grassroots human rights education and activism. However, trust in Amnesty's "brand" is higher than trust in most corporations at least partially because it is *not* like a corporation: "Profits are not a goal; altruism and goodwill rule" (Dauvergne & LeBaron, 2014, p. 111).

Therefore, associating human rights with "Amnesty International" via a branding or outreach campaign makes someone interested in human rights more likely to visit the website, join a group, or take an Amnesty-directed political action than if they do not associate the product with an organization at all. It is also likely to lead to more funding for Amnesty through membership dues, grants from foundations, and other sources of income, which make decisions based on trust in organizational partners. At the very least, simple product placement should lead to increased visibility for the organization itself: Amnesty will become better recognized as a leading human rights advocacy group.

Second, depending on the context in which it is placed, it is possible to make a product "cool." Take, for example, James Bond and the Aston Martin (Cooper, Schembri, & Miller, 2010). This enhanced reputation makes the product, and the organization promoting it, more likely to be chosen over a competing brand. If someone associates both Human Rights Watch and Amnesty with human rights, but one is perceived as "cooler" than the other, all other things being equal that person is more likely to direct their attention to the "cooler" organization, giving Amnesty a distinct advantage over its peers in recruiting and funding. If the opposite, Human Rights Watch receives the benefits.[4]

Some types of placements may lead to results beyond a perception of trendiness. One particular goal, for Amnesty and for those who engage in principled action, is to create *affect*: an emotional connection with the issues presented that drives action in a way that dry numbers or facts cannot (Slovic, 2007). From viewing human-rights-related stories and incorporating the informational and

---

[2]A number of studies show that product placement increases brand recognition and that viewers do not really mind seeing brands in entertainment, as long as they do not feel that their attitudes toward that brand are being directly influenced (Russell, 2002; La Ferle & Edwards, 2006; Yang & Roskos-Ewoldsen, 2007). However, because much of the data on product placement effectiveness are proprietary, there has not been much scholarly analysis of the causal mechanisms or different success rates of different types of product placements.

[3]One well-known example of successful product placement is that of Reese's Pieces in the movie *E.T. The Extra-Terrestrial* (Kennedy & Spielberg, 1982). In the film, the protagonist (Elliott) uses the candies to lure E.T. out of the forest and into the house. Although the label on the bag is never seen, the candy's bright orange color is distinctive, and sales of Reese's Pieces reportedly increased by 65% within a month of the film's release (Babin, 1996).

[4]This particular competition, between Amnesty and Human Rights Watch, has been the subject of some concern by Amnesty since the late 1990s brought Human Rights Watch increased media presence (Hopgood, 2006, pp. 136–142).

emotional cues available about both the issue and the types of people affected by it, viewers will probably learn at least something about the specific issue (the global arms trade, conflict diamonds) with which they are presented. They will also be able to link that information to the physical and emotional experience of those whose rights are being violated. If viewers become both educated and emotionally involved with an issue they feel they can positively impact through personal action, even on a part-time basis (be it political letter writing, voting, or consumer-based methods), that person is presumably more likely to do so than one who is educated on an issue but not emotionally impacted by it. The nature of storytelling and the framing of issues have the ability to make us *want* to act; perhaps that may be possible if we seek out the organization mentioned in the story itself.

Last, and also depending on placement, products may end up seen as "normal." This is the simplest expression of a norm cascade, whereby standards of appropriate behavior are adopted because key influential actors have already done so, and new norm adopters wish to emulate their behavior. Slowly, such attitudes and behavior are internalized, and the specific reasons for belief and practice cease to be actively contested (Finnemore & Sikkink, 1998). On a general level, simple product placement in otherwise nonpolitical film and television may "normalize" or "mainstream" human rights, whereas previously the average viewer may have relegated them to a separate sphere of "political" activity. This is the essence of the "human rights culture" that Amnesty is trying to build: a more sustained involvement in human rights activism in general, beyond issue-related or "trendy" political action.

How does it work?

In controlling where and how an organization such as Amnesty is portrayed in fictional entertainment, I argue that each product placement decision becomes an act of strategic communication. Placements can be refused if the content of the entertainment does not fit Amnesty's desired image, but they can also be solicited in pieces that appeal to the audiences that it would like to reach. This section details the process of securing and agreeing to placements, as well as its forms and intended effects.

The actual placement of a name, logo, or product can occur via three pathways. First, if writers, costumers, or set designers, or even actors, desire to use Amnesty's name or products (T-shirts, posters, mugs, etc.) in a for-profit production, they must ask Amnesty for permission to use its copyrighted materials. Second, AIUSA receives volunteered services from a company called Hero Entertainment Marketing to push for the inclusion of Amnesty products when someone on the production has not specifically asked for it already. Hero performs the same services for regular companies such as LEGO, Cuisinart, and the *Financial Times* (Hero Entertainment Marketing, n.d.). Third, and most like traditional information politics or advocacy efforts, Amnesty works with interested writers and producers in the film industry to create entertainment content that reflects human rights issues and values. In the first two types, because Amnesty does not pay for the placement (either directly or indirectly), the Federal Communications Commission does not require that it be disclosed. In the third case, the fee for this consultancy can come in the form of a product placement or mention of the organization in the final product, or inclusion of experts on additional DVD materials, and must be made public. However, these sponsorship disclosure requirements are for television shows and do not currently apply to films produced for theatrical release (Fujawa, 2012).

There are two basic forms of product placement: simple visual and auditory placements (referred to as product placement or prop placement) and featuring products heavily within a plot (product integration). Each has the potential to affect both recall and positive attitudes toward the product in question, although this potential varies depending on clarity, placement, timing and repetition, reaction, integration with character identity or character development, and other factors (Russell, 2002).

Studies on representation and modality have shown a difference between visual and auditory delivery of signals. In a film and television context, the visual mode sets the tone and makes an environment feel realistic, whereas the auditory mode actually delivers the content—the story itself— via the script. Therefore, seeing a candle-and-barbed-wire logo and hearing the words "Amnesty

International" will have different effects on both recall and preference. Whereas seeing the logo might set a scene, that is, explain preferences or provide cues as to character development, hearing the words "Amnesty International" might instead serve a specific character or plot arc, and in terms of advertising effectiveness would be considered "more meaningful" than a mere visual cue (Russell, 2002).

The second form, plot integration, is potentially the most meaningful form of placement. It incorporates the organization or product (in this case, human rights) directly and meaningfully into the storyline. If connection with the plot positively influences informational recall from films, it stands to reason that a film with "nonprofit product" integration, and therefore concerned with issues relevant to Amnesty, might generate interest in the group or at least a desire for further issue-related research.

The majority of placements in television are of the first kind and are both fleeting and unobtrusive: They appear onscreen for generally fewer than 5 s and are either visual or verbal, but not usually both. Visual cues tend to be prominent and uncluttered, but in the background, and do not necessarily interact with characters or with plot. Auditory cues, on the other hand, tend to be spoken by a lead or supporting character and have direct significance as to their role in the scene (La Ferle & Edwards, 2006). I suggest that they may affect efforts at brand management but are unlikely to spur either greater subject knowledge of, or emotional response to, human rights in general.

However, for plot integration, questions of story and character are both potentially important to human rights organizations. What exactly is explained or discussed in a story, and in what terms, helps frame discussions about whether issues are human rights related or not in the first place. A fictional character can function in the same manner as a real-life representative of an issue or a normative perspective; by humanizing an abstract concept, readers or viewers may imagine themselves and their reactions to such a situation, and their emotional responses may lead to greater attachment to the political issue or actor.[5]

It should be noted that the nature of the creative process makes the results of placements uncertain. Even if they manage to get into a script or onto a set (which depends on production staff choosing objects as set or costume pieces), several production or postproduction processes (editing, camera angles, acting decisions, etc.) may intervene, resulting in a placement that disappears in production or is unintelligible to the viewer. Nonprofits, unlike traditional companies that use product placement, are not providing funding for the creative process in return for the successful placement of their product. Their inclusion in the finished film or show is therefore dependent upon creative, rather than financial, decision-making processes and is therefore much less secure.

The content and context of AIUSA product placements

Many viewers of popular television and film have seen Amnesty product placements, even if they were not aware of it at the time. Some of Amnesty's representative placements are examined next to help illustrate their expected effect on viewers' recognition of, and feelings about, Amnesty as an organization (the "brand") and human rights activism in general (the "product").

Visual: Set dressing and costume

Visual placements could be part of a set or as a character's wardrobe. Considerations for the placement's effectiveness might include whether the place is public—a school or work hallway—or private, such as a character's home or office, as well as the relative prominence of the character wearing the logo. Also to be considered is the "loudness" of the logo or item itself.

Set dressing. On the television series *The West Wing*, in the office of Toby Ziegler, White House communications director and a committed civil liberties advocate, hangs an Amnesty poster (Caddell, O'Donnell, & Lehmann, 1999; see Figure 1). It is a visually striking poster, in a bright color with contrasting

---

[5]"Actor" here is used in the political science sense of the word, rather than the Oscars/Emmys/Golden Globes sense of the word.

Figure 1. Amnesty International placement in *The West Wing*.

text that includes human-rights-related terms such as "oppression," "torture," and "abuse." It is designed to catch the viewer's eye. However, the poster is never quite seen in full: Over the course of at least four seasons the words "Amnesty International" are never actually seen onscreen. This is seemingly a problem for Amnesty, as the lack of name or logo recognition would negate any influence the poster might have. However, themes that might eventually lead a viewer to Amnesty are easy to recall given the poster's "loudness" and association with a specific character with human-rights-oriented politics.

A more directly informative placement occurs on a large screen in the office of a magazine in the film *Friends with Benefits* (Glotzer, Gluck, Shafer, Zucker, & Zucker, 2011; see Figure 2). Both the distinctive logo and the name "Amnesty" are easily identified by the viewer. However, the poster appears only once in a 2-hr film, rather than repeatedly over the course of multiple television episodes. This means that viewers have less of a chance of noticing the poster in the first place. Recall may be more specific to Amnesty, but it is less likely to happen overall.

Both of these posters are seen in the offices and buildings of fictional politically aware figures (a Democratic White House and a progressive magazine office), and a viewer would not be particularly surprised to see such a poster in a politically liberal setting.[6] Viewers who are interested in politically engaged

Figure 2. Amnesty International placement in *Friends With Benefits*.

---

[6]Although *Friends with Benefits* is not a politically oriented film, the particular office in question is.

Figure 3. Amnesty International placement in *The Avengers*.

forms of entertainment are more likely both to notice the poster and to agree with Amnesty's general positions. Thus the placement achieves brand recognition but does not necessarily change viewers' beliefs about the "normalcy" of human rights activism in politically neutral settings. If human rights NGOs wish to be viewed as nonpartisan, they must broaden their visual messaging beyond partisan placements.

For example, there is a fleeting image of an Amnesty logo in *The Avengers* (Feige & Whedon, 2012; see Figure 3). Set on top of a taxi in downtown Manhattan, this logo does not have a political placement and, like *Friends with Benefits*, is not even placed in the context of a politically engaged film. For any viewers who manage to catch this placement, human rights activism (and Amnesty in particular) is portrayed as a normal part of everyday life—that is, if one is able to actually see the image, much less process it: The logo is visible for less than 1 s in the middle of an action sequence.

Another typical space without necessarily political connotations, especially for young viewers, is high school. The placement of Amnesty posters in high school hallways and classrooms shows the group as active in a nonpolitical setting that both is highly recognizable to youth audiences and specifically encourages youth participation. Such placements occur in both *21 Jump Street* (Cannell, Moritz, Lord, & Miller, 2012; see Figure 4) and *Mean Girls* (Michaels & Waters, 2004; see Figure 5). Perhaps just as important, the subject matter of the productions is not remotely political: Both are comedies set in high schools. Viewers are more likely to be young but not more likely to be politically aware than the average population or predisposed to certain political leanings.

Seeing an Amnesty poster in a high school setting, then, offers an example of youth-oriented human rights activism as a normal activity, like any other after-school club. Amnesty sections in high schools are relatively common; in 2013 there were more than 1,000 registered youth and high school AIUSA groups, and the organization offers a starter kit as well as numerous communication tools and activity guides for young people (Amnesty International, n.d.). Seeing an Amnesty poster on film might just inspire a student to organize an Amnesty group at school.

Costume. The first poster discussed earlier, in Toby Ziegler's office, helps inform his character, as presumably the character would have chosen his own office decorations. But set dressing is not the only way to inform character: Sometimes the most direct route is by dressing the actor.

Two television doctors on two shows have sported Amnesty T-shirts: John Carter on *ER* (see Figure 6), played by Noah Wyle, and Christopher Turk on *Scrubs* (see Figure 7), played by Donald Faison. The effect on the viewer of seeing these two characters wearing Amnesty T-shirts is different due to the amount of knowledge viewers already have of these characters' political beliefs.

Figure 4. Amnesty International placement in *21 Jump Street*.

Figure 5. Amnesty International placement in *Mean Girls*.

The medical drama *ER* did not shy away from political, international, or human rights issues over its 15-year run, and the character of Dr. Carter was particularly engaged in these topics within the show environment. In 2001, Dr. Carter wore an Amnesty T-shirt (Crichton, Gemmill, Hunter, & Thorpe, 2001). Although wearing the shirt was the actor's choice out of a number of other wardrobe choices, and although Amnesty would have had the shirt on screen worn by an extra if actor Noah Wyle had not chosen it (Calvo, 2002), in this case an Amnesty logo being worn by a main character helps inform the viewer of that character's personal beliefs by tying him to a real-world organization that mirrors those beliefs. That Dr. Carter would be an Amnesty supporter is not surprising: This placement does not necessarily add anything to the plot or character development of Dr. Carter, nor does it surprise viewers that he would be wearing such a T-shirt. In an expected environment, on what many believe is the stereotypical Amnesty supporter, this placement is basically just for brand recognition.

Dr. Turk, on the other hand, is a political unknown—until he wears an Amnesty shirt (Lawrence, Fordham, & Trilling, 2002). *Scrubs* was a half-hour comedy set in a hospital, and the episodes rarely

Figure 6. Amnesty International placement in *ER*.

Figure 7. Amnesty International placement in *Scrubs*.

discussed political issues. If previous studies on nonpolitical placements are correct, the incongruous nature of the placement might actually lead to a negative perception of the product (Couldry & Markham, 2007). However, because this placement is on a character, it also informs character development: When an apolitical character on an apolitical show appears onscreen in a political T-shirt, viewers are presented with an anomaly and learn something about that character that they did not already expect. They could potentially discount it. However, might they instead learn something else: If people can be politically aware and active without it being overtly apparent, even if you know someone fairly well (as the audience believes it knows Turk), perhaps the people in the viewer's everyday life are more politically active than originally thought. Such activity—in this case, through Amnesty—becomes more "normal."

Auditory: **About a Boy** *versus* **Slumdog Millionaire**

The context in which Amnesty is referred to with an auditory placement, complete with differences in tone, has a potential effect on how viewers perceive the organization: Is it to be taken seriously or not? Is Amnesty's earnestness to be praised and emulated or smiled at indulgently? Two examples of auditory placements help to illuminate this dilemma: the romantic comedy *About a Boy* and Mumbai-based drama *Slumdog Millionaire*.

About a Boy (Felner et al., 2002) is a romantic comedy revolving around the relationship between a man and the son of the woman he is attempting to date. The male lead, Will (Hugh Grant), is initially presented as immature, shallow, and cynical. It is he who mentions Amnesty:

> That's the problem with charity. You must mean it. You have to mean things to help people. Like the time I volunteered to help out at a soup kitchen … and very nearly made it. Or the time at Amnesty International. … Wait a minute. You say you haven't got a boyfriend? Talk about a human rights violation.

In this context, Amnesty is presented as an ideal: Only "good," earnest people engage with it, but many if not most of us aren't passionate enough about the subject to really get involved. To add insult to injury, only moments later Will, in an attempt to be witty, actually trivializes the core of Amnesty's work by comparing being single to having one's human rights violated. Such a placement, although probably leading to name recognition for viewers, creates the impression that Amnesty is perhaps too serious for its own good.

In Danny Boyle's Oscar-winning film *Slumdog Millionaire* (Boyle & Tandan, 2008), the viewer also hears mention of Amnesty, this time by a police inspector (Irrfan Khan) worried about the exposure of torture:

> Inspector of Police: He's unconscious, *chutiya*. What good is that? How many times have I told you—?
> Sergeant Srinivas: Sorry, sir.
> [The door opens and a constable walks in.]
> Constable: The Englishman is here, sir.
> [The inspector turns to Sergeant Srinivas with heavy irony.]
> Inspector: *Aré wa*, Srinivas! Now, we'll have Amnesty International in here peeing their pants about human rights. Get him down for God's sake and clean him up.

In this case, although the character himself is dismissive of Amnesty, the viewers have just witnessed someone being tortured on screen. The police inspector is the "bad guy" in this situation, and his rejection of Amnesty may create a positive impression for viewers of both the organization and its effectiveness. Its use here, within the story, actually serves the purpose that Amnesty wishes to serve in the real world: ending human rights abuses.

Plot integration: **Lord of War** *and* **Blood Diamond**

The most intense insertion of Amnesty and human rights issues into popular media comes in the form of plot integration. In this case, the story told uses a major human rights issue as its backdrop, and writers and producers have worked with Amnesty and other human rights NGOs to make sure that their information is as accurate as it can be in a fictional piece. I suggest that, as a form of edutainment rather than simple brand recognition or association, this integration affords the opportunity for issue-specific advocacy and to call upon all four of Keck and Sikkink's (1998) advocacy tactics: information politics, symbolic politics, leverage politics, and accountability politics.

Information politics present viewers with facts and other usable information that they did not have and that might cause a change in belief or behavior. Symbolic politics uses symbols (such as logos), persons, or stories to help audiences both make sense of a situation and become sensitized to the moral issue at hand. Leverage politics involves using those who have power, and can thus effect change, to help those who do not and cannot. Last, accountability politics attempts to hold powerful actors to the promises they have made about their actions. All four tactics, in combination, are routinely used in human rights activism over a variety of media and nonmedia platforms (Isaacs, 2003; Keck & Sikkink, 1998; Ron, Ramos, & Rodgers, 2005; Thrall, Stekula, & Sweet, 2014; Vestergaard, 2008).

The 2005 film *Lord of War* brought light and dramatic flair to the issue of illicit global arms sales (Niccol, 2005). The main character is Yuri Orlov (Nicolas Cage), an arms dealer who gains and loses fortune, power, and family over the course of his life and career. The viewer also sees the nature and workings of the global arms trade and the harms it produces. One is presented with relevant information and a symbolic frame within which to understand its importance: "Nine out of ten war victims today are killed with assault rifles and small arms. ... That's the real weapon of mass destruction" (Niccol, 2005). Viewers are informed and made passionate about an issue through the use of symbolic and information politics. But one is not presented with an option for Keck and Sikkink's third tactic, leverage politics: There is no apparent action to take to fix that statistic, no one to lean on to change the policy.

> While the biggest arms dealer in the world is your boss—the President of the United States, who ships more merchandise in a day than I do in a year—sometimes it's embarrassing to have his fingerprints on the guns. Sometimes he needs a freelancer like me to supply forces he can't be seen supplying. So. You call me evil, but unfortunately for you, I'm a necessary evil. (Niccol, 2005)

This may be an attempt at Keck and Sikkink's fourth tactic, accountability politics: showing there is a disconnect between discourse and practice, particularly for governments, and therefore "shaming" them into action. However, one does not get the impression that such attempts will work. Although one might be educated on and emotionally invested in the issue presented, the story line of the film leaves the viewer pessimistic about the chances for that issue's resolution and the ability of the average person to impact it. This person would be less likely to take concrete action (in the form of a petition or other political message) than one who thought he or she could actually make a difference. Rather than empowering individuals to act, the film makes a systemic problem seem impervious to citizen-based political activism. This film may actually lessen Amnesty's perceived ability to affect systemic change.

Blood Diamond (Herskovitz, King, Weinstein, & Zwick, 2006), on the other hand, offers a clear way for viewers to take individual action, even if Amnesty itself is not identified in the film. Set amidst the brutal Sierra Leonean civil war in 1999, the story follows the partnership of a diamond smuggler (Leonardo DiCaprio) and a poor fisherman (Djimon Hounsou) as they journey to find a valuable diamond and a kidnapped son. They are aided by a journalist (Jennifer Connelly), whose work provides a convenient way to place facts and exposition into the script. Those facts include both a verbal mention of the NGO Global Witness and its long-standing work on conflict diamonds and an explanation of exactly how the conflict diamonds system works. The connection between issue-specific information and Global Witness as the issue expert (provider of that information) aids both the organization and its work on the issue. In this case, although Amnesty also works on conflict diamonds and has provided advice to the film's writer and producers, it is another NGO that captures the spotlight, as they were the authors of a report seen early in the screenwriting process that changed the trajectory of the film's development (Faye, n.d.).

Although the problem is dire, the journalist sees potential for change: "The people back home wouldn't buy a ring if they knew it cost someone else their hand" (Herskovitz et al., 2006).[7] Both a frame and a leverage point are presented. Viewers are informed about an issue, shown why it is important, and presented with an action that they, as consumers, can take: Don't buy conflict

---

[7]This is essentially the same frame used earlier, by Global Witness and others, in a print marketing campaign in the early 2000s. Repeating the frame might create resonance with preexisting advocacy efforts, therefore enhancing recall.

diamonds. The film ends on a hopeful note, which includes an expression of successful account-ability politics: the boycotting of a diamond company and the signing of the Kimberley Accord. The viewer is left informed, emotionally connected, empowered to act, and hopeful that his or her action will be helpful to the cause.

Neither of the preceding examples explicitly mentions Amnesty; indeed, one even mentions a different organization. If Amnesty were judging the effectiveness of its product placement efforts solely on whether its name or logo showed up on screen, then its efforts failed for these two films. However, this is the key difference between nonprofit and for-product placement. Whereas the corporation's goal is to attract consumers to its brand, AI has a secondary goal: to create awareness of specific human rights issues and potentially spur action to confront them. AIUSA offered expert commentary to the media and created educational materials to coincide with the release of each film, generating numerous opportunities for a newly interested public to engage with both the topic and the organization. In addition the DVD edition of *Lord of War* contained a special message from star Nicolas Cage that directed viewers to Amnesty for more information and ways to act (AIUSA, n.d.; Niccol, 2005). For both these films, the way to Amnesty was through human rights issues themselves rather than Amnesty brand recognition.

The ethics of corporatized advertising and fictional representation

In an increasingly corporatized and consumption-centered world, Amnesty is not alone in struggling with the question of whether to embrace corporatized institutional structures and advocacy strate-gies. Dauvergne and LeBaron (2014) argued that the turn toward "branding" is reflective of a larger shift in political activism, moving away from community- or issue-oriented groups that challenge the existing world order to movements that are centrally organized, managed from the top-down, and frequently work with and within (and thus implicitly accept and help to reproduce) the corporate order they are trying to change. They argued that political activism has largely become "deradica-lized" and that NGO "branding" has become a necessary tool in the search for organizational funding and visibility. Although brand management is seen as essential for Amnesty's financial stability, serious concerns have been expressed about "contamination of the image" and the values associated with it. Amnesty has been reluctant to overtly embrace a language of branding and corporatized advertising strategy even though it has been engaging in it (in various forms) since the 1980s (Hopgood, 2006).

This turn to brand-sensitive, corporatized operations can be seen in other aspects of NGO practice, by no means unique to Amnesty, such as website design, the use of celebrity advocates, and partnerships with corporate sponsors to sell ethically branded goods. I argue that it is far from clear, however, that this is necessarily a bad thing. If the use of successful advertising techniques enables NGOs to do better issue-oriented work, they should be seen as enabling, as well as limiting, the scope of possible political action. If new participants are sensitized to issues and given ways to participate in human rights processes, either politically or economically, such campaigns may be more immediately effective than campaigns that depend on long-term engagement from strongly committed activists. Furthermore, if involvement in a campaign through weak social ties (such as engaging in the popular culture) leads some of these individuals to maintain and deepen their ties to human rights organizations, then spreading a "culture" of human rights through superficial outlets may lead to an increase in long-term committed human rights activists who have fully internalized the human rights message. Whether this actually happens, and whether the concern of deradicaliza-tion and the benefit of increased cultural relevancy balance out in terms of improvements in global human rights practices, is unclear.

Another ethical question involves the accusation of "commodity activism," in which campaigns are targeted at the identity of the campaigner rather than the needs of the victims. By shifting the focus from those who need it most to those who are likely to consume the media in question, commodity activism removes agency from the beneficiaries of human rights policies, who need it most, and gives it to the activists themselves. It also risks trivializing the very real and very dangerous work that human rights defenders do around the world by linking activism with entertainment. In addition, by making human rights activism cool rather than necessary, this type of marketing strategy "risks reinforcing the public's skeptical consumerism towards human rights appeals as well as their moral apathy towards distant suffering" (Waldorf, 2012, p. 472).

On the other hand, the use of fiction as a method of relaying information and creating affect has some potential advantages, especially as regards risk to human rights defenders on the ground. By dramatizing, rather than directly relaying, stories of oppression, fiction can help to preserve the anonymity and safety of sources. Although Amnesty and other groups take much care to protect their networks of informants, it is an ongoing struggle to make sure that the detail presented in reports does not reveal informants' identities and make them, or their families and villages, targets. In addition, by amalgamating multiple experiences and making connections between processes and victims of oppression, a single fictional story may also impart more information than a single real story. Last, it is of course in the interests of the filmmakers to tell a story in such a way that it makes profits, but the goals of clear conveyance of information, the production of affect, and a profitable final product are not necessarily opposed. A well-told story that produces an emotional response is also one that is more likely to garner positive reviews and increased viewership, exposing more people to human rights stories and the embedded names and logos contained within them.

As regards the specific ethics of embedded advertising, another ethical problem arises. The very act of product placement involves a certain amount of purposeful deception. The intent is to sink messages "subconsciously" so that the consumer may not even be aware that a product is being marketed at her. For organizations that praise and generally practice transparency unless it would endanger those on the ground, the use of potentially deceptive practices may cross ethical boundaries. Tellingly, this particular advertising strategy is not mentioned anywhere on AIUSA's website. Rather than calling visitors' attention to some of the more overt forms of cultural marketing such as tribute CDs, film festivals, and rock concerts, AIUSA neither publicly celebrates nor even mentions its successful product placements. Hackley et al. (2008) suggested that some of the ethical murkiness surrounding embedded advertising may be alleviated by making such strategies more explicit, such as publicizing the fact that such placements are pursued. However, such overt identification of strategy may create other problems: In one study on stealth advertising, the knowledge that a company engaged in such efforts diminished participants' brand loyalty, but this effect was moderated somewhat depending on brand familiarity and the sense that the marketing tactic was "appropriate" (Wei, Fischer, & Main, 2008).

These ethical considerations about Amnesty's media strategy have been the subject of a certain amount of disagreement between the International Secretariat and AIUSA, which is both Amnesty's largest national section and the instigator of most product placements (Hopgood, 2006, pp. 136–142). Other national sections have not used product placement to the extent that AIUSA has, although this may also be related to the different rules surrounding the practice in different countries. On the other hand, this difference in preferences on media advocacy strategies is also similar to research demonstrating differences in the relative acceptance of corporatized marketing, particularly within the arts, between American and other global entertainment consumers (Gould, 2000; Khalbous, Vianelli, Domanski, Dianoux, & Maazoul, 2013; Sung & Lee, 2011). This suggests that AIUSA may be the most enthusiastic about the use of product placement because Americans in general are the most receptive to it.

American audiences are also the largest financial contributors to Amnesty's operations. Although Amnesty strives to be a global, multicultural human rights organization, the vast majority of its funding comes from rich Western states. The International Secretariat receives nearly 25% of its funding from the U.S. section alone (Hopgood, 2006, p. 197). Financial stability and growth are dependent on states for which entertainment-based advertising is widely accepted as normal. In addition, each national section holds ownership of the Amnesty logo (the candle and barbed wire) in their own country, meaning that the Secretariat is dependent on funding from states that are particularly receptive to this form of advertising and relatively helpless to stop it without financial risk.

These ethical critiques of product placement in general, and for NGOs in particular, suggest that different organizations will come to different conclusions regarding their own entry into the field of product placement. For many organizations, the decision may ultimately rest on the perceived need to "not be left behind" in the fight for visibility and funding.

Conclusion

This article has presented a somewhat paradoxical human rights practice: placing brand names, logos, and issues that are serious, political, and normatively important into the generally lighter, sometimes fantastical, and profit-driven world of mass entertainment. Although the contradiction may seem strange to some, the human rights movement has always operated via multiple moving parts: Some do dangerous in-country work, whereas others lobby governments and stand up for activists at risk, and still more educate and raise awareness around the world. As Keck and Sikkink (1998) argued, the work of many actors and strategies is necessary to advance and promote human rights. Product placement, although a relatively new tool in the advocacy repertoire, deserves to be analyzed and understood not just for its novelty but for its potential to contribute positively to organizations' recruitment and outreach activities.

Evaluating the impact of subconscious advertising on political engagement, rather than product identification and consumption, is difficult to accomplish without experimental studies or detailed viewer/participant tracking. Do viewers learn about an issue or see an Amnesty poster on a set, go to Amnesty's website, and keep coming back? Do they sign up for a mailing list, make a financial contribution, or join a group? If they are brought to Amnesty by an issue film like *Blood Diamond*, does that single-issue passion lead to a greater general interest in human rights? It is hoped that this article may serve as a catalyst to future studies of political culture that engage the arts themselves.

The interplay between politics and culture is exactly what Amnesty is hoping to exploit: "We're about building a culture of human rights … and in order for us to do that, we have to be at the epicenter of pop culture" (Calvo, 2002). From specific issues and specific organizations to a general culture of rights, the potential for cultural products to influence the practice of political activism in a number of traceable or measurable ways most certainly exists and deserves to be further explored.

References

Amnesty International. (2016). Amnesty International: Who we are. Retrieved from http://www.amnesty.org/en/who-we-are

Amnesty International. (n.d.). Human rights friendly schools network: About us. Retrieved from http://friendly schools.tiged.org/?about=hrfsn

Amnesty International USA. (n.d.). *Lord of War education guide.* Available from http://www.amnestyusa.org/pdfs/lordofwar_edguide.pdf

Babin, L. A. (1996). Advertising via the box office: Is product placement effective? *Journal of Promotion Management, 3*, 31–52.

Boyle, D. (Producer & Director), & Tandan, L. (Producer). (2008). *Slumdog millionaire* [Motion picture]. United States: Warner Brothers.

Caddell, P. (Writer), O'Donnell, L. (Writer), & Lehmann, M. (Director). (1999). Five.votes down [Television series episode]. In J. Wells (Executive producer), *The west wing.* Los Angeles, CA: NBC.

Calvo, D. (2002, January 6). Amnesty's new cause. *The Los Angeles Times.* Retrieved from http://articles.latimes.com/2002/jan/06/entertainment/ca-amnesty06

Cannell, S. J. (Producer), Moritz, S. H. (Producer), Lord, P. (Director), and Miller, C. (Director). (2012). *21 Jump Street* [Motion picture]. United States: Columbia Pictures.

Carlson, G. S. (2012). *Channel surfing knowledge: A narrative criticism of edutainment television programming* (Unpublished doctoral thesis). University of Illinois, Chicago, IL.

Cmiel, K. (1999). The emergence of human rights politics in the United States. *Journal of American History, 86*, 1231–1250.

Cooper, H., Schembri, S., & Miller, D. (2010). Brand-self identity narratives in the james bond movies. *Psychology & Marketing, 27*, 557–567.

Couldry, N., & Markham, T. (2007). Celebrity culture and public connection: Bridge or chasm? *International Journal of Cultural Studies, 10*, 403–421.

Crichton, R. (Creator), Gemmill, R. S. (Writer), Hunter, E. (Writer), & Thorpe, R. (Director). (2001). Blood, sugar, sex, magic [Television series episode]. In M. Crichton & J. Wells (Executive Producers), *ER*. New York, NY: NBC.

Dauvergne, P., & LeBaron, G. (2014). *Protest inc.* Cambridge, UK: Polity Press.

Faye, D. (n.d.). Diamond scribe: Interview with Charles Leavitt. Retrieved from http://www.wga.org/content/default.aspx?id=3136

Feige, K. (Producer), & Whedon, J. (Director). (2012). *The Avengers* [Motion picture]. United States: Marvel Studios in association with Paramount Pictures.

Felner, E. (Producer), Rosenthal, J. (Producer), De Niro, R. (Producer), Bevan, T. (Producer), Weitz, C. (Director), & Weitz, P. (Director). (2002). *About a boy* [Motion picture]. United States: Universal Pictures.

Finnemore, M., & Sikkink, K. (1998). International norm dynamics and political change. *International Organization, 52*, 887–917. doi:10.1162/002081898550789

Fujawa, J. (2012). The FCC's sponsorship identification rules: Ineffective regulation of embedded advertising in today's media marketplace. *Federal Communications Law Journal, 64*(3), 550–575.

Glotzer, L. (Producer), Gluck, W. (Producer & Director), Shafer, M. (Producer), Zucker, J. (Producer), & Zucker, J. (Producer). (2011). *Friends with benefits* [Motion picture]. United States: Screen Gems and Castle Rock Entertainment.

Gould, S. J. (2000). Product placements in movies: A cross-cultural analysis of Austrian, French and American consumers' attitudes toward this emerging, international promotional medium. *Journal of Advertising, 29*(4), 41–58.

Hackley, C., Tiwsakul, R. A., & Preuss, L. (2008). An ethical evaluation of product placement: A deceptive practice? *Business Ethics: A European Review, 17*, 109–120. doi:10.1111/j.1467-8608.2008.00525.x

Hero Entertainment Marketing. (n.d.). Clients. Retrieved from http://www.heropp.com/category/client/

Herskovitz, M. (Producer), King, G. (Producer), Weinstein, P. (Producer), & Zwick, E. (Producer & Director). (2006). *Blood diamond* [Motion picture]. United States: Warner Brothers.

Holbert, R. L., Pillion, O., Tschida, D. A., Armfield, G. G., Kinder, K., Cherry, K. L., & Daulton, A. R. (2003). *The West Wing* as endorsement of the U.S. presidency: Expanding the bounds of priming in political communication. *Journal of Communication, 53*, 427–443.

Hopgood, S. (2006). *Keepers of the flame: Understanding Amnesty International*. Ithaca, NY: Cornell University Press.

Isaacs, A. (2003). Book review: Like water on stone: The story of Amnesty International. *Common Knowledge, 9*(1), 166. doi:10.1215/0961754X-9-1-166

Keck, M. E., & Sikkink, K. (1998). *Activists beyond borders: Advocacy networks in international politics*. Ithaca, NY: Cornell University Press.

Kennedy, K. (Producer), & Spielberg, S. (Producer & Director). (1982). *E.T. The extra-terrestrial* [Motion picture]. United States: Universal Pictures.

Khalbous, S., Vianelli, D., Domanski, T., Dianoux, C., & Maazoul, M. (2013). Attitudes toward product placement: A cross-cultural analysis in Tunisia, France, Italy, and Poland. *International Journal of Marketing Studies, 5*(2), 138–153.

Krain, M. (2012). J'accuse! Does naming and shaming perpetrators reduce the severity of genocides or politicides? *International Studies Quarterly, 56*, 574–589. doi:10.1111/j.1468-2478.2012.00732.x

La Ferle, C., & Edwards, S. (2006). Product placement: How brands appear on television. *Journal of Advertising, 35*(4), 65–86.

Lawrence, B. (Creator), Fordham, D. (Writer), & Trilling, L. (Director). (2002). My lucky day [Television series episode]. In B. Lawrence (Executive Producer), *Scrubs*. New York, NY: NBC.

Michaels, L. (Producer), & Waters, M. (Director). (2004). *Mean girls* [Motion picture]. United States: Paramount Pictures.

Niccol, A. (Producer & Director). (2005). *Lord of war* [Motion picture]. United States: Entertainment Manufacturing Company.

Ramos, H., Ron, J., & Thoms, O. N. T. (2007). Shaping the northern media's human rights coverage, 1986–2000. *Journal of Peace Research, 44*, 385–406. doi:10.1177/0022343307078943

Ron, J., Ramos, H., & Rodgers, K. (2005). Transnational information politics: NGO human rights reporting, 1986–2000. *International Studies Quarterly, 49*, 557–588. doi:10.1111/j.1468-2478.2005.00377.x

Russell, C. A. (2002). Investigating the effectiveness of product placement in television shows: The role of modality and plot connection to congruence on brand and memory attitude. *Journal of Consumer Research, 29*, 306–318.

Slovic, P. (2007). "If I look at the mass I will never act": Psychic numbing and genocide. *Judgment and Decision Making, 2*(2), 79–95.

Sung, Y., & Lee, T. D. (2011). Cross-cultural challenges in product placement. *Marketing Intelligence & Planning, 29*, 366–384. doi:10.1108/02634501111138545

Thrall, A. T., Stekula, D., & Sweet, D. (2014). May we have your attention please? Human-rights NGOs and the problem of global communication. *The International Journal of Press/Politics, 19*(1), 1–25.

van Zoonen, L. (2007). Audience reactions to Hollywood politics. *Media, Culture & Society, 29,* 531–547.

Vestergaard, A. (2008). *Humanitarian branding and the media: The case of Amnesty International.* Amsterdam, the Netherlands: John Benjamins. doi:10.1075/jlp.7.3.07ves

Waldorf, L. (2012). White noise: Hearing the disaster. *Journal of Human Rights Practice, 4,* 469–474. doi:10.1093/jhuman/hus025

Wei, M., Fischer, E., & Main, K. J. (2008). An examination of the effects of activating persuasion knowledge on consumer response to brands engaging in covert marketing. *Journal of Public Policy & Marketing, 27*(1), 34–44.

Yang, M., & Roskos-Ewoldsen, D. R. (2007). The effectiveness of brand placements in movies: Levels of placements, explicit and implicit memory, and brand-choice behavior. *Journal of Communication,* 469–489.

Promoting the people's surrogate: The case for press freedom as a distinct human right

Wiebke Lamer

European Inter-University Centre for Human Rights and Democratisation

ABSTRACT
Liberal theory regards a free press as vital not only to political processes, but also to the development and maintenance of personal autonomy and the right to self-determination. Yet, press freedom receives very little attention in the wider debate on international human rights and in the academic literature on the subject. This article submits that press freedom matters in its own right and not merely as a means to secure other human rights like free speech and freedom of information. This article places press freedom at the center of how we think about democracy and human rights promotion. If the goal is to promote Western liberal ideals, press freedom should be the centerpiece of human rights advocacy and democracy promotion in international relations, not merely a side note to freedom of expression or freedom of information.

Introduction

Historically and philosophically, press freedom has closely been linked to the fight against tyranny and the advancement of human rights. An opponent of Napoleon's, Mme de Staël, called it "the right on which all other rights depend" (Holmes 1990: 27). The American Founding Fathers established a specific press clause in the First Amendment. Churchill praised the free press as "the unsleeping guardian of every other right that free men prize; it is the most dangerous foe of tyranny" (The Leveson Inquiry 2012: 56). Yet, as evidence in this article shows, when it comes to human rights, press freedom is at best a marginal concern in debates focused on freedom of expression or at worst is absent from the debate altogether. This article makes the case for a clearer distinction between these two concepts and argues that press freedom deserves a more central role within the international human rights framework—one that corresponds to the vital political and social functions a free press serves in guarding and promoting a system of government that responds to the will of the people.

The current state of press freedom and its neglected status in the human rights debate

It is not difficult to find statistics on the deteriorating state of press freedom across the world. This section will summarize those trends briefly and highlight the more unreported reality that press freedom is also declining in the developed world. What follows is a survey of academic human rights books, reference works, and articles, which shows that press freedom has been ignored almost entirely in this context. The research also finds that the two concepts of press freedom and freedom of expression are closely connected, but that much more emphasis is placed on the latter, while the press, or media more generally, tends to be addressed primarily with regard to their human rights coverage.

Press freedom around the world has increasingly come under attack in recent years. A recent Freedom House report found that global press freedom fell to its lowest level in over a decade (Dunham et al. 2015). Less than 14% of the world's population now live in countries with a press that earns the Freedom House status "Free." There are, of course, the usual offenders like Russia and China, and the war in Syria, along with unrest across the Middle East, also contributed to bringing up the death toll of journalists killed over the last few years. But in the West, press freedom is also experiencing worrying setbacks. This year, the United States ranks forty-ninth in the Reporters Without Borders World Press Freedom Index due to increasing crackdowns on investigative journalists and their sources, and the events in Ferguson, Missouri, which included detentions, harassment, and rough treatment of journalists by police (Reporters Without Borders 2015).

Across the Atlantic, the United Kingdom is still embroiled in a crisis over media regulation following the revelations of the Murdoch phone-hacking scandals. Several other European countries saw a weakening of press freedom in recent years, most notably Hungary and Greece, which both have seen dramatic declines since 2014 and are no longer categorized as Free but as Partly Free in the latest Freedom House Press Freedom rankings (Dunham et al. 2015). And while press freedom is being curtailed across the continent, the European Union is seriously entertaining the introduction of legislation that would install media councils with enforcement powers to impose fines, to order apologies, and to fire journalists (European Commission High Level Group on Media Freedom and Pluralism 2013).

There is no shortage of reports compiling the atrocities committed against media personnel worldwide, and recent efforts have been made through the UN Plan of Action on the Safety of Journalists and Impunity to draw more attention to the terrible dangers that many journalists in crises situations face. The issue of journalist safety has also been taken up by the International Association for Media and Communication Research, which hosted a special session on this topic at its annual convention in June 2015. In May 2015, the UN Security Council stressed the importance of protecting journalists in the context of humanitarian law by adopting Resolution 2222 (United Nations Security Council 2015), which calls on member states to comply with their obligations regarding the protection of journalists in armed conflicts.

While this resolution marks a significant milestone in recognizing the important role of journalists and protecting them, it is still limited in its scope. A mechanism for monitoring the implementation of the resolution is still lacking. What is more, the resolution does not address the obligations of states to protect journalists outside of war zones and in nonconflict situations.

In this equally important respect, press freedom enjoys only limited attention from the international human rights community. If anything, the press freedom debate is often subsumed by the debate on freedom of expression, given that there is no explicit provision for freedom of the press in the context of human rights. For the UN, press freedom falls under

Article 19 of the Universal Declaration of Human Rights: "Everyone has the right to freedom of opinion and expression; this right includes freedom to hold opinions without interference and to seek, receive and impart information and ideas through any media and regardless of frontiers" (United Nations 1948). The emphasis here is clearly on the individual right to freedom of expression. It does not, however, protect the press in a structural sense.

The UN framework does not treat press freedom as an end in itself. Instead, the media are treated as a means to an end, and that end comes in different variations: to protect the right to information; to guarantee freedom of expression; to foster understanding and friendly cooperation among people and states; to publicize and mitigate humanitarian disasters; or to promote human and economic development. In other words, the media, or press freedom, are treated as a channel to secure other human rights. They are not treated as an institution that requires its own protection.

Since the International Bill of Rights does not include any provisions for protecting the press specifically, there is no legally binding instrument on press freedom in international law. If anything, the International Covenant on Civil and Political Rights puts more emphasis on restrictions on the press, rather than its protections. There are, of course, the declarations of Windhoek (UNESCO 1991), Alma-Ata (UNESCO 1992), Santiago (UNESCO 1994), and Sana'a (UNESCO 1996) to promote an independent and pluralistic press in Africa, Asia, Latin America and the Caribbean, and the Arab world, respectively. None of these are legally binding, however. The same applies to the United Nations Education, Scientific, and Cultural Organization (UNESCO)'s 1978 Mass Media Declaration, which observers have described as so ambivalent and inconsistent that it is pointless (McPhail 2010).

General usage trends of terms such as "press freedom" and "freedom of expression" also confirm that historically debates about the latter have garnered more attention. Figure 1 shows the rise of the phrase "press freedom" compared to the phrase "freedom of expression" in the English language from 1900 to 2008 based on the Google Books database of more than eight million digitized books. Interestingly, while the usage of the term "human rights" has increased drastically since 1945, usage of press freedom did not grow. This gap is highlighted in Figure 2.

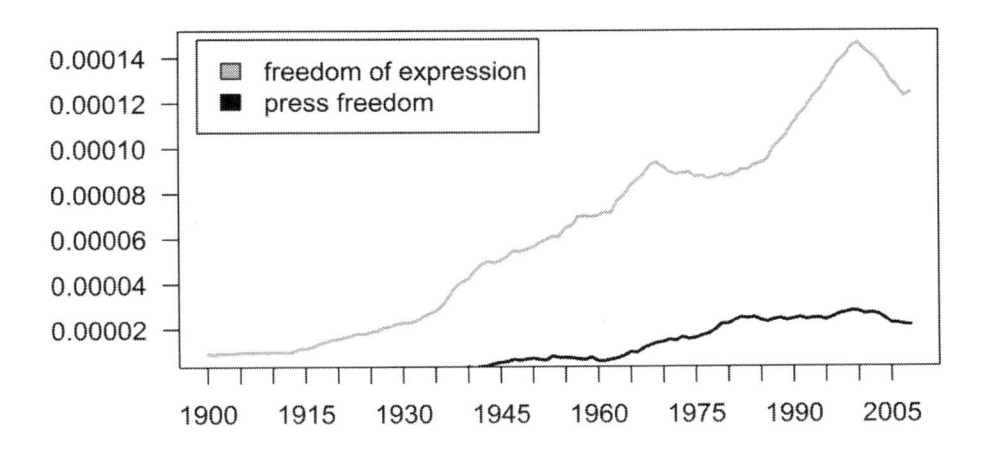

Figure 1. Usage of "press freedom" vs. "freedom of expression" in print, 1900–2008 (Google Books n.d.).

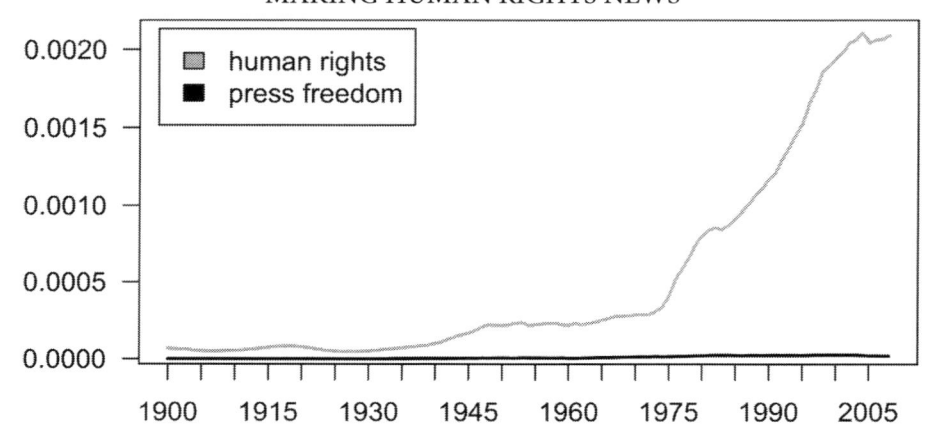

Figure 2. Usage of "press freedom" vs. "human rights" in print, 1900–2008 (Google Books n.d.).

This general trend and the lack of focus on press freedom in international law is reflected in the human rights literature. Plenty of prominent human rights volumes only mention press freedom in passing.[1] Many do not feature any references to it at all. Jack Donnelly's *Universal Human Rights in Theory and Practice* (2003) does not mention press freedom or free press at all and mentions free speech only once. Similarly, David Forsythe's latest edition of *Human Rights in International Relations* (2012) does not bring up freedom of the press or expression or anything on media more generally.[2]

As far as human rights reference works are concerned, press freedom fares only marginally better. Lawson's *Encyclopedia of Human Rights* (1996) counts a handful of references to press freedom and a free press or media. However, the discussion of the topic is far from comprehensive. The 2000 *International Encyclopedia of Human Rights* by Maddex features a short entry on press freedom that places it within the general context of the media's responsibilities and shortcomings for the protection of human rights. The 2009 *Encyclopedia of Human Rights* edited by David Forsythe addresses whether the right to a free press is a human right but does so only briefly, mostly because this point is featured under the entry "Media" that quickly moves on to concerns of how the advent of the Internet is affecting traditional media potential for political socialization, and how media exert influence through agenda setting and framing. In fact, the media entry strikes a cautionary note overall, warning of the dangers of the media rather than highlighting its necessity for democracy and human rights.

Other notable human rights books that mention press freedom superficially are *Which Rights Should Be Universal* by William Talbott (2005), who makes the case that press freedom should be one of nine universal rights but at no point in the book elaborates on why press freedom is on his list. The other is Beth Simmons' *Mobilizing for Human Rights*. While she acknowledges the importance of a free press for democratic governance and government adherence to human rights domestically, she has nothing to say about press freedom as a human right per se (Simmons 2009).

In a similar vein, human rights journals have not paid much attention to press freedom either. From 2002 until 2015, only three articles on press freedom appeared in the *Journal of Human Rights*. Between 1981 and 2015, *Human Rights Quarterly* published only six articles directly related to press freedom. Five of these are case studies of the status of press freedom in developing countries, while one addresses the question whether free speech and press is an absolute right (Jeffery 1986). With the exception of one article on confining press freedom in Singapore, all of these articles date back to the 1980s. Even worse is the record of *Human Rights Review*, which did not feature a single article on press freedom between 1999 and 2015 and only one on free speech.

Data from the Human Rights Citation Database Project, indexing close to 7,000 academic articles written on the topic of "human rights" from Web of Science, the Social Science Citation Index, and the Arts and Humanities Citation Index (1975–present) and ranking them according to the number of times these articles have been cited, also show astonishing results (Gaubatz 2013).[3] Out of these nearly 7,000 articles, only one carries the term press freedom in its title and is only cited twice (Peksen 2010). Freedom of expression or free speech comes up eight times. A search for "media" returns 17 results, although some of those overlap with related search terms like journalism/journalists (three), news/newspapers (two), and fourth estate (one). Out of all media and press freedom-related human rights articles, the highest score goes to "Shaping the Northern Media's Human Rights Coverage, 1986–2000" with 19 citations (Ramos and Thoms 2007). It provides a case study of the human rights reporting of *The Economist* and *Newsweek*, overall drawing positive conclusions with regard to the media being a potentially useful ally in the fight against human rights violations but also highlighting the media's gatekeeper role.

On the whole, however, what these findings show is that older texts on human rights do not feature much discussion on press freedom, free press, or free media. In the cases that they do, it is in the context of the right to free speech and mostly perfunctory. Newer texts acknowledge the importance of the media and particularly the Internet but do not address press freedom in depth, if at all. The general emphasis is on taking the power of the press for granted in the context of other human rights, on the one hand, and on highlighting the drawbacks of the free media and how they do not adequately report on human rights abuses on the other. However, this approach is undermining the vital role of the press in preserving civil and political rights, as the next section outlines in more detail.

Press freedom versus freedom of expression

Protecting the free press goes beyond protecting the individual right to freedom of expression. Free speech and free press should not be blindly equated. The free press is a political and social institution, which guarantees that the government draws its authority from the will of the people, a concept to which the International Bill of Rights is clearly committed. The following sections will discuss the distinctions between freedom of expression and press freedom, in the process outlining why press freedom deserves a more central role in the realm of human rights.

The political importance of the press can be broken down into two parts. The first highlights the oversight role of the press, while the second underlines the fact that the press draws its power from its audience. These two aspects are closely intertwined, as the following quote shows:

> Burke said there were Three Estates in Parliament; but in the Reporter' Gallery yonder, there sat a Fourth Estate more important than they all. It is not a figure of speech, or a witty saying; it is a literal fact [...]. Whoever can speak, speaking now to the whole nation, becomes a power, a branch of government, with inalienable weight in lawmaking, in all acts of authority. It matters

not what rank he has, what revenues or garnitures: the requisite thing is that he have a tongue which others will listen to; this and nothing more is requisite. The nation is governed by all that has tongue in the nation. Democracy is virtually there. (Carlyle 1841: 141)

The Fourth Estate represents another branch of government, one that is responsible to exercise oversight over the others in the name of the people, while it derives its power from being able to speak "now to the whole nation."

Since the Founding Fathers included an explicit provision for the free press in the First Amendment to the US Constitution, the debate over the legal status of press freedom has been fraught with difficulties, particularly when it comes to the distinction between press freedom and freedom of speech. The First Amendment states "Congress shall make no law... abridging the freedom of speech, or of the press," which indicates that the Founding Fathers regarded these two concepts as separate. Nonetheless, legal experts continue to debate whether the press clause is redundant or whether the press indeed deserves constitutional protection (West 2011). The difficulty mostly stems from the close relationship between the concepts of free speech and free press. Indeed, it is no easy task to disentangle freedom of expression from freedom of the press, which is underlined by the fact that the US Supreme Court did not touch the subject of press freedom in any significant way until 1919 and has continued to deflect decisions on the status of press freedom vis-à-vis freedom of expression.

Some historians even argue that the Founding Fathers did not differentiate between the two either but rather that they equated free speech with free press. But, as Melville Nimmer points out: "As nature abhors a vacuum, the law cannot abide a redundancy. The presumption is strong that language used in a legal instrument, be it a constitution, a statute, or a contract, has meaning, else it would not have been employed" (Nimmer 1975: 640). Indeed, there is plenty of evidence that suggests that the Founding Fathers were well aware of the connection between guaranteeing a free press and preventing the abuse of power, or even overthrowing tyranny. After all, the fourth article of the original draft of the Bill of Rights states:

The people shall not be deprived or abridged of their right to speak, write, or to publish their sentiments; and the freedom of the press, as one of the great bulwarks of liberty, shall be inviolable. (Annals of Congress, 1st Cong., 1st session, p. 451)

First Amendment historian Leonard Levy goes even further and argues that the free speech clause was a result of the perceived importance of an unrestricted press: "It developed as an offshoot of freedom of the press, on the one hand, and on the other, freedom of religion—the freedom to speak openly on religious matters" (Levy 1960: 5). Rather than being an addition to the free speech clause, there is a strong case to be made that the press was important to the Founding Fathers from the beginning. According to Levy, they might not have had a clear idea of what precisely they were doing by including the press clause, but they were nonetheless implying that the press should have a Fourth Estate function as an unofficial part of the checks and balance system (Levy 1985: 273).

In short, it is clear that there is a strong link between protecting the free press and creating a democratic society that was recognized by the American Founding Fathers. Subsequent Supreme Court rulings safeguarded this idea by expanding freedom of the press and widening the First Amendment protection for journalists, most critically in the 1964 *New York Times Co. v. Sullivan* case.

The Sullivan case established the active malice standard, which dictates that government officials trying to sue publishers must show that the published information was untrue and that the publishers knew that the information was false or acted in reckless disregard of the truth. This ruling imposed a much heavier burden on public officials pursuing slander or libel cases against the media and was celebrated by the *New York Times* on the fiftieth anniversary of the ruling as the "clearest and most forceful defense of press freedom in American history" (The Uninhibited Press 2014). The court made it clear that even at the cost of erroneous information being reported, open debate and discussion about government conduct and policy had to be preserved, and that the press must be able to report about public issues in an uninhibited way.

New York Times Co. v. United States (1971) was also a landmark case for journalists. After a secret government report on the Vietnam War was leaked to the *New York Times* and *Washington Post*, the US government attempted to prohibit the newspapers from publishing documents of this report known as the Pentagon Papers. The government argued that publication of the study could pose a threat to national security, but the Supreme Court ruled that the newspapers had a right to publish the documents and supported the view that the principle of prior restraint on freedom of speech is almost never justified. Although the ruling is based on the free speech clause rather than the free press clause of the First Amendment, the case is important because it addresses the difficulty of striking the balance between press freedom and national security. The Pentagon Papers case reinforced the responsibility of the press as the Fourth Estate, or fourth branch of government, that holds public officials accountable and acts as a distributer of information that is relevant to important public debates, even if public officials would prefer this information to remain secret.

The issue of striking the difficult balance between informing the public and protecting sensitive information that might affect national security was reignited in 2013 with the Edward Snowden leaks on government surveillance activities, which were published in the *Guardian* and other mainstream newspapers worldwide. This incident highlights the very important impact the press has on initiating public debates and legitimizing information. This is even truer in the digital age that is characterized by a constant stream of information flow. Snowden made the choice to work with the journalists Glenn Greenwald and Laura Poitras on publishing the National Security Agency (NSA) surveillance documents because he wanted the revelations to have a lasting impact and to inform the public. Glenn Greenwald writes: "In the very first online conversation I had with Edward Snowden, he told me he had only one fear about coming forward: that his revelations might be greeted with apathy and indifference, which would mean he had unraveled his life and risked imprisonment for nothing" (Greenwald 2014: 248). But he was also determined to publish the stories journalistically, so that the materials could be provided with context and the public could process the information in a more rational way: "If I wanted the documents just put on the Internet en masse, I could have done that myself. [...] I want you to make sure these stories are done, one by one, so that people can understand what they should know" (Greenwald 2014: 53).

This shows that even today, when anyone with a computer and Internet access can publish information and can benefit from the right to freedom of expression, the press still carries out a political role that not every ordinary citizen with information or Internet access can perform. The press provides an editorial role by offering context, filtering information, and raising to political relevance issues that might otherwise be nothing more than a passing story in the 24/7 stream of news. The next section looks at the power and functions of the press in more detail, but first it deserves to be stressed once more that even in the United States, press freedom is far from being treated as a vital requirement for democratic politics.

The Founding Fathers included the press clause in the First Amendment, but the debate about the legal importance of the press clause continues. The Sullivan and Pentagon Papers cases established some rights for journalists that go beyond those of ordinary citizens. However, in other cases, like *Branzburg v. Hayes* (1972), the courts decided that journalists do not have a special privilege to protect their sources and can be compelled to testify before a grand jury. More recently, the Obama administration has turned out to be the most hostile administration in US history towards government leaks, investigative journalism, and the reporter's privilege. Shield laws and informal rules exist in many US states to protect reporters from having to give up their sources and thus to be able to do their job of obtaining information on matters of public importance (Reporters Committee for Freedom of the Press n.d.). But the Department of Justice under President Obama has intimidated government employees from speaking to reporters and journalists from doing their work.

In 2012, the Department of Justice (DOJ) seized phone records of 20 journalists at the *Associated Press* in an effort to investigate leaked classified information (Savage and Kaufman 2013). In 2013, James Rosen, a *Fox News* Washington correspondent, was accused by the DOJ of violating the Espionage Act and acting as an "aider and abettor and/or co-conspirator" in leaking information, in effect accusing him of breaking the law for simply doing his job of reporting on government secrets (Lizza 2013). For years, *New York Times* reporter James Risen had been embroiled in a legal battle with the Department of Justice, defending his right to protect his source's confidentiality and avoiding having to testify in the trial of a former Central Intelligence Agency (CIA) intelligence officer, who had been charged with leaking classified government information to Risen. Risen continued to refuse to give up his source until, in December 2014, Attorney General Eric Holden, following his promise that he would not put any reporters in jail, gave in and declared that the DOJ would not force Risen to reveal his source.

These incidents demonstrate the precarious state of press freedom in the United States. But what is more, the legal debates also show that even in the United States with its separate provision for press freedom in its Bill of Rights, the distinction between freedom of the press and freedom of expression is muddled, a situation that the government is exploiting and the judiciary is not touching. The Supreme Court, for example, refused to hear the Risen case and effectively sided with the government, placing the need for securing evidence in a national security prosecution above the violation of press freedom (Liptak 2014).

Given these recent controversies and crackdowns on investigative journalism and the free flow of information, it is time to pay more attention to the vital role of press freedom for protecting and promoting democracy and human rights and to draw a clearer distinction between the concept of press freedom and freedom of expression, both in the domestic legal context as well as in the global human rights debate.

The current tendency in the human rights debate to focus on the right to freedom of expression ignores the historical context in which these rights developed, since there is evidence to support the view that the Founding Fathers regarded press freedom as more important than free speech, rather than vice versa. Within the current discussion, however, freedom of expression or free speech carries more weight, while press freedom is often not more than an afterthought. As a result, what is forgotten are the functions that are unique to the press, which cannot be fulfilled by simply guaranteeing everyone the right to freely express themselves. Focusing on the political power of the press and its societal roles helps distinguish press freedom from freedom of expression and highlights why a free press is often incompatible with government interests.

The power of the press

The key to understanding press freedom in its own right is the fact that it makes information available to the masses. If one person expresses a view critical of the government, this exercise of free speech is unlikely to cause public officials to take note. If, however, the mass media publicize the same issue, the government faces more pressure than from one person or a small group of people. In fact, the importance of press freedom vis-à-vis free speech is today more pronounced than it was at the time the Founding Fathers drafted the Bill of Rights. Newspapers were a driving force behind the revolution, but it was also easier for a person in the market square of Philadelphia to reach a critical audience.

In an age of ever-expanding government bureaucracies and capabilities and changing social fabrics, the press holds a bigger responsibility for ensuring government oversight than ever. Critics may point out that the rise of the Internet is reversing this trend, but recent events in the Arab world tell a different story. To reach and mobilize the masses, traditional news outlets are still indispensable. The Arab Spring originated with a few hundred or thousand activists who organized protest movements through new and social media, but only after *Al Jazeera* and other traditional media outlets started reporting about the protests, did the movement scale upwards to mobilize millions (Alterman 2011). The trajectory of the protests that erupted on September 11, 2012, in the Middle East in response to the controversial video "The Innocence of Muslims" tells a similar story. The video was published on YouTube in July 2012 without garnering much attention. Only after the video was sent to reporters in the United States, Egypt, and elsewhere on September 6, did it become widely publicized and caused outraged responses from Muslims (Chayes 2012).

Furthermore, Eleanor Townsley and Ronald Jacobs argue that the traditional media outlets are "increasingly central to the large and densely networked public sphere" because blogs or other alternative media pick up the debates that are conducted in the opinion sections of the elite national newspapers and by commentators of the mainstream television programs (Jacobs 2011). A Pew survey finds, for instance, that it is not true that large percentages of Americans now get their news mainly from recommendations from their friends via social media (Mitchell et al., 2012). Online news consumption has increased dramatically over the last few years, but the top news sites continue to be legacy news outlets (Mitchell and Rosenstiel 2012).

Despite a greater availability of channels of communication, politicians still turn primarily to the newspapers and major TV networks to sell their policies to the people. The Internet offers a place for everyone to voice their opinions and thus serves a self-fulfilling purpose. It is also easy to find like-minded people online who share the same political opinions, however rare they might be. But in terms of serving the political process, new media cannot easily replace the press, because the latter also acts as a facilitator of forming majorities (Garry 1990: 76). "Democratic government," Patrick Garry writes, "must come from what is common among its citizens" (1990: 81). The press is well suited to pick up the central debates that are of concern to everyone and to present them to a wider audience in their role as "well-organized, well-financed, professional critics to serve as a counterforce to government" (Blasi 1977: 541).

Indeed, the notion that press involvement in political reporting and debate leads to political participation and progress of democratic politics is not new. Thomas Leonard contends that it was not necessarily the republican style of government that created the democratic process in the United States. Instead, it was the press because it created a "common language in both words and pictures for political interests to be expressed and shared" (Leonard 1986: 4). To this day, this is true of the press as it dominates the way public debate and opinion is framed.

The power of the press, in short, lies with its ability to reach a mass audience. Freedom of expression, on the other hand, is not defined in terms of audience. On the contrary, it is focused on the individual. But the fact that everyone is allowed to express their opinion or to spread their ideas through any medium does not guarantee government oversight. An unrestricted press that is not hampered in gathering, transmitting, and explaining relevant information to the masses does.

The role of the press

The institution of a free press is the greatest safeguard the public has against government abuses and for ensuring that they receive the information they need in order to make government accountable to them. This is the basis of democracy, as James Madison put it: "The people, not the government, possess the absolute sovereignty" (Lewis 1991: 60–61). A government that is checked by a free press is more accountable and less likely to become corrupt (Dworkin 1996). This goes back to the likes of Kant and Montesquieu, who argued in favor of the principle of publicity to prevent the abuses of power. Or, to use Justice Brandeis' words, "Publicity is justly commended as a remedy for social and industrial diseases. Sunlight is said to be the best of disinfectants; electric light the most efficient policeman" (1914: 92). This highlights the status of the press as the stand-in for the people, using its powers to ensure that those in office work in the public interest.

Given the fact that the people possess the absolute sovereignty in a democracy and that the elected officials are mere representatives of the public will, their government needs a way of staying in touch with the wants and needs of the citizenry. Simply granting free expression to every citizen does not fulfill this vital function. After all, it is the press through which public opinion, "the public expression of agreement or dissent concerning institutions," circulates (Bobbio 1989: 26). Consequently, the democratic dialogue function is best served by the press due to this circumstance and the fact that it exerts a unique "informing and opinion-shaping" influence (Nimmer 1975: 654).

The press does much more than merely provide information. These days, governments have ways of making information public directly through their Web sites or social media channels. But the availability of information does not automatically increase the number of informed citizens. Most people do not have time to spend hours online going through hundreds of pages of meeting minutes or draft legislation. The press is needed to make sense of the vast amount of information that the government and other institutions release every day. Media expert Jay Rosen makes this key point when writing that "Journalists build up the world because their reports about it contain more than 'information,' that superabundant commodity. Headlines and the stories that follow are guides to what's important, cues to what's current" (1999: 3).

The press thus plays a vital role not just in informing the public and the government but also by putting this information into context. Granting the right to freedom of expression does not automatically safeguard this vital political function and neither does the right to freedom of information. Even in a system in which both of these rights are upheld and the government is fully transparent, a lot of important information might end up in the vast depths of the Internet without a free press that combs through the terabytes of data and presents it to the public in an accurate way that the audience can understand.

Although the lines between individual speech and journalism are becoming increasingly blurry as a result of the digital revolution, having a press that provides an editorial function and adheres to professional standards, like objectivity, accuracy, and confidentiality, is vital. Edward Snowden deliberately chose to work with journalists, who could put the information he revealed into context, rather than simply making the information available online. Reaching a mass audience is critical for having a political impact, but explaining information, so that the public can make sense of it, is just as important.

This applies even more in light of the fact that authoritarian regimes are becoming more and more adept at creating an "alternate universe of faux democracy," where they not only create fake political parties but also pseudo news media that disseminate the messages and ideas of faux nongovernmental organizations (NGOs), think tanks, and election monitors (Walker 2015). Given the global flow of information, it is not surprising that these messages spread to audiences abroad and become increasingly difficult to disentangle from normal news, particularly online:

> Popular aggregators of information on Russia [...] seamlessly include RT [formerly known as Russia Today, a government-funded Russian cable, satellite and online news channel] and other Kremlin-backed media alongside sources such as the Associated Press and the German broadcaster Deutsche Welle. Slick Web sites with phony, misleading news reports appear increasingly in the new democracies of Central Europe to offer a Kremlin spin on events. As China, Iran and other ambitious, undemocratic regimes scale up their global media activities, the challenge of distinguishing between authentic and phony information will become only more complicated. (Walker 2015)

In order to fight this onslaught of propaganda, it is vital to have trained reporters and reputable journalistic outlets that can help legitimize information. They have the knowledge and tools to sift through much of the material that is disseminated by authoritarian propaganda machines and can thus give the public a better idea of what information and sources can be trusted and which ones cannot.

In addition to its political oversight role, the press also fulfills social functions. The social and political are closely intertwined, of course, particularly when it comes to concepts such as the democratic dialogue or the opinion-shaping purpose of the press and thus deserve to be noted here.

One of these functions of the press is the fostering of a sense of community. The 2011 National Newspaper Association community newspaper readership survey reflects an encouraging reality in this regard. It found that three quarters of respondents read a local newspaper every week. Their primary reason to do so is to find out about local news or local information (National Newspaper Association 2011). The role of the local paper to connect people to their communities is invaluable, even if they do not uncover major scandals on a regular basis (Muller 2011). Even though local newspapers increasingly expand their online content and readership is shifting away from the traditional paper format, the fact remains that local journalists and editors provide community-building services that are not readily replaced by bloggers or other individuals freely expressing themselves.

After all, democracy starts at the grassroots level where the press is counteracting what Rosen calls the "disappearing public" through community newspapers and local TV and radio news (Rosen 1999). With social fabrics changing and more and more of our day-to-day interaction replaced by online activities, the threat of the disappearing citizen is becoming more troubling. The argument about declining social capital and the loss of a sense of community in Western societies has been made for some time now (Putnam 2000). It is thus particularly important to highlight the values of the press both for sustaining democracy at home and in our efforts at promoting it internationally.

There are two other arguments in favor of promoting a free press. On the one hand, keeping the public channels of communication open will enable society to be able to adapt to changing circumstances and to develop new ideas (Garry 1990). On the other hand, allowing all forms of speech, even the extremist kind, fosters a sense of tolerance, which is vital for any society (Bollinger 1986). Both of these are arguments highlighting the role of the press as promoting a certain type of society that goes beyond the notion of the press as a political watchdog (Garry 1990). Accordingly, the 1947 Commission on Freedom of the Press framed the role of the press in broad terms:

> Today our society needs, first, a truthful, comprehensive, and intelligent account of the day's events in a context which gives them meaning; second, a forum for the exchange of comment and criticism; third, a means of projecting the opinions and attitudes of the groups in the society to one another; fourth, a method of presenting and clarifying the goals and values of the society; and, fifth, a way of reaching every member of the society by the currents of information, thought, and feeling which the press supplies. (Commission on Freedom of the Press 1947: 20–21)

The role of the press in democratic societies is thus varied. It functions as a political institution that checks public officials for abuses of power; it also provides information and content that contributes to the democratic dialogue between citizens and their government representatives; and it plays an important role in fostering social cohesion. However, the right of the individual to be able to say and write whatever he or she wants does not protect from tyranny, corruption, or incompetence by itself. Only if there is a press able to report without restrictions to the public at large can government oversight by the people truly be guaranteed.

The importance of the press therefore stems from a combination of two things: The press holds power due to its mass audience and as a result carries out vital social and political functions. As pointed out in this section, both of these factors underscore the difference between free speech and free press. The fact that governments have a different relationship with the Googles, Facebooks, and Verizons of the media landscape further highlights the distinction between press freedom and freedom of expression. These companies, although providing people with the tools to freely express themselves and to access information, are not tasked with providing a government oversight role and can even be abused by the government, as recent revelations surrounding American and British data surveillance programs have shown. The very idea behind having a free press, on the other hand, is to safeguard the people's interests by widely publicizing government policies and behavior. Freedom of expression is not necessarily a thorn in the side of governments that aim to pursue their interests, but press freedom is. Even in advanced democracies, government interests and promoting a free press are at odds, since the very goal of press freedom is to keep the government in check and to protect civil and political liberties.

In fact, when it comes to recognizing the political power of the press, governments have been beating the human rights community to the punch for decades. They are apt at drawing distinctions between freedom of expression and press freedom on a regular basis, thus able to circumvent the more damaging effects of press freedom on their own power, while claiming to uphold the cherished human right to freedom of expression. Russia under Putin has provided ample evidence of this.

In a 2010 article on the status of press freedom in Russia, Maria Lipman makes the case that freedom of expression is possible without a free press. "Today's Kremlin," she writes, "doesn't mind free and critical voices as long as they remain politically irrelevant and have no impact on decision-making" (Lipman 2010: 158). She concludes that Russia enjoys freedom of expression but no press freedom, if one understands press freedom "as one of the elements in an institutionalized democratic polity" (Lipman 2010: online abstract). More recently, President Putin summed up his government's approach to freedom of expression: "Citizens' right to freedom of speech is unshakable and inviolable—however, no one has the right to sow hatred, to stir up society and the country, and put under threat the life, welfare and peace of millions of our citizens" (Barry 2013). In other words, speech is free until it poses dangers to the state as defined by the government. Putin draws a clear distinction between the right to free speech, which every Russian citizen is granted, and the channels that can render speech politically relevant, in this case the Internet: "It is necessary to block attempts by radical groups to use information technologies, Internet resources and social networking Web sites for their propaganda" (Barry 2013), as Putin goes on to state his policy.

This definition of free expression is, of course, a very narrow one. People have to live in fear of saying something that might become politically relevant are less likely to say anything at all. At the very least, they are more likely to self-censor what they are saying. Neither of these scenarios is in accordance with the idea of free speech that lets people express themselves without fear whatever the political repercussions might be. What is more, none of this is in line with the idea that people are the masters of their government.

Because authoritarian regimes draw these distinctions, the human rights community needs to distinguish between freedom of expression and press freedom as well. Only if the vital political functions and power of the free press are appreciated to their full extent, can press freedom be promoted accordingly in the context of human rights.

The importance of press freedom as a human right

Free press supporters point to Article 19 of the Universal Declaration of Human Rights (UDHR) as a home for press freedom. As outlined in the previous section, however, the benefits of press freedom extend far beyond the realms of guaranteeing free speech as a channel of individual self-fulfillment. In fact, most human rights actually depend on a right to a free press.

Human rights are first and foremost aimed at protecting the individual from abuses of government power. Article 5 of the UDHR protects freedom from torture and cruel, inhuman treatment or punishment (United Nations 1948: art. 5). Article 9 grants the right to freedom from arbitrary arrest and detention (United Nations 1948: art. 9). Article 12 states that no one shall be subjected to arbitrary interference with his privacy and home (United Nations 1948: art. 12). It is the government, however, which is most likely to interfere with these freedoms to begin with. The government holds the monopoly on legalized violence and therefore requires an oversight mechanism that can protect citizens from undue exercise of such government power.

Like the US Constitution and Bill of Rights, the Universal Declaration of Human Rights is an attempt at safeguarding people against tyranny. But unlike the Founding Fathers, the makers of the International Bill of Rights ignored the "great bulwark of liberty" (Annals of Congress, 1st Cong., 1st session, p. 451). Westerners might think that this does not affect them, since our constitutions tend to prescribe systems of checks and balances to prevent the abuse of power. But even in these systems, action against the government is taken only if there is a high level of public dissatisfaction with official actions and a demand to look into the actions of one branch of government (Blasi 1977). Whether it is the president or a member of parliament who is guilty of misconduct, they are both subject to the same kind of power dynamics that drive them and give them access to subpoena powers, citizen data, or law-enforcement personnel. In the absence of any other channel through which public dissatisfaction can be expressed in a way that puts pressure on those in government, the press remains the only viable protection mechanism against official misconduct.

This fact alone justifies a more central role of press freedom in the human rights debate than it currently holds. Everyone who is not a journalist, publisher, or owner of the press deserves the right to benefit from the advantages of a free press and the work of these individuals. To frame the debate within the context of freedom of expression ignores the wider social and political consequences of protecting the free press as a structural necessity of the modern state and underestimates its significance as the basis of other political and civil rights.

Although the significance of the free press as the basis for human rights is neglected in international law, scholars have recognized its value in recent years, not just in the context of political and civil rights, but even for the most fundamental human needs and the right to life itself. In 2008, a statistical report found that there is a good correlation between press freedom and different indicators of development, poverty, and governance (Guseva 2008). Amartya Sen makes the powerful case that a free press encourages good governance and emphasizes public concerns. He finds that "in the terrible history of famines in the world, no substantial famine has ever occurred in any independent and democratic country with a relatively free press" (Sen 1999: 5–6).

Similarly, several studies have shown that a free press has positive effects on human development (Norris 2008). More recently, Mohamed Keita from the Committee for the Protection of Journalists made a similar case for the importance of journalistic oversight on issues like malnourishment and other humanitarian crises. Not only does a lack of reporting on such matters prevent the local government from adequately taking action but it also hinders the ability of aid groups to quickly and effectively provide support (Keita 2012).

At the systemic level, scholarship has also highlighted the importance of press freedom, particularly since Hallin's and Mancini's 2004 comparative analysis of Western media systems that created a systematic approach to studying the relationship between media and politics. Studies employing the community approach, for example, have shown that the media are also influenced by society and can be agents of social change in that they have a greater capacity to criticize established institutions and traditions than other institutions (Demers and Viswanath 1999; Winston 2015). In a recent study on the media coverage of HIV/AIDS in Sub-Saharan Africa, a group of researchers found that in countries with more democratic press–state relations, the coverage was framed towards heightened governmental responsibility and progress in fighting HIV/AIDS, meaning that the news agenda in more democratic media systems pushes policymakers harder to address HIV/AIDS than in more authoritarian systems (D'Angelo et al. 2013). This provides another example of the importance of press freedom for society and politics and supports the idea that a free press is more conducive to facilitating human development than repressive media systems.

Press freedom is also more important than simply establishing multiparty elections. A 2009 study, for example, found that impunity, that is, failure of governments to guarantee that their representatives comply with the same laws that apply to the rest of the citizenry, drastically decreases in the presence of higher levels of press freedom (Jorgensen 2009). "Formal democracy," the author contends, "results in episodic rather than constant pressure on abusive and poorly controlled military and police forces" (Jorgensen 2009: 385).

In this context, the democratic dialogue function of the press is also important. Article 21 of the Universal Declaration of Human Rights states that "Everyone has the right to take part in the government of his country" and that "The will of the people shall be the basis of the authority of the government" (United Nations 1948: art. 21). Elections are not the only mechanism through which the public will is expressed, and, if it is, it happens only periodically. However, the public expresses its will constantly through the channels of the free press thus, aiding the democratic dialogue. If everyone is entitled to participate in the collective decision-making process, everyone is entitled to a free press.

The societal role of the press cannot be left out in this context. A recent study examining the relationship between civil society and press freedom in the fight against corruption concludes that "claims of civil society's anticorruption impact must acknowledge its significant dependence on civil society's ability to generate public pressure against corruption and that, in turn, the public pressure mechanism is strongly conditioned by the extent of press freedom" (Themudo 2013: 82). In other words, corruption stands a much better chance of being weeded out if civil society is strong, which depends on the presence of a free press.

To be fair, the relationship between civil society and a free press is one of the few aspects to which the UN draws attention in the rare case press freedom is brought up at all, most often in the context of World Press Freedom Day. But as the previous section outlines, there is more to press freedom than simply being a means to secure the right to freedom of expression. Despite the vital social and political functions a free press fulfills, this idea of press freedom as a common or human right, has not taken hold in the established discourse.

This might ultimately go back to the assumption that because the right to freedom of expression covers journalists and other media workers just like every other individual, a specific protection for the press is not necessary. While this might be an acceptable notion in theory, the reality looks very different. The fact that journalists are more prominent precisely because they have more power as a result of reaching a bigger audience than regular citizens means that they are the first ones to be arrested or killed. The many reports on journalist mistreatment seem to suggest that the international community recognizes this circumstance to some degree, but plans to anchor press freedom more firmly within the human rights framework are nonetheless lacking. Surely, the fact that journalists in theory enjoy the same right to freedom of expression should not detract from extending special safeguards for press freedom. Equal rights for women are not specifically spelled out in most domestic legislation, and yet the human rights community considers it a priority to promote equal rights for women and to monitor and admonish those that violate them. Press freedom, however, enjoys a neglected status at the international level and often has to give way to human rights considerations of Internet freedom, despite the fact that those two concepts diverge as well.

Press freedom versus internet freedom

In his 1991 book *Images of the First Amendment*, Lee Bollinger makes the point that freedom of the press, in its central and widely accepted image, is about the state not being allowed to coerce the press in order for the public to receive the information they need to make up their minds on their own and ultimately to be the sovereign. But Bollinger also outlines another press freedom image that tends to be downplayed in US domestic considerations, namely the fact that if unfettered, the press can also be a gatekeeper with influence over which voices get heard (Bollinger 1991). This has become more of a concern after the advent of radio and television news and has led to the implementation of regulations aimed at guaranteeing fair and balanced access to a plurality of voices.

At the international level, it is the second image of press freedom that dominates, while Bollinger's central image is mostly ignored. The human rights community is primarily concerned with the dangers of the gatekeeper role of the press. This is hardly surprising considering that in the majority of states the government has control over most, if not all, broadcasting channels. But this state of affairs has also had the unfortunate consequence of reducing the positive functions of the press as guardian of the people as sovereign to the notion of the press as a mere tool of the government.

This reality is reinforced by the fact that the Internet, particularly social media, is currently treated as the cure-all to the gatekeeper problem. Because the Internet eliminates access barriers, everyone can be heard. Consequently, the freedom of expression community is concerned with keeping the Internet free from restrictions. While this is undoubtedly an important cause, one that should not be at odds with promoting press freedom, it tends to neglect the role of journalists and the wider implications of a free press.

Recently, Article 19, an NGO dedicated to the promotion of freedom of expression, published a policy brief in which it makes the case for the international community to recognize the right to blog. Again, this is a laudable cause since bloggers are targeted and prosecuted by many governments for their political views. However, Article 19 also calls for a functional definition of journalism, meaning it is "an activity that can be exercised by anyone" (Article 19 2013: 1). While in theory this might be workable, in practice it is not. The functions of the press cannot simply be replaced by access to Blogger or Twitter. For one, 61% of the world's population is still without Internet access (International Telegraph Union 2013).

Furthermore, what is published on blogs and social media is primarily information, not necessarily context. There are bloggers that investigate, fact-check and explain. But there is no guarantee that they will be heard. It is easy to get published online but it is difficult to be heard and even more difficult to be heard by a critical mass. Traditional or professional journalists are still needed to sift through the vast amounts of information we are bombarded with and give it meaning, particularly for those people who do not spend their time searching for information online on their own initiative. Even though journalism *can* be exercised by anyone, it does not mean that it *will* be exercised by everyone; or that everyone will have the time or incentive to actively pursue the efforts of citizen journalists. Those people, too, have a right to a political institution that makes sure their government responds to their interests. And that institution is the press.

What the Internet is good at, among many other things, is making traditional journalism more accountable, since it is much easier to spot errors in reporting with an added layer of online fact-checkers who have the tools to spread the news about these errors more quickly. It is one way of bringing the press closer to the people and making them more responsive to the public's interests, which is what the press is supposed to look out for in the first place. It also shows how press freedom and Internet freedom are two sides of the same coin and work best together. It does not show, however, that focusing exclusively on Internet freedom will solve the problem of securing an unrestricted, independent press. If anything, political and civil rights would benefit if in addition to the gatekeeper concern, the human rights community would invest more resources in highlighting what Bollinger calls the central image of press freedom: that a free press protects the status of the people as the masters of their government.

There are more roadblocks on the way to a more visible place for press freedom in human rights, however. These will be addressed briefly in the next section.

Common sources of resistance to press freedom as a human right

Of course, the different roles of the press described above are mostly best-case scenarios, ones that only rarely translate into reality in their idealized theoretical understanding. The press and the systems in which it operates have many flaws. In some cases, as in the UK News of the World phone-hacking scandal, the press abdicates its responsibilities entirely and thus opens itself up to criticisms from those who would like to see the power of the press checked. However, politicians are not the only ones who emphasize the problems of a free press at the expense of its merits. All too often observers and the public alike forget about the vital role the press plays in the protection of democracy and human rights.

Granted, dealing with the press in legal and political terms is often complicated. Below are a few excuses that are commonly brought up in discussions of press freedom and its special status in the political system. This is not an argument to ignore any of these concerns but rather a reminder that we should not let them drown out the reasons for giving the "great bulwark of liberty" (Annals of Congress, 1st Cong., 1st session, p. 451) its rightful place in the context of human rights.

Problems for press freedom usually start with definitions. Much of the First Amendment literature, and many of the US Supreme Court rulings, are concerned with the difficulty of defining the term "the press." This is further complicated by considerations of what the Founding Fathers meant by the term and the fact that the media landscape has drastically changed since the creation of the Bill of Rights and even since the drafting of the Universal Declaration of Human Rights. Things become even thornier when considering the fact that these days "the press" has practically disappeared in common usage. Instead, it has been replaced by "media" to be all inclusive and nondiscriminatory, when in fact some discrimination in this context might be helpful (Rosen 2003).

By trying to protect any and all media, the unique functions of the press outlined above are diluted and downplayed. Most movies do not serve a political oversight purpose. Nor do dance competition shows on television or food blogs, for instance. The key is to differentiate between the all-encompassing media and the press that is engaged in newsgathering activities, that provides government oversight, and that facilitates the democratic dialogue. This is not to say that food bloggers and screenwriters have no right to freedom of speech. Of course they do. But their rights are guaranteed by the right to freedom of expression, whereas the special political functions of the press are rarely recognized within the human rights debate and even more rarely legally protected.

Others have argued that it is possible to determine who and what constitute being part of the press and thus deserve protection that goes beyond the general free speech rights (West 2011). Arguing that it is difficult to define the press should not be an excuse for not treating it as the important right that it is.

Furthermore, if press freedom is recognized as a distinct human right, the fact that media systems differ dramatically from one country to the next, even within the West, will not pose any more obstacles to addressing press freedom more uniformly at the international level. In this case, it will not matter if the press in Britain and France developed differently, or whether one system is market oriented in one country and government subsidized in another. As long as the press is recognized for playing these important structural roles and protected for it, other differences will become less of an obstacle in framing press freedom as a human right.

Another reason that is often brought up in negative reference to the media is its status as an economic actor. At the international level global media corporations are often seen within the debate of Western cultural and economic dominance and exploitation of other countries. While this is an important debate, the narrow focus on the media's economic status and the resulting drawbacks often lead to the political and social functions of the press being overlooked.

Another concern is that many people think of the press as an elite club, rubbing shoulders with political insiders instead of being in touch with the needs of the public. Related to this is Anthony Lewis' (1991) argument that it makes people apprehensive to talk about the press as a political institution or watchdog, because referring to it as such invokes the notion of outside checks. The question that arises, then, is who is supposed to check the press?

This is certainly a valid concern, but it is also a somewhat hypocritical question. It puts much more confidence in the other branches of government to exercise oversight over each other, although they have vastly more capabilities to affect the lives of its citizens in harmful ways than the press does. While presidents or members of parliament can abuse their access to law enforcement and legislation, the press has no such power. It can fail in its task of informing the citizenry adequately, as in the case of the 2003 invasion of Iraq, when the US press neglected to ask policymakers tough questions on behalf of the public.

Overall, however, the benefits of a free press far outweigh the disadvantages. Without it, democracy would be unthinkable because it is the only way to ensure that the government ultimately remains responsive to the people, the sovereign. The final arbiter is the public and as such, if the public does not want a free press, there will not be one (Altschull 1990). The first step on the way to secure the birthright to a free press for everyone, therefore, is to stop focusing on the alleged dangers of a free press and instead concentrate on the good it brings.

Conclusion

The evidence shows that press freedom is not receiving adequate attention in the context of human rights; that it is, for the most part, neglected in the human rights literature and subsumed by other debates, mostly by those on freedom of expression. Historically and philosophically, however, press freedom is closely linked to protecting civil and political rights, even more so than freedom of expression. The central difference to freedom of expression is the fact that the press possesses power that it draws from its mass audience and its resulting status as the people's surrogate. Its role is to protect the masses from the age-old conviction that power corrupts and implement the notion that those in charge of running the government consequently require an outside checking mechanism that holds them accountable to the public whose interests they are representing.

However, the human rights community tends to neglect this vital function of the press, while governments from Beijing to Washington, DC, know how to conveniently draw the lines between the broader but not necessarily political concept of free speech and the notion of a free press whose role is to exercise political oversight. But as press freedom is increasingly coming under threat worldwide, it is time for the human rights community to rethink its current treatment of the press and reinstate it as a fundamental ingredient to securing political and civil rights and start promoting it as the guardians of the human rights movement's central goal of making the people the masters of their own governments.

Notes

1. Sohn and Buergenthal's 1973 classic *International Protection of Human Rights* only addresses press freedom violations in Haiti, while freedom of expression and information receive considerably more prominent coverage.
2. There are plenty of other human rights texts that do not mention press freedom either, such as L. J. MacFarlane's *The Theory and Practice of Human Rights* from 1985, *Human Rights in the World Community* by Claude and Weston from 2006, Haas' *Improving Human Rights* from 1994, and Philip Alston's *The United Nations and Human Rights* from 1992, for example.
3. The 10 most prominent human rights articles have between 100 and 492 citations each.

References

ALSTON, Philip (ed.). (1992) *The United Nations and Human Rights: A Critical Appraisal* (Oxford: Clarendon Press).
ALTERMAN, Jon B. (2011) The revolution will not be tweeted. *The Washington Quarterly*, 34, 103–116.
ALTSCHULL, J. Herbert. (1990) *From Milton to McLuhan: The Ideas behind American Journalism* (New York: Longman).
ARTICLE 19. (2013) *The Right to Blog* (London: Article 19).

BARRY, Ellen. (2013, February 14) Russia seeks the arrest of a politician from Georgia. *New York Times.* [Online]. Available: http://www.nytimes.com/2013/02/15/world/europe/russia-seeks-arrest-of-georgian-politician-givi-targamadze.html?_r=0 [2 January 2016].

BLASI, Vincent. (1977) The checking value in First Amendment theory. *American Bar Foundation Research Journal,* 2(3), 521–649.

BOBBIO, Norberto. (1989) *Democracy and Dictatorship: The Nature and Limits of State Power* (Minneapolis: University of Minnesota Press).

BOLLINGER, Lee C. (1986) *The Tolerant Society* (New York: Oxford University Press).

BOLLINGER, Lee C. (1991) *Images of a Free Press* (Chicago, University of Chicago Press).

BRANDEIS, Louis D. (1914) *Other People's Money: And How the Bankers Use It* (New York: F.A. Stokes).

BRANZBURG V. HAYES. (1972) 408 U.S. 665.

CARLYLE, Thomas. (1841) *On Heroes, Hero-Worship, and the Heroic in History* (London: James Fraser).

CHAYES, Sarah. (2012, September 18) Does "innocence of Muslims" meet the free-speech test? *Los Angeles Times.* [Online]. Available: http://articles.latimes.com/2012/sep/18/opinion/la-oe-chayes-innocence-of-muslims-first-amendment-20120918 [2 January 2016].

CLAUDE, Richard P., and WESTON, Burns H. (2006) *Human Rights in the World Community: Issues and Actions* (Philadelphia: University of Pennsylvania Press).

COMMISSION ON FREEDOM OF THE PRESS. (1947) *A Free and Responsible Press* (Chicago: University of Chicago Press).

D'ANGELO, Paul, POLLOCK, John C., KIERNICKI, Kristen, and SHAW, Donna. (2013) Framing of AIDS in Africa: Press-state relations, HIV/AIDS news, and journalistic advocacy in for sub-Saharan Anglophone newspapers. *Politics and the Life Sciences,* 32(2), 100–125.

DEMERS, David, and VISWANATH, K. (eds.). (1999) *Mass Media, Social Control, and Social Change: A Macrosocial Perspective* (Ames, IA: Iowa State University Press).

DONNELLY, Jack. (2003) *Universal Human Rights in Theory and Practice* (Ithaca, NY: Cornell University Press).

DUNHAM, Jennifer, NELSON, Bret, and AGHEKYAN, Elen. (2015) *Press Freedom in 2014: Harsh Laws and Violence Drive Global Decline* (Washington, DC: Freedom House).

DWORKIN, Ronald. (1996) *Freedom's Law: The Moral Reading of the American Constitution* (Cambridge, MA: Harvard University Press).

EUROPEAN COMMISSION HIGH LEVEL GROUP ON MEDIA FREEDOM AND PLURALISM. (2013, January) *A Free and Pluralistic Media to Sustain European Democracy* (Brussels: European Commission).

FORSYTHE, David P. (2009) *Encyclopedia of Human Rights* (Oxford: Oxford University Press).

FORSYTHE, David P. (2012) *Human Rights in International Relations* (Cambridge: Cambridge University Press).

GARRY, Patrick M. (1990) *The American Vision of a Free Press* (New York: Garland Publishing, Inc.).

GAUBATZ, K. T. (2013) *Human Rights Citation Database* [ongoing research project] (Old Dominion University).

GOOGLE BOOKS. (n.d.) *Ngram Viewer.* [Online]. Available: https://books.google.com/ngrams [3 March 2014].

GREENWALD, Glenn. (2014) *No Place to Hide: Edward Snowden, the NSA, and the U.S. Surveillance State* (New York: Metropolitan Books).

GUSEVA, Marina E. A. (2008) *Press Freedom and Development* (Paris: UNESCO).

HAAS, Michael. (1994) *Improving Human Rights* (Westport, CT: Praeger).

HALLIN, Daniel C., and MANCINI, Paulo. (2004) *Comparing Media Systems: Three Models of Media and Politics* (Cambridge: Cambridge University Press).

HOLMES, Stephen. (1990) Liberal constraints of private power? Reflections on the origins and rationale of access regulation. In *Democracy and the Mass Media,* J. Lichtenberg (ed.) (Cambridge: Cambridge University Press).

INTERNATIONAL TELEGRAPH UNION (ITU). (2013) *The World in 2013: ICT Facts and Figures* (Geneva: ITU).

JACOBS, Ronald N., and TOWNSLEY, Eleanor. (2011) *The Space of Opinion: Media Intellectuals and the Public Sphere* (New York: Oxford University Press).

JEFFERY, Anthea J. (1986) Free speech and press: An absolute right? *Human Rights Quarterly*, 8(2), 197–226.

JORGENSEN, Nick. (2009) Impunity and oversight: When do governments police themselves? *Journal of Human Rights*, 8(4), 385–404.

KEITA, Mohamed. (2012, April 15) Africa's free press problem. *New York Times*. [Online]. Available: http://www.nytimes.com/2012/04/16/opinion/africas-free-press-problem.html [2 January 2016].

LAWSON, Edward. (1996) *Encyclopedia of Human Rights* (Washington, DC: Taylor & Francis).

LEONARD, Thomas C. (1986) *The Power of the Press: The Birth of American Political Reporting* (New York: Oxford University Press).

THE LEVESON INQUIRY. (2012, November) *An Inquiry into the Culture, Practices and Ethics of the Press* (London: The Stationary Office).

LEVY, Leonard W. (1960) *Legacy of Suppression: Freedom of Speech and Press in Early American History* (Cambridge, MA: Belknap Press of Harvard University Press).

LEVY, Leonard W. (1985) *Emergence of a Free Press* (New York: Oxford University Press).

LEWIS, Anthony. (1991) *Make No Law: The Sullivan Case and the First Amendment* (New York: Random House).

LIPMAN, Maria. (2010) Rethinking Russia: Freedom of expression without freedom of the press. *Journal of International Affairs*, 63(2), 153–169. [Online]. Available: http://jia.sipa.columbia.edu/freedom-expression-without-freedom-press/ [2 January 2016].

LIPTAK, Adam. (2014, June 2) Supreme Court rejects appeal from Times reporter over refusal to identify source. *New York Times*. [Online]. Available: http://www.nytimes.com/2014/06/03/us/james-risen-faces-jail-time-for-refusing-to-identify-a-confidential-source.html?_r=0 [2 January 2016].

LIZZA, Ryan. (2013, May 20) The D.O.J. versus James Rosen. *The New Yorker*. [Online]. Available: http://www.newyorker.com/news/news-desk/the-d-o-j-versus-james-rosen [2 January 2016].

MACFARLANE, Leslie J. (1985) *The Theory and Practice of Human Rights* (New York: St. Martin's Press).

MADDEX, Robert L. (2000) *International Encyclopedia of Human Rights: Freedoms, Abuses, and Remedies* (Washington, DC: CQ Press).

MCPHAIL, Tom L. (2010) *Global Communication: Theories, Stakeholders, and Trends* (Malden, MA: Wiley-Blackwell).

MITCHELL, Amy, and ROSENSTIEL, Tom. (2012) *The State of the News Media 2012: Key Findings* (The Pew Research Center's Project for Excellence in Journalism). [Online]. Available: http://stateofthemedia.org/2012/overview-4/key-findings/ [30 January 2013].

MITCHELL, Amy, ROSENSTIEL, Tom, and CHRISTIAN, Leah. (2012) *What Facebook and Twitter Mean for News* (The Pew Research Center's Project for Excellence in Journalism). [Online]. Available: http://stateofthemedia.org/2012/mobile-devices-and-news-consumption-some-good-signs-for-journalism/what-facebook-and-twitter-mean-for-news/ [30 January 2013].

MULLER, Judy. (2011, September 13) Where newspapers thrive. *Los Angeles Times*. [Online]. Available: http://articles.latimes.com/2011/sep/13/opinion/la-oe-muller-weeklies-20110913 [2 January 2016].

NATIONAL NEWSPAPER ASSOCIATION. (2011) *2011 Community Newspaper Readership Survey* (Falls Church, VA: National Newspaper Association).

NEW YORK TIMES CO. V. SULLIVAN. (1964) 376 U.S. 254.

NEW YORK TIMES CO. V. UNITED STATES. (1971) 403 U.S. 713.

NIMMER, Melville B. (1975) Introduction — Is freedom of the press a redundancy: What does it add to freedom of speech? *Hastings Law Journal*, 639–658.

NORRIS, Pippa. (2008) *Driving Democracy: Do Power-Sharing Institutions Work?* (Cambridge: Cambridge University Press).

PEKSEN, Dursen. (2010) Coercive diplomacy and press freedom: An empirical assessment of the impact of economic sanctions on media openness. *International Political Science Review*, 31(4), 449–469.

PUTNAM, Robert D. (2000) *Bowling Alone: The Collapse and Revival of American Community* (New York, Simon & Schuster).

RAMOS, Howard, RON, James, and THOMS, Oskar N. T. (2007) Shaping the Northern media's human rights coverage, 1986–2000. *Journal of Peace Research*, 44(4), 385–406.

REPORTERS COMMITTEE FOR FREEDOM OF THE PRESS. (n.d.) *The Reporter's Privilege Compendium: An Introduction.* [Online]. Available: https://www.rcfp.org/browse-media-law-resources/guides/reporters-privilege/introduction [23 May 2015].

REPORTERS WITHOUT BORDERS. (2015) *2015 World Press Freedom Index.* [Online]. Available: https://index.rsf.org/#!/ [2 January 2016].

ROSEN, Jay. (1999) *What Are Journalists For?* (New Haven: Yale University Press).

ROSEN, Jay. (2003, September 1) *PressThink: An Introduction.* [Online]. Available: http://archive.pressthink.org/2003/09/01/introduction_ghost.html [30 January 2013].

SAVAGE, Charlie, and KAUFMAN, Leslie. (2013, May 14) Phone records of journalists seized by U.S. *New York Times.* [Online]. Available: http://www.nytimes.com/2013/05/14/us/phone-records-of-journalists-of-the-associated-press-seized-by-us.html?pagewanted=all&_r=0 [2 January 2016].

SEN, Amartya. (1999) Democracy as a universal value. *Journal of Democracy*, 10(3), 3–17.

SIMMONS, Beth A. (2009) *Mobilizing for Human Rights: International Law in Domestic Politics* (Cambridge: Cambridge University Press).

SOHN, L. B., and BUERGENTHAL, T. (1973) *International Protection of Human Rights* (New York: Bobbs-Merrill).

TALBOTT, William J. (2005) *Which Rights Should Be Universal?* (Oxford: Oxford University Press).

THEMUDO, Nuno S. (2013) Reassessing the impact of civil society: Nonprofit sector, press freedom, and corruption. *Governance: An International Journal of Policy, Administration, and Institutions*, 26(1), 63–89.

THE UNINHIBITED PRESS, 50 YEARS LATER. (2014, March 8) *New York Times.* [Online]. Available: http://www.nytimes.com/2014/03/09/opinion/sunday/the-uninhibited-press-50-years-later.html?_r=0.

UNESCO. (1991, May 3) Declaration of Windhoek. [Online]. Available: http://www.unesco.org/webworld/fed/temp/communication_democracy/windhoek.htm [2 January 2016].

UNESCO. (1992, October 19) Declaration of Alma Ata. [Online]. Available: http://www.unesco.org/webworld/fed/temp/communication_democracy/almaty.htm [2 January 2016].

UNESCO. (1994, May 6) Declaration of Santiago. [Online]. Available: http://www.unesco.org/webworld/fed/temp/communication_democracy/santiago.htm [2 January 2016].

UNESCO. (1996, January 11) Declaration of Sana'a. [Online]. Available: http://www.unesco.org/webworld/fed/temp/communication_democracy/sanaa.htm [2 January 2016].

UNITED NATIONS. (1948) Universal Declaration of Human Rights.

UNITED NATIONS SECURITY COUNCIL. (2015, May 27) Resolution 2222.

WALKER, Chris. (2015, April 17) Welcome to the alternate universe of faux democracy. *Washington Post.* [Online]. Available: http://www.washingtonpost.com/opinions/welcome-to-the-alternate-universe-of-faux-democracy/2015/04/17/e1569526-d7e9-11e4-8103-fa84725dbf9d_story.html [2 January 2016].

WEST, Sonja R. (2011) Awakening the press clause. *UCLA Law Review*, 58, 1025–1070.

WINSTON, Morton. (2015) Preface. In *Journalism and Human Rights: How Demographics Drive Media Coverage*, John C. Pollock (ed.) (New York: Routledge).

News about her: The effects of media freedom and internet access on women's rights

Jenifer Whitten-Woodring

University of Massachusetts Lowell

ABSTRACT
Human rights organizations have long heralded media freedom as critical to holding government accountable and thereby improving a wide range of human rights. Similarly the Internet and social media are assumed to empower citizens by enabling them to document repression and thereby discourage future abuse. So what does this mean for women's rights? I propose that, when it comes to women's rights, the combination of media freedom and Internet access will make a difference and that the effect of media freedom will depend on Internet access. I test my hypotheses across countries and over time and find that the interaction of Internet access and media freedom has positive effects on women's rights regardless of regime type.

The world is starting to grasp that there is no policy more effective in promoting development, health, and education than the empowerment of women and girls. And I would venture that no policy is more important in preventing conflict, or in achieving reconciliation after a conflict has ended. — Kofi Annan, Secretary-General of the United Nations (2006: para 3)

The reality of Dalit women and girls is one of exclusion and marginalization.... They are often victims of civil, political, economic, social and cultural rights violations, including sexual abuse and violence. — Rashida Manjoo, UN Special Rapporteur on Violence against Women, Its Causes and Consequences (2013: para 2)

#dalitwomenfight (2015)

Repression of women is prevalent across cultures and over history. In fact, it is so fundamental that it is often overlooked. Yet, as evidenced by Kofi Annan's speech heralding Women's Day in 2006, there is increasing recognition that addressing and ameliorating women's rights might just be critical to improving the human condition (Hudson et al. 2014). Harnessing the power of the media to bring attention to violations of women's rights is seen by many to be a first step. Indeed human rights organizations have long heralded media freedom as critical to holding government accountable and thereby improving a wide range of human rights. Similarly, globalized digital media, especially the Internet and social media, are assumed to empower citizens by enabling them to document government repression and to transmit information about the abuses around the world, thereby discouraging future repression. Yet, media are a product of the culture in which they exist, and gender-based repression is often deeply rooted within that culture. Thus, there are many challenges to using media to eradicate the repression of women. The question I seek to answer here is the following: Can a free press make a difference in women's rights, and, if so, under what conditions are free media more or less effective? Moreover, can Internet access, especially access to social media lead to improvements in women's rights?

I propose that, when it comes to women's rights, the ability of media to serve as a fourth estate depends on the combination of media freedom and Internet access. There is evidence that media freedom is not always associated with improved human rights. Whitten-Woodring (2009) found that in an autocracy, free and independent news media were associated with lower government respect for physical-integrity rights (the rights to be free from political imprisonment, murder, torture, and disappearance), but this study was conducted on data for 1980 to 1995, before the widespread availability of online media.[1] Apodaca (2007) found that media freedom and access to radio and television had positive effects on physical-integrity rights, but that Internet availability did not have a significant effect; however, this study was conducted using data for limited years (1989 to 2002 for broadcast media and 1996 to 2002 for the Internet). Moreover, given the cultural roots of gender-based repression, it is unclear whether the findings regarding politically based physical-integrity rights have implications for women's rights. In this study, I build on past research on the role of media in human rights and hypothesize that when it comes to women's rights, media freedom in conjunction with Internet access can be used to create a boomerang effect like that theorized by Keck and Sikkink (1998). In this scenario, marginalized women are able to harness the power of transnational activism through the use of social media and international media to pressure their government to improve their situation. I test this proposal across countries on women's physical security and across countries and over time on women's economic rights and women's political rights and find that the interaction of media freedom with Internet access has a statistically significant and positive effect on women's rights.

In the first section, I discuss the distinct characteristics of women's rights and hypothesize about how accessibility of digital media and media freedom might influence societal and government respect for these rights. In the second section, I detail the data and methods used to develop a multivariate model to test these hypotheses and to identify patterns in the relationship between media accessibility and media freedom across countries and over time. I then present the findings from the statistical analyses, which reveal that the interaction of media freedom and Internet access has a significant, positive, and substantial effect on women's rights. In the concluding section, I discuss the implications of these findings for policy development and future research.

What makes rights women's?

MEERUT: The Baghpat village of Sankrod is suddenly in the limelight for all the wrong reasons. A 23-year-old resident has sought Supreme Court intervention against the Khap panchayat order that a Dalit woman and her sister be raped and paraded naked as payback for their brother's alleged elopement with a married woman from the Jat community. (Rai 2015: para 1)

Though the quote above is from a 2015 *Times of India* article, repression of Dalit women is nothing new. As Dalits or "untouchables," they are at the bottom of India's caste system, and as women they have historically been victims of sexual violence. Yet, the Dalit women are not alone. In fact, repression of women may well be the original oppression. Citing research by anthropologists and evolutionary biologists, Hudson et al. (2014) assert that repression of women—from domestic violence to economic, legal, and political inequalities—was probably the first form of systematic structural violence among humans and may be a root cause of human conflict at the civil and international levels. Indeed, one of the challenges in detecting repression of women is that gender inequalities are so widespread and so common that they are often the norm rather than the exception.

Unlike physical-integrity rights, which tend by definition to be determined by political factors, women's rights (or the lack thereof) are frequently linked to social and economic issues (Bunch 1990). Additionally, with violations of physical-integrity rights, the government is generally the perpetrator, whereas violations of women's rights are often carried out at the microlevel by nongovernment actors and tolerated at a societal level. With physical-integrity rights, the government is usually directly involved; with women's rights, the government is generally culpable of a lack of enforcement or, to put it plainly, looking the other way. Of course, one way government can improve women's rights is by instituting laws protecting women from violence and discrimination, but laws are only effective to the degree that they are enforced (Richards and Haglund 2015). Women's rights are violated in both the public and private spheres, at the personal level and the systemic level, and these violations can range from discriminatory practices to physical violence. "Women face violence both in the context of the home (perpetrated by family or an intimate partner) and outside the home (perpetrated by various individuals including government agents, employers, coworkers, and teachers)" (Richards and Haglund 2015: 4–5).

Deciding which rights are women's rights can also be challenging. Pollock (2014) argues that a number of issues, such as human trafficking, HIV/AIDS, access to clean water, and child labor, should also be considered women's rights because they affect women in developing countries more than men. Furthermore, many of these gender disparities are deeply rooted in cultural and religious traditions (Coleman 2004). Consider, for example, female genital mutilation/cutting (FGM/C). Though the international community has condemned FGM/C as a violation of women's physical security, it is still widely practiced in 29 countries in Africa and the Middle East (United Nations Children's Fund [UNICEF] 2013). Yet, with FGM/C, the health risks to women have helped to unify people across cultures in the effort to eradicate the practice, but, in other cases, practices that one culture might deem oppressive are seen by another culture as empowering. Take, for example, the debate over hijabs (headscarves that cover the hair), niqabs (full facial coverings), and burqas (full body coverings). Some have argued that women should have the right to wear these garments as a form of religious expression, but "In Western countries with sizable Muslim citizen minorities or with large-scale Muslim immigration, the question of women's dress was sometimes used to assert so-called national values, such as secularism and gender equality" (Howard-Hassman 2011: 441).

Human rights are generally divided into two categories: negative and positive. Women's physical-integrity rights are negative in that they exist on a fundamental level and can be maintained as long as they are not violated; whereas rights like women's economic and political rights are positive in that their establishment and maintenance require programs and government investment. Of course, as Landman (2006) posited, there are positive and negative dimensions to all human rights. For example, protection of civil liberties and political rights requires government investment in legal systems and electoral institutions; likewise, the protection of social and economic rights requires antidiscrimination policies (Landman 2006). The Convention on the Elimination of All Forms of Discrimination against Women (CEDAW), which was adopted by the United Nations General Assembly in 1979, defines such discrimination as the following:

> [A]ny distinction, exclusion or restriction made on the basis of sex which has the effect or purpose of impairing or nullifying the recognition, enjoyment or exercise by women, irrespective of their marital status, on a basis of equality of men and women, of human rights and fundamental freedoms in the political, economic, social, cultural, civil or any other field. (United Nations 2009: para 2)

While few would contest that women's rights are human rights, there are many reasons to consider the effect of media on these rights independently from their impact on other human rights. In particular, "many violations of women's human rights are distinctly connected to being female—that is, women are discriminated against and abused on the basis of gender" (Bunch 1990: 486). Although the Western concept of human rights tends to emphasize political and civil rights, those who study women's rights consider socioeconomic rights as well because gender discrimination often has socioeconomic impacts. In fact, some have posited that advocating for women's rights will have economic benefits in developing countries. Coleman (2004) argued that, though gender discrimination exacts a heavy toll on women, "ultimately all of society pays a price for them. Achieving gender equality is now deemed so critical to reducing poverty and improving governance that it has become a development objective in its own right." In fact, some have argued that security of women is crucial to security of the state and world peace (Hudson et al. 2014). Yet, there remain significant gender disparities in many parts of the world, in part because this discrimination is still accepted in many cultures (Coleman 2004).

Where the media come in

In August 2015, the story of two Dalit sisters threatened with a rape order made headlines around the world, prompting some members of the British Parliament to call for their government to put pressure on the Indian government. Amnesty International circulated a petition calling on the Indian Supreme Court to protect the sisters. Though questions emerged about the facts of the story, the Supreme Court did eventually order police protection for the family (Basu 2015). Although it is unlikely this incident will lead to any long-term improvements for the Dalit, it does illustrate how news about violence against women can quickly spread around the world.

Some scholars suggest that globalization in general and globalized communication in particular will help to improve the condition of women. Howard-Hassman (2011) contends that globalization has facilitated the international women's movement because "Easier travel and communication enable women from across the globe to unite and work on common concerns" (445) and that this in turn has helped the movement to minimize potential harmful effects of globalization such as sex trafficking. Yet, Hertel cautions that the effects of globalization require that states take steps to prevent marginalization of women:

> [I]f women improve their temporary condition by engaging in globalized production in the formal sphere but the state opts out of its regulatory responsibilities in that sphere or fails to

support women's reproductive and informal sector work, then women's long-term position will not change and can even be eroded by globalization. (2011: 454)

Amnesty International and Human Rights Watch have advocated for media freedom and increased access to online media, arguing that independent news media and online media will improve human rights by letting citizens know and spread the word about repression (Amnesty International 2006). Certainly news media and social media can serve as mechanisms to spread information, and the Internet, in particular, makes it easy to transmit information around the world. If journalists are truly able and willing to provide a voice to the voiceless, it stands to reason that by drawing attention to the plight of marginalized women, journalists and news media might be able to make a difference.

Yet, just because news media have the capacity to function freely and to criticize those in power, does not mean they will do so.[2] In fact, there may need to be a certain level of respect for women's rights in place before news media would consider covering issues that matter to women. For example, Pollock (2014) found that female empowerment (a measure based on indicators including female literacy, life expectancy, and education) was associated with increased newspaper support for nongovernment intervention to address issues of particular importance to women such as access to clean water. Similarly, access to the Internet and social media do not guarantee that people will use these tools to bring about change or that anyone will pay attention if they try to do so.[3] In fact, the prevalence of gender-based repression often goes undetected and unreported because it has been "normalized" (Hudson et al. 2014). Certainly media (including traditional news media and social media) have been complicit in this normalization. Yet, because many, including journalists themselves, believe a key role of the news media is to provide a voice for the voiceless (Kovach and Rosenstiel 2001), the ability of a news media to improve government and societal respect for women's rights is a reasonable test of effective media. Similarly, while much has been made of the potential of the Internet to facilitate communication and to improve human rights, little is known about the effect of Internet access on women's rights.

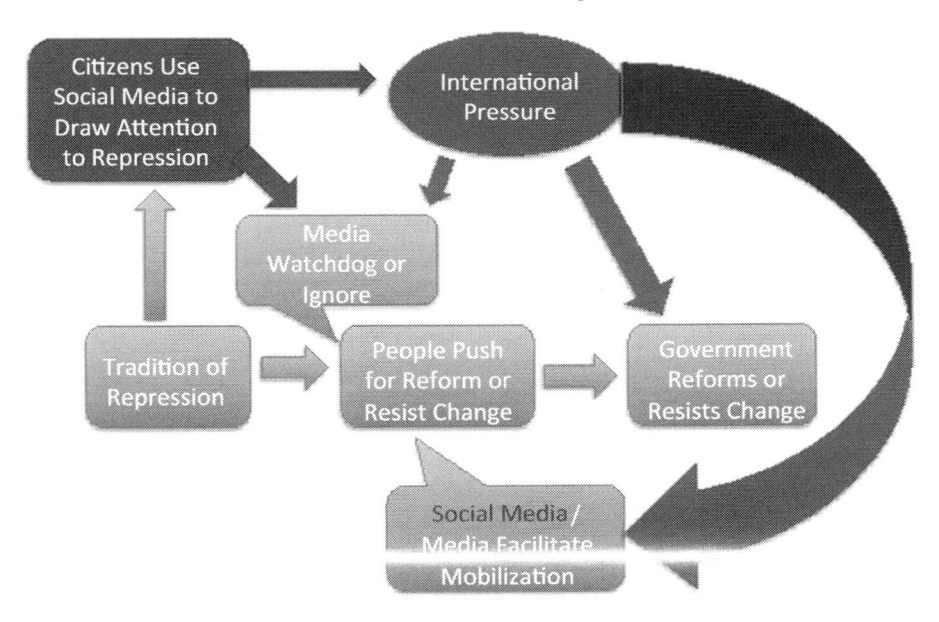

Figure 1. The role of news media and new media on women's rights.

The potential intervening role of traditional news media and social media in the repression of women is depicted in Figure 1. I propose that it is unlikely that the news media will cover violations of women's rights in states where there is a tradition of repression because there is probably a cultural tolerance for such violations. Thus, I expect that *news media will not cover the repression until the violations breach cultural tolerance or there is some sort of external pressure on news media.* This external pressure could come from citizens (international or domestic) using social media to draw attention to the violations. This social-media-generated pressure could also garner attention from international groups and international news media, which, in turn could lead to international governments and nongovernment organizations pressuring the domestic government to stop the repression. Both domestic media and social media could also be used to mobilize protest at the domestic level, which could also lead to reform. This is, in short, a media-driven and Internet-fueled version of Keck and Sikink's (1998) boomerang effect.[4]

Additionally, I posit that cultural attitudes toward gender equality are likely to influence not only whether women's rights are respected but also the amount of attention and quality of news coverage the media provide. For example, in Burkina Faso in 1975, the practice of FGM/C was common and widely accepted as an important coming-of-age ritual for young women. Because most Burkinabe believed the cutting was appropriate, they were unreceptive to negative messages about it. Therefore, a radio campaign against excision was met with great hostility (Triendregeogon 1982). Of course cultural attitudes can shift over time. As a case in point, attitudes towards female employment began to change in the United States during World War I when women stepped into jobs traditionally held by men. To encourage women to work in factories during the war, the government launched the "United War Work Campaign," which featured posters showing women at work. These images were widely spread through the media and contributed to a shift in attitudes about the role of women (although certainly many disparities remained in place) and likely led to the passage of the Nineteenth Amendment in 1920, which gave women voting rights.

Thus, I propose that media are more likely to report on violations of women's rights when there is some sort of pressure to do so. This pressure could come from a government program (as in the case of the campaigns encouraging women to work in factories during World War I and World War II), but it could also come in the form of international pressure from transnational activist groups and organizations like Amnesty International and/or conditions for foreign assistance. Additionally, I suspect, when they do get involved, news media and social media are more likely to focus on the most egregious and most obvious violations of women's rights. Both news media and social media are drawn to issues and stories that are dramatic, shocking, and unexpected. Therefore, public violence against women and overt political discrimination are far more likely to garner news media and social media attention than private violence against women and ongoing economic discrimination.

As depicted in Figure 1, if there is a tradition of repression of women's rights, it may take international pressure to spur the media to cover women's issues, and it may well take citizens themselves using social media to focus that international attention on the repression. Moreover, social media decrease the costs for citizens to draw international attention to domestic problems and can facilitate the formation of networks of activists seeking to improve women's rights (Keck and Sikkink 1998). Both news media and social media may play intervening roles by serving as mechanisms to facilitate and mobilize protest movements as long as news media are able to function freely and citizens have Internet access. Thus, I propose that it is the interaction of media freedom and Internet access that could help to mitigate gender-based repression.

Based on the propositions outlined above, this study tests the following hypotheses:

H1: Media freedom is positively related to women's rights.

H2: Internet access is positively related to women's rights.

H3: The effect of media freedom on women's rights depends on Internet access and vice versa.

Research design, data, and methods

To explore the relationship between media (especially media freedom and access to digital media) and women's rights and to test my hypotheses across countries and over time, I developed several statistical models of women's rights. To create these models, I merged data from several datasets. In each model, the unit of analysis is a country-year. In this section, I provide details about these datasets and the selected variables, starting with the dependent variables for women's rights, followed by the primary independent variables of media freedom and Internet access, and a number of additional variables that have been identified from previous research as potentially influencing women's rights.

Dependent variables: Measuring women's rights

As evidenced from previous studies, repression of women takes on many forms. Because I suspect that media will be a more effective mechanism in mitigating violations of political and physical-security rights rather than economic rights, I test my hypotheses on these three types of women's rights using three different dependent variables from two publicly available datasets, the CIRI Human Rights Dataset (Cingranelli et al. 2014a) and the Woman-Stats Database (WomanStats Project 2015). The CIRI Human Rights Dataset, which focuses on government practices regarding a broad range of human rights, including women's economic and political rights, provides annual coding for about 200 countries from 1980 to 2011.[5] In contrast, the WomanStats Database focuses exclusively on women's rights and issues and provides comprehensive information about the status of women in 175 countries. For this study, I use the Physical Security of Women Scale for all available countries in the year 2009.[6] Table 1 shows the distribution of these three women's rights variables for the samples used in this study. Details about these variables and how they were gathered are provided below.

Women's economic rights from the CIRI Human Rights Dataset

CIRI coders assessed all available countries from 1980 to 2011 on several dimensions related to the economic freedom of women, including equality in compensation, hiring and promotion practices, freedom to choose profession without male consent, freedom from discrimination and sexual harassment, and the right to work in the military, law enforcement, and other dangerous occupations. Based on this assessment, each country-year is rated on a scale ranging from 0 (no rights) to 3 (full rights) using two primary considerations, "one, the extensiveness of laws pertaining to women's economic rights; and two, *government practices* towards women or how effectively the government enforces the laws" (Cingranelli et al. 2014b: 77). As shown in Table 1, the majority country-year cases have middle to low levels

Table 1. Measuring women's rights.

Women's Economic Rights 1980–2011 (148 Countries in sample) Source: CIRI Human Rights Database	Code	Frequency	Percentage
No economic rights for women; discriminatory laws may exist	0	334	8
There are some laws protecting women's economic rights, but they are not enforced	1	2192	56
There are some laws protecting women's economic rights and these are enforced, but there a low level of discrimination remains	2	1233	31
All or nearly all women's economic rights are guaranteed in law and practice	3	181	5

Women's Political Rights 1980–2011 (148 Countries in sample) Source: CIRI Human Rights Database	Code	Frequency	Percentage
No laws protecting women's political rights	0	152	4
There are laws protecting women's political rights, but these are severely prohibited in practice	1	688	17
There are laws protecting women's political rights, but these are somewhat prohibited in practice	2	2831	71
Women's political rights are guaranteed in law and practice	3	309	8

Physical Security of Women for 2009 (143 Countries in sample) Source: WomanStats Database	Code	Inverted Code	Frequency	Percentage
No or weak laws protecting women's physical security; honor killings/femicide ignored or accepted	4	0	40	28
Laws protecting women's physical security are rarely enforced; honor killings/femicide generally not accepted	3	1	71	50
Laws protecting women's physical security sporadically enforced; honor killings/femicide rare and condemned by society	2	2	23	16
Laws protecting women's physical security usually enforced, but there are norms against reporting related crimes; no honor killings/femicides	1	3	9	6
Laws protecting women's physical security are enforced; there are no norms against reporting related crimes; no honor killings/femicides	0	4	0	0

of government respect of women's economic rights. In 56% of the cases, there are some laws protecting women's economic rights, but these are not enforced in practice. Only 5% of the cases had full respect for women's economic rights.

Women's political rights from the CIRI Human Rights Dataset

CIRI coders assessed all available countries from 1981 to 2011 on aspects related to the political freedom of women including voting rights and the rights to petition government officials, to join political parties, to run for political office, and to hold government positions, as well as representation (Cingranelli et al. 2014b). As with the indicator for women's economic rights, the coding for this variable ranges from 0 (no rights) to 3 (full rights) and centers on the "extensiveness of laws" pertaining to women's political rights as well as enforcement of those laws and practice. As depicted in Table 1, in most country-year cases (71%), respect for women's political rights was at Level 2, meaning that there were laws protecting women's political rights, but these were somewhat prohibited in practice.

The physical security of women from the WomanStats Database[7]

Coders for WomanStats assessed the physical security of women in 175 countries based on the country's laws and practices regarding domestic violence, rape and sexual assault, marital rape, femicide (meaning the targeted killing of women), and honor killings (WomanStats Project 2015).[8] Based on this assessment, each country is rated on a scale that ranges from 0 (meaning there are laws against these crimes that are enforced and these crimes are rare) to 4 (meaning there are no laws against these crimes or that existing laws are not enforced, and honor killings and femicide go unpunished). In 2009, there were no countries at the 0 level; thus, in practice, from a women's rights perspective, the best score in 2009 was a 1, meaning that, while there are laws against domestic violence, marital rape, rape and sexual assault, and femicide and these laws are usually respected in practice, "there are taboos or norms against reporting these crimes (or ignorance that these are reportable crimes)" (WomanStats Project 2015: para 2). Only 6% of the country-year cases reached this level of physical security for women. In fact, most cases had low (50%) or no (28%) physical security for women (see Table 1). For ease of interpretation, I have inverted this scale so that higher values mean higher levels of physical security for women. Thus, this inverted scale ranges from 0 (meaning there are no laws or there is no enforcement of laws against the crimes related to women's physical security) to 3 (meaning there are laws protecting the physical security of women that are usually respected in practice, but there are some norms or taboos that sometimes prevent the reporting of these crimes). Using this inverted version of the Physical Security of Women scale keeps it consistent with the two CIRI variables, such that higher values mean higher levels of women's rights.

Independent variables: Media freedom and internet access

When analyzing the effect of media freedom, it is important to use a clearly defined measure of media freedom that is consistent over time. To that end, I use the Global Media Freedom Dataset (GMFD) gathered by Whitten-Woodring and Van Belle (2014). The GMFD is a definition-driven dataset that provides codes for the media environment of all available countries from 1948 to 2012.[9] Rather than measuring media restrictions, the GMFD categorizes the media environment for each country-year based on a conceptualization of media freedom as the ability of media to hold those in power accountable.

Media freedom from the Global Media Freedom Dataset (GMFD)

Coders for the GMFD project assessed the media environment for each country-year and placed it in one of the following categories: Free, meaning criticism of government and officials is a common part of the political dialogue; Imperfectly Free, meaning there are costs (social, legal, and/or economic) related to criticism of government or officials that limit criticism, but investigative journalism and criticism does occur; Not Free, meaning it is not possible to safely criticize government or officials and media are either indirectly controlled or directly controlled (Whitten-Woodring and Van Belle 2015). This is a categorical coding rather than an interval scale; the difference between media environments coded Imperfectly Free and those coded Not Free is far more substantial than the differences between those coded Free and Imperfectly Free. Therefore, I have combined the Free and Imperfectly Free categories because media in both of these categories function freely.

Internet access from the International Telecommunication Union (ITU)

The ITU (2014) provides an estimate of the percentage of individuals using the Internet based on surveys conducted in each country-year based on guidelines from the ITU. This measure incorporates Internet access via all devices, including smartphones. In my sample, the percentage of Internet users ranges from less than 2 (Liberia in 2000) to 94 (Sweden in 2011) with a mean of about 22. While smart phones are a growing and strikingly important means of accessing online media, particularly in developing countries (Aker and Mbiti 2010), the ITU Internet-penetration dataset incorporates Internet access obtained through mobile technology. Thus, I do not include mobile phone penetration in these analyses.

Control variables

Of course there are factors other than media freedom and Internet access that might influence women's rights. Previous studies have identified democracy and international law as well as a variety of domestic features as factors that might shape human rights. Chief among these is democracy. In fact, when studying the effects of media freedom across a range of regime types, a common question is whether media freedom can exist independent of democracy. While most free media occur in highly democratic countries, there are also cases of free media in nondemocratic settings, and there are cases of democracies in which the media are not free (Whitten-Woodring and Van Belle 2014).

In measuring regime type for an analysis that includes both women's rights and media freedom, it is critical to restrict the definition and measurement to institutional democracy, because definitions and measurements of democracy that incorporate civil liberties might also incorporate freedom of speech and of the press as well as human rights. In order to avoid a tautology, to test my hypotheses, and to account for the variation of media freedom across regime types, it is important to keep these measurements discrete. Though the Polity IV dataset does not incorporate civil rights (Marshall and Jaggers 2002; Choi and James 2006), to address any lingering concerns that some aspect of the Polity scale might inadvertently incorporate media freedom or women's rights, I use the executive constraints variable, the component of the Polity scale found to be the most influential (Gleditsch and Ward 1997).

Executive constraints from the Polity IV dataset

Coders for the Polity IV dataset assessed the level of executive constraints, meaning the degree to which the executive's decision-making powers are limited by accountability groups (these may take the form of a legislative body, an independent judiciary, or a military) such that there are checks and balances on the executive's decision-making process. This variable ranges from 1 (meaning "Unlimited Authority") to 7 (meaning "Executive Parity or Subordination") (Marshall, Gurr and Jaggers 2013: 24–25).

Findings regarding the effects of international law on human rights are mixed. Most studies have found that United Nations human rights treaties have little or no effect on human rights practices (Camp Keith 1999; Hathaway 2002; Hafner-Burton and Tsutsui 2007; Englehart 2009), but a couple of recent studies have found that the Convention on the Elimination of All Forms of Discrimination Against Women (CEDAW) has a positive effect on women's rights (Hill 2010; Englehart and Miller 2014). Yet, Richards and Haglund (2015) find that over time participation in the CEDAW had mixed effects on laws protecting women, that it was associated with increased legal protections against domestic violence but decreased protections against rape. Therefore, following Englehart and Miller (2014), I include a dummy variable that indicates whether the country (for the year) in question has ratified CEDAW.

In addition to the CEDAW, I expect the same factors that influence government behavior regarding physical-integrity rights will have similar effects on government respect for women's rights, although not always for the same reasons. I predict that violations of women's rights, as with physical-integrity rights, are more likely to occur when a government is facing a threat of either interstate or internal armed conflict (Poe et al. 1999). Although in the case of women's rights, I expect that violations increase because the government is too distracted by the threats posed by the civil conflict and international conflict on women's rights. To control for conflict, I use the Major Episodes of Political Violence (MEPV) and Conflict Regions, 1945–2012, dataset (Marshall 2013). Specifically, I use the CIVTOT variable to measure the presence and intensity of civil conflict (including civil and ethnic violence and war) and the INTTOT variable to measure presence and intensity of international conflict and war. To qualify as a major episode of violence or war, there must be a minimum of 500 directly related deaths over the entire episode and the magnitude of each episode is coded 0 (no conflict) to 10 (highest magnitude of conflict) and this score is entered for each related country/year. If there is more than one episode for a given country/year, the impact scores are summed (Marshall 2013).

I expect the level of economic development to be important with women's rights. Regarding physical-integrity rights, the rationale is that governments with strong economies enjoy more security from the threat of domestic rebellion; therefore, the healthier the economy, the less likely a government will feel the need to engage in repression (Poe et al. 1999). In the case of women's rights, I expect that in less-developed countries where there are fewer jobs to be had, men may feel more threatened by the prospect of women entering the workforce. Inglehart et al. (2002) hypothesized that modernization drives democratization, which in turn encourages female participation in politics. Moreover, "economic development also brings unforeseen cultural changes that transform gender roles" (Inglehart et al. 2002: 4–5). Of course, the argument has been made that the causal arrow runs in the other direction and that a country's level of development depends on women's economic rights (Coleman 2004). Additionally, Richards and Haglund (2015) find that economic globalization has a negative effect on laws aimed at preventing violence against women. Thus, there is evidence that development and trade have mixed effects on women's rights. Moreover, preliminary analyses indicate that economic development is highly correlated with Internet access. This makes sense intuitively—the more developed a country, the more likely it is to have the infrastructure and resources to facilitate Internet access. Unfortunately, because they are highly correlated, it is not possible to include both Internet access and economic development in the same model because doing so can lead to spurious results. Therefore, I control for economic development only in models that do not include Internet access. To measure economic development, I use the gross domestic product (GDP) per capita. Specifically, I use the RGDPE variable from Penn World Tables Version 8 (Feenstra et al. 2015), which is the expenditure-side GDP chain series that has been adjusted for purchasing power parity (PPP) to compare standards of living across countries and over time. Because GDP per capita has a trend of exponential growth, I transform this variable by taking a natural log.

Previous studies have found that population is negatively related to government respect for human rights because the larger the population the greater the opportunity for rebellion and repression (Poe and Tate 1994; Poe et al. 1999). Therefore, I include a log of population for each country/year from the Penn World Tables Version 8 (Feenstra et al. 2015).

Since there is no consistent measure of cultural attitudes toward gender equality that is consistent across countries and over time, I use religion as a proxy for cultural attitudes toward gender equality. My justification for doing so is based on research indicating that there is a strong correlation between religion and attitudes toward gender equality (Inglehart and Norris 2003). Inglehart and Norris (2003) found that Orthodox and Muslim faiths were negatively related with support for gender equality and that Catholic and Protestant faiths were positively related to support for gender equality. Specifically, I use variables for the percentage of Christians, Muslims, Hindus, and people with no religious affiliation for each country-year. These are the four largest religious groups, according to the Pew Research Center's Forum on Religion and Public Life (2012). These percentages were obtained from the World Religion Dataset (Maoz and Henderson 2013).

Finally, when analyzing human rights over time, it is standard practice to control for previous levels of human rights (Davenport and Armstrong 2004; Poe and Tate 1994; Poe et al. 1999). The theoretical reason for doing so is that previous respect for human rights (or the lack thereof) may reflect the cultural intolerance (tolerance) for such violations and also may account for persistence in government behavior regarding human rights. Methodologically, this models any autoregression (the effect of past values of human rights on current values of human rights) in the time-series data. Therefore, I use a one-year lag of the dependent variable.

Statistical methods

Using these measures for the dependent and independent variables, I conducted a series of multivariate analyses. Since the dependent variables each had distinct categories that could be placed in a meaningful order but the distance between the categories is unknown, I chose to use ordered logistic regression. Ordered logistic regression is a nonlinear model that estimates the change in the probability of different categories of the outcome variable for a given change in one of the independent variables with the magnitude of this change in probability depending on the levels of all of the independent variables.

Because media freedom can change overnight and Internet penetration has increased dramatically from one year to another in many countries, I use contemporaneous versions (as opposed to lagged versions) of the independent variables. Since the models using the CIRI variables include cases for each country for each year between 1981 and 2011, I suspect there may be unspecified effects for each of these countries. To control for these effects, I employ robust standard errors, clustering on country identification. For the models using the WomanStats data for the year 2009, I do not control for previous physical security of women, because this study has a limited number of cases (143), and including the lag of physical security would likely mask the effects of the other independent variables (Achen 2000).

Results: The effects of media freedom and internet access on women's rights

Overall the interaction of media freedom and Internet access had significant and positive effects on women's rights. These effects are more substantial for women's political rights and the physical security of women than for women's economic rights. Here I present the findings for each type of women's rights.

Table 2. Women's economic rights: The Internet makes a difference.

	Model 1 1981–1995 141 Countries	Model 2 2000–2011 148 Countries	Model 3 2000–2011 148 Countries
Previous Women's Economic Rights	0.000145	0.00152	0.00146
	(0.000459)	(0.00134)	(0.00138)
Media Freedom	0.653	−0.04022	−0.742*
	(0.33)	(0.27739)	(0.301)
Executive Constraints	0.1299	0.3217***	0.286***
	(0.0959)	(0.0842)	(0.0854)
Percent with Internet Access	—	0.0374***	0.0115
		(0.00544)	(0.0130)
Media Freedom* Internet Access	—	—	0.0328* (0.0143)
CEDAW Ratification	0.3293	0.147	0.229
	(0.274)	(0.536)	(0.529)
International Conflict	0.0376	0.497	0.454
	(0.244)	(0.482)	(0.495)
Civil Conflict	−0.0776	−0.2802**	−0.295**
	(0.0711)	(0.0878)	(0.0900)
GDP/Capita (logged)	0.7089***	—	—
	(0.1887)		
Population (logged)	−0.1513	−0.1231	−0.117
	(0.0865)	(0.08)	(0.0800)
Percent Christian	−0.113	−0.4339	−0.512
	(0.753)	(0.752)	(0.766)
Percent Muslim	−1.612	−1.5329	−1.529*
	(0.839)	(0.79)	(0.780)
Percent Hindu	−1.246	1.2836	1.466
	(1.16)	(1.098)	(1.187)
Percent No Religion	0.852	0.2764	0.0393
	(1.498)	(1.167)	(1.187)
Cut 1	2.457**	−1.538	−1.868*
	(1.013)	(0.841)	(0.852)
Cut 2	6.69***	2.191	1.818*
	(1.107)	(0.869)	(0.867)
Cut 3	10.061***	5.078	4.830***
	(1.597)	(0.915)	(0.900)
Observations	1598	1674	1674
Pseudo $R2$	0.131	0.213	0.221
BIC	2712.5	3034.1	3014.9

Note. These are results from a series of ordered logistic regressions estimated using Stata 14; Standard errors in parentheses.
$^*p < .05$, $^{**}p < .01$, $^{***}p < .001$.

Findings for women's economic rights

The results for women's economic rights are shown in Table 2.[10] Model 1 gives us a picture of the influences on women's economic rights before the Internet became widely available. It includes information for 141 countries from 1981 to 1995. In Model 1, controlling for other factors, only GDP per capita has a statistically significant and positive effect on women's economic rights. Specifically, on average, a one standard deviation increase in GDP per capita increases the probability of having full women's economic rights (Level 3) by about .04 and high women's economic rights (Level 3) by .1 and decreases the probability of having no women's economic rights (Level 0) by .04.[11] In this model, media freedom does not make a difference. In Models 2 and 3, which include 148 countries for the years 2000 to 2011, the story changes with the addition of Internet access. In Model 2, media freedom does not have a

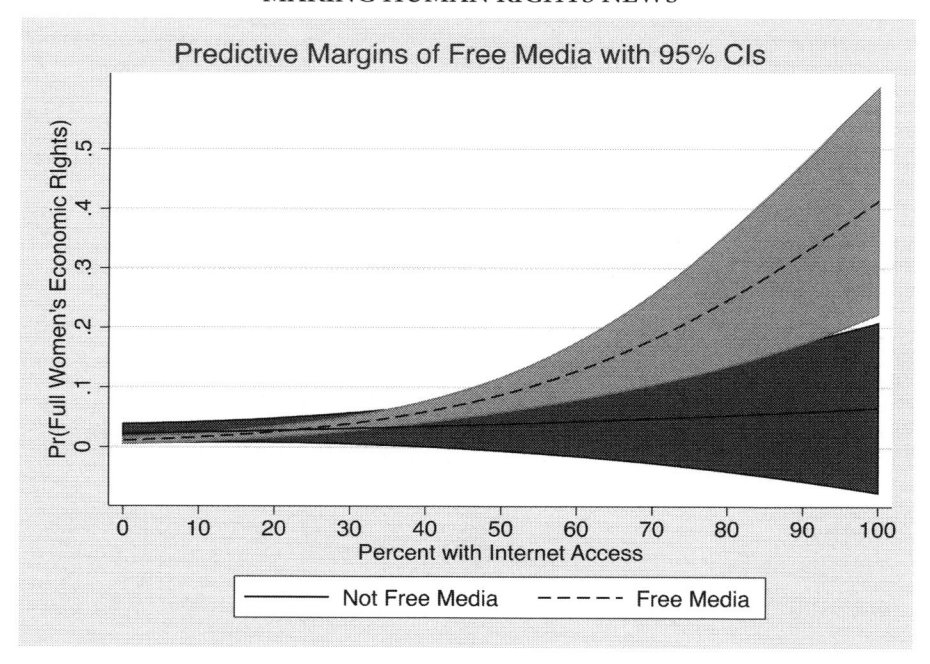

Figure 2. The marginal effects of media freedom and Internet access on the predicted probability of full respect for women's economic rights.
Note. This figure depicts the predicted probability of full respect for women's economic rights as Internet access shifts from 0 to 100% in countries with and without media freedom.

significant independent effect, but Internet access does have a statistically significant and positive effect on women's economic rights. However, fit statistics indicate that Model 3, which includes the interaction of media freedom and Internet access, does a better job of explaining the variation in women's economic rights.[12] In Model 3, the coefficient for the interaction of media freedom with Internet access is statistically significant and positive but because it must be considered in conjunction with the coefficients for media freedom and Internet access, the substantive effects of this interaction are best interpreted graphically. Figure 2 depicts the predicted probability of full respect for women's economic rights in states with free media and not free media as Internet access increases from 0% to 100% while other variables are held constant. The dashed line shows that this probability increases in countries with free media as Internet access increases, whereas the solid line shows that the probability remains close to zero in states with not free media, regardless of the level of Internet access; however, the

Table 3. Average marginal effects of executive constraints, civil conflict, and religion on the predicted probability of different levels of women's economic rights (from Model 3).

	No Rights (0)	Low Rights (1)	High Rights (2)	Full Rights (3)
Executive Constraints(1 standard deviation increase)	−.039***	−.05**	.055***	.034**
Civil Conflict (1 standard deviation increase)	.032**	.019**	−.035**	−.016**
Percentage Muslim (1 standard deviation increase)	.052	.025*	−.053*	−.024*

Note. These are the average marginal effects of changes in the values of the independent variables estimated using SPost13 (Long and Freese 2014).
*$p < .05$, **$p < .01$, ***$p < .001$.

confidence intervals overlap until Internet access exceeds 90%, indicating that media freedom does not have a statistically significant effect until this level of Internet access is achieved and then the probability of full women's economic rights ranges from about .2 to above .5. Executive constraints have a statistically significant and positive effect on women's economic rights. As reported in Table 3, on average a one standard deviation increase in executive constraints increases the probability of full women's economic rights by 0.34. Holding other factors constant, civil conflict and the percentage of Muslims have statistically significant and negative effects on women's economic rights (Table 3 reports the average marginal effects of these variables). Previous women's economic rights, international conflict, CEDAW ratification, population, and other religions did not have statistically significant effects on women's economic rights.

Table 4. Women's political rights: Media freedom and the Internet make a difference.

	Model 4 1981–1995 141 Countries	Model 5 2000–2011 148 Countries	Model 6 2000–2011 148 Countries
Previous Women's Political Rights	0.00124*	0.00144*	0.00147*
	(0.000559)	(0.000724)	(0.000697)
Media Freedom	0.892**	0.403	−0.00144
	(0.337)	(0.503)	(0.537)
Executive Constraints	0.0239	0.043	−0.00221
	(0.094)	(0.137)	(0.136)
Percent with Internet Access	—	0.0234**	−0.0101
		(0.0075)	(0.0105)
Media Freedom* Internet Access	—	—	0.0408**
			(0.0124)
CEDAW Ratification	0.599*	1.201*	1.298*
	(0.246)	(0.523)	(0.511)
International Conflict	0.0643	−0.388	−0.443
	(0.235)	(0.322)	(0.318)
Civil Conflict	0.0156	−0.134	−0.157
	(0.0737)	(0.097)	(0.0971)
GDP/Capita (logged)	0.048	—	—
	(0.185)		
Population (logged)	0.099	0.189	0.192
	(0.105)	(0.107)	(0.106)
Percent Christian	0.607	1.675**	1.660*
	(0.606)	(0.627)	(0.671)
Percent Muslim	−1.235	−1.72**	−1.707**
	(0.638)	(0.594)	(0.643)
Percent Hindu	−0.9	−0.476	−0.144
	(1.233)	(1.309)	(1.281)
Percent No Religion	1.333	−0.039	−0.472
	(1.837)	(1.27)	(1.309)
Cut 1	−1.594	−2.793	−3.230***
	(1.285)	(0.871)	(0.883)
Cut 2	0.704	−0.326	−0.759
	(1.364)	(0.781)	(0.820)
Cut 3	5.478***	5.596	5.226***
	(1.348)	(0.924)	(0.948)
Observations	1623	1675	1675
Pseudo $R2$	0.131	0.216	0.229
BIC	2712.5	2032	2009.7

Note. These are results from a series of ordered logistic regressions estimated using Stata 14; Standard errors in parentheses.
*$p < .05$, **$p < .01$, ***$p < .001$.

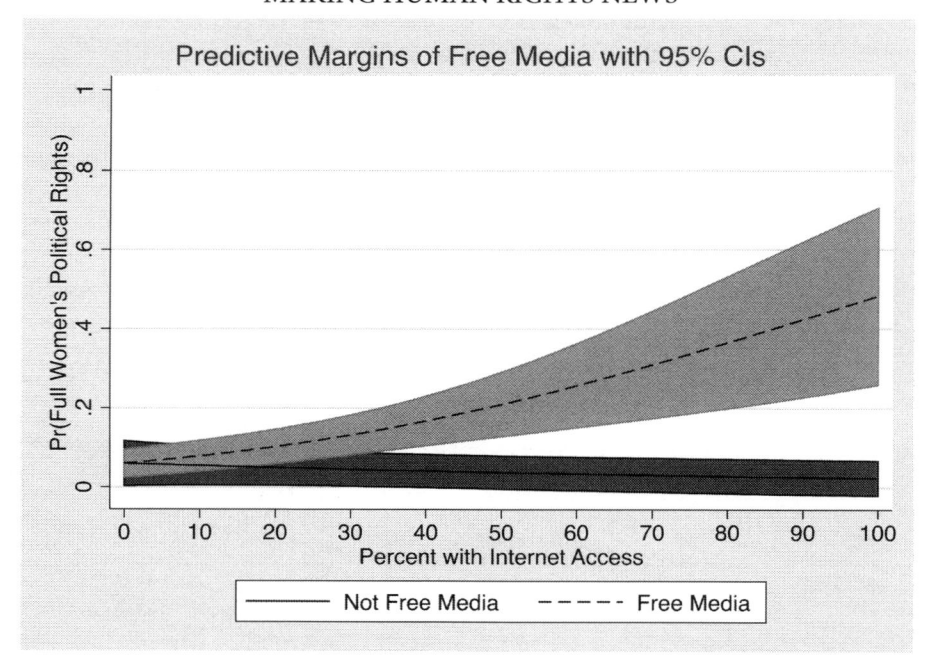

Figure 3. The marginal effects of media freedom and Internet access on the predicted probability of full respect for women's political rights.

Note. This figure depicts the predicted probability of full respect for women's political rights as Internet access shifts from 0 to 100% in countries with and without media freedom.

Findings for women's political rights

Unlike women's economic rights, media freedom does appear to have made a substantive difference in women's political rights, even in the absence of the Internet (see Model 4 of Table 4). Specifically, compared to countries without media freedom, for those with media freedom, the probability of a high level (Level 2) of respect for women's political rights was on average .14 higher, but the effect of media freedom on full respect was not statistically significant. With the addition of the Internet, the effect of media freedom on women's political rights is more pronounced. As shown in Model 5, the Internet has a statistically significant and positive effect, and media freedom does not have independent effect, but, as with

Table 5. Average marginal effects of previous rights, CEDAW ratification, and religion on the predicted probability of different levels of women's political rights for 2000–2011 (from Model 6).

	No Rights (0)	Low Rights (1)	High Rights (2)	Full Rights (3)
Previous Women's Political Rights (1 standard deviation increase)	−.001	−.003*	−.001	.005
CEDAW Ratification	−.023	−.094	.03	.088**
Percentage Christian (1 standard deviation increase)	−.005	−.030**	−.029	.064*
Percentage Muslim (1 standard deviation increase)	.009	.04*	0	−.049**

Note. These are the average marginal effects of changes in the values of the independent variables estimated using SPost13 (Long and Freese 2014).

*$p < .05$, **$p < .01$, ***$p < .001$.

women's economic rights, fit statistics indicate that Model 6 with the interaction of media freedom and Internet access is a better model for women's political rights. Again the effects of this interaction are best interpreted graphically. Figure 3 depicts the predicted probability of full respect for women's political rights in states with free media and not free media as Internet access increases from 0% to 100% while other variables are held constant. The dashed line shows that this probability increases in countries with free media as Internet access increases, whereas the solid shows that the probability remains close to zero in states with not free media, regardless of the level of Internet access. In particular, as Internet access exceeds 30%, media freedom makes a statistically significant difference in the probability of full respect for women's political rights and when Internet access approaches 100%, this predicted probability ranges between .25 and .7.

Also in Model 6, previous women's political rights have a positive and statistically significant effect, indicating that once women have political rights in a state, they have a higher chance of keeping them. CEDAW ratification had a statistically significant and positive effect; on average, the probability of full respect for women's political rights was .088 higher in countries that had ratified the CEDAW (this and other average marginal effects are reported in Table 5). The percentage of Muslims had a statistically significant and negative effect, and the percentage of Christians had a statistically significant and positive effect. Population, the percentage of Hindus, and the percentage of people with no religion were all insignificant. Interestingly executive constraints did not have a statistically significant effect in any of the models of women's political rights.

Findings for women's physical security

The effects of media freedom and Internet access on women's physical security are similar to those for women's political rights. As shown in Table 6, while media freedom does not have

Table 6. Women's physical security: The effect of media freedom depends on Internet access.

	Model 7	Model 8
Media Freedom	−0.350 (0.621)	−1.338 (0.731)
Percent with Internet Access	0.0506*** (0.0101)	0.00502 (0.0188)
Media Freedom* Internet Access	—	0.0617** (0.0225)
Executive Constraints	0.498** (0.182)	0.420* (0.187)
CEDAW Ratification	0.971 (1.204)	1.141 (1.220)
International Conflict	0.281 (0.695)	0.257 (0.713)
Civil Conflict	−0.608** (0.211)	−0.660** (0.207)
Population (logged)	0.0762 (0.132)	0.0956 (0.132)
Percent Christian	0.372 (0.844)	0.381 (0.863)
Percent Muslim	−1.899* (0.921)	−1.565 (0.924)
Percent Hindu	1.233 (2.009)	2.304 (2.045)
Percent No Religion	−1.361 (1.876)	−1.785 (1.906)
Cut 1	2.457 (1.454)	1.686 (1.496)
Cut 2	6.850*** (1.606)	6.297*** (1.642)
Cut 1	9.182*** (1.703)	8.899*** (1.751)
Observations	143	143
Pseudo $R2$	0.345	0.368
BIC	288.9	286.3

Note. These are results from a series of ordered logistic regressions estimated using Stata 14. Standard errors in parentheses.
$^*p < .05, ^{**}p < .01, ^{***}p < .001.$

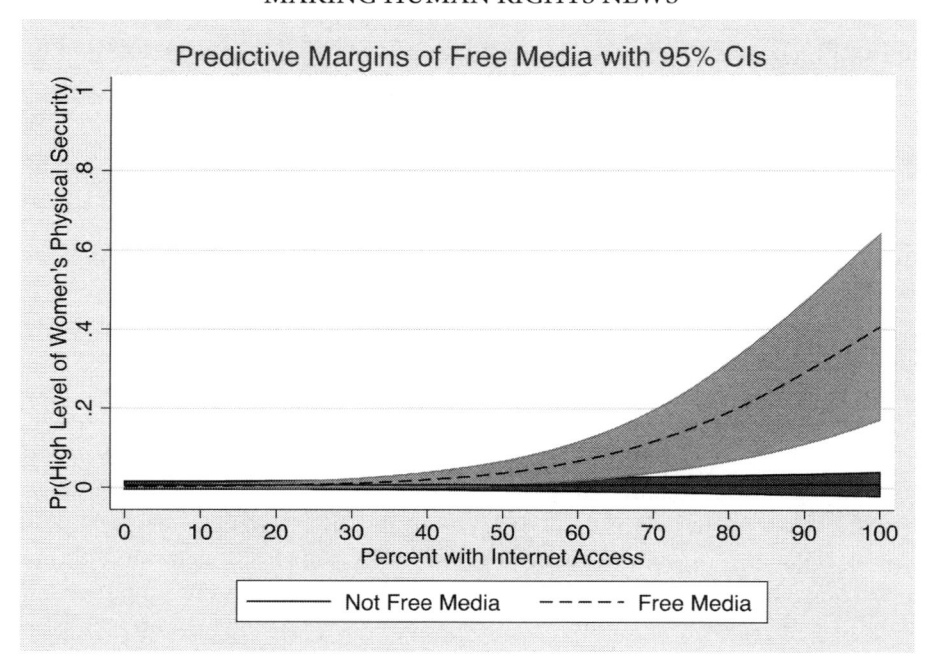

Figure 4. The marginal effects of media freedom and Internet access on the predicted probability of a high level of women's physical security.
Note. This figure depicts the predicted probability of a high level of women's physical security as Internet access shifts from 0 to 100% in countries with and without media freedom.

an independent effect on women's physical security (see Model 7), the interaction of media freedom and Internet access (see Model 8) does have a statistically significant and positive effect on women's physical security. Once again, fit statistics indicate that the model with this interaction is the better model for women's physical security. Figure 4 depicts the effect of media freedom on the predicted probability of a high level of women's physical security as Internet access increases to 100% while other variables are held constant. As indicated by the dashed line, this probability increases in countries with free media as Internet access increases, whereas the solid line shows that the probability remains close to zero in states with not free media, regardless of the level of Internet access. As Internet access approaches 70%, media freedom makes a statistically significant difference in the probability of a high

Table 7. Average marginal effects of executive constraints and civil conflict on the predicted probability of different levels of women's physical security (from Model 8).

	No Security (0)	Low Security (1)	Medium Security (2)	High Security (3)
Executive Constraints (1 standard deviation increase)	−.093**	−.023	−.028	.042
Civil Conflict (1 standard deviation increase)	.098***	−.038**	−.033*	−.027**

Note. These are the average marginal effects of changes in the values of the independent variables estimated using SPost13 (Long and Freese 2014).
*$p < .05$, **$p < .01$, ***$p < .001$.

level of women's physical security and, when Internet access approaches 100%, this probability ranges from about .2 to .6.

Executive constraints have statistically significant and positive effects on women's physical security. As reported in Table 7, on average, a standard deviation increase in executive constraints was associated with a .093 decrease in the probability of no physical security for women, but the same increase did not have a significant effect on other levels of women's physical security. Civil conflict has a statistically significant and negative effect. On average, a standard unit increase in civil conflict was associated with a .098 increase in the probability of having no physical security for women (see Table 7). Ratification of the CEDAW, international conflict, population, and religion did not have statistically significant effects on women's physical security once I controlled for the interaction of media freedom with Internet access.

In summary, while there is mixed support for H1, the hypothesis that media freedom will have a positive effect on women's rights, and H2, the hypothesis that Internet access will have a positive effect on women's rights, there is strong support for H3, the hypothesis that the effect of media freedom depends on Internet access. Media freedom had an independent, positive, and significant effect on women's political rights but only in the pre-Internet model. While Internet access had an independent, significant, and positive effect on women's economic rights, political rights, and physical security, this effect was not significant once I controlled for the interaction of media freedom and Internet access. For all three types of women's rights, media freedom had a positive effect as Internet access increased, and Internet access had a positive effect in free media environments. In the next section, I consider the implications of these findings.

Discussion

Overall, these findings indicate that the emergence of the Internet makes a difference in women's rights and that this difference is more pronounced when media freedom is present. Similarly, media freedom is associated with improved women's rights, but only as Internet access increases. Additionally, this interactive effect is more substantive for women's physical security and women's political rights than for women's economic rights. It is really not all that surprising that media freedom and Internet access would have less of an effect on women's economic rights, after all economic issues are generally more complicated and difficult to cover in news media and social media, whereas physical security (especially overt violence) and political issues are more common fodder for news stories and social media posts. Recent coverage of the violence against Dalit women is certainly a case in point.

Though repression of Dalit women has been going on for centuries, their struggle has made headlines in recent years, especially in India, a country with imperfectly free (meaning functionally free) media and an estimated 237.3 million Internet users (about 20% of the population). This coverage comes generally in the form of stories about particular atrocities, for example, the 2014 story of two teenage girls who were gang raped and then hanged from a mango tree in Uttar Pradesh (the same state where a village council is alleged to have ordered the rape of two sisters in 2015). Human rights organizations have sought to leverage this attention to bring about change for the Dalit women (Amnesty International 2015). In March of 2014, hundreds of Dalit women marched across India demanding justice. Throughout the month of marching, they posted updates on Facebook, Instagram, and

Twitter using #dalitwomenfight. In 2015, #dalitwomenfight launched a tour of campuses across North America to raise awareness and international support for their cause. News organizations around the world have covered this movement. Whether these latest efforts will be successful in bringing about change remains to be seen, but certainly #dalitwomanfight is an example of survivors and activists using social media and news media to draw attention to their cause and to pressure their government to improve women's physical security.

In regards to other factors influencing women's rights, it is interesting that the findings for executive constraints were mixed. They had positive effects on women's economic rights and women's physical security but did not have a significant effect on women's political rights. It could be that controlling for previous women's political rights masked any effect of executive constraints. CEDAW ratification was associated with higher levels of women's political rights, but it did not have a significant effect on women's economic rights or women's physical security. Perhaps the CEDAW's lack of an effect on women's physical security should not be surprising, since it does not include violence against women (Richards and Haglund 2015). Findings were also mixed for civil conflict and religion. As expected, civil conflict had significant and negative effects on women's economic rights and physical security but, surprisingly, did not appear to make a difference in women's political rights. International conflict did not have any significant effects. The percentage of Muslims in the population had negative and significant effects on women's economic and political rights but did not have a significant effect on women's physical security. This negative effect could be related to the increased prevalence of more fundamentalist versions of Islam. This effect is similar to that identified by Inglehart and Norris (2003), and it is also in line with the findings of Richards and Haglund (2015). The percentage of Christians in the population had a statistically significant and positive effect on women's political rights but was otherwise insignificant. The percentage of Hindu and no religion did not have significant effects. Finally, population did not have a significant effect on any type of women's rights. In general because these analyses covered a limited number of years in order to focus on the years since the Internet became widely available, it is possible that there simply is not enough data to capture the effects of some of the variables that appear to be insignificant here—in particular executive constraints, civil conflict, and international conflict. Other variables such as population simply may not have an effect on women's rights. Further research is needed as more data become available.

Conclusion

This study presents a first look at the effects of media on women's rights. The findings point to the potential for both media freedom and Internet access to make a difference, particularly in women's political rights and the physical security of women; however, it is the interaction of two that is associated with this positive effect. This makes sense intuitively. Just as media freedom makes it possible for news media to serve as a voice for the marginalized, the Internet makes it possible to spread the news and information about repression around the world. Similarly, Internet access makes it possible for activists at both the domestic and international levels to use social media to pressure local journalists to cover domestic repression, getting around the gate-keeping role of traditional media. Furthermore, activists and journalists alike can employ social media to mobilize international support for women's issues and to pressure governments to bring about reform. Thus, media freedom and Internet access could be the mechanisms necessary to bring about a boomerang effect (Keck and Sikink 1998).

Of course this is an optimistic view, and it is also true that social media campaigns tend to encourage passive participation; liking or retweeting a post on social media does not often lead to protest or reform. Yet consistent use of Facebook, Twitter, and old fashioned print and broadcast media may help to build awareness and potentially to shift cultural attitudes over time. Take, for example, the multimedia campaign to eradicate the practice of FGM/C in Burkina Faso, a nondemocracy that has had imperfectly free media since 1991. Initially the government-led campaign met with great resistance and public anger because, although the practice was widespread, discussion of it was taboo. Yet, over time the media campaign has made progress to the extent that the subject of FGM/C is no longer taboo (IRIN 2005). Additionally, though the practice of FGM/C remains common, according to a report by UNICEF (2013) less than 10% of women and girls now support the practice of FGM/C. In spite of this apparent change in the cultural acceptance of FGM/C in Burkina Faso, more than 75% of women and girls have been cut and their physical security remains quite poor. Yet Internet access in Burkina Faso remains quite low, with less than 5% of the population estimated to have access in 2014. As the Internet becomes more prevalent, perhaps women's rights will improve.

Finally, the significant and positive effect of Internet access on women's rights has important policy implications. Certainly it is far easier to increase Internet availability, especially through the introduction of smart phones, than it is to bring about changes in executive constraints and development. However, the evidence here indicates that this positive effect of the Internet depends on a free media environment. This would suggest that programs fostering media freedom might also benefit women's rights. Though previous research has found that, in the absence of democratic institutions, media freedom might have a negative effect on physical-integrity rights (Whitten-Woodring 2009), this study suggests that, when it comes to women's rights, it is the combination of media freedom and Internet access that matters. Perhaps it is because this combination fosters the communication and transmission of information necessary to instigate changes in cultural attitudes, which, in turn, could lead to improvements in women's rights.

Acknowledgments

I am grateful to Celin Carlo-Gonzalez for her excellent research assistance, and to John Cluverius, David Faris, Chris McKallagat, Ken Rogerson, the Gender and Violence Writing Group (Chris Allen, Jana Sladkova, and Rebecca Stone) and the associates at the University of Massachusetts Lowell Center for Women and Work for their thoughtful suggestions. This article was also substantially improved thanks to the helpful comments from the editors and two anonymous reviewers. Any mistakes are completely my own.

Notes

1. Whitten-Woodring (2009) theorized that media freedom would have different effects on physical-integrity rights in different regime types and tested this proposition with a multiple regression analysis using a pooled cross-sectional time series including 93 countries for the years 1980 to 1995.
2. A case in point is the failure of the mainstream news media in the United States to question the build up to the Iraq war (Bennett et al. 2007).
3. As Tsui (2010: viii) puts it, "The Internet presents a unique opportunity as well as a radical challenge: in a world where everybody can speak, who will listen?"
4. Pollock (2015a, 2015b) also finds evidence of a media-driven boomerang effect. In particular, foreign direct investment was associated with an increase of domestic media coverage emphasizing government responsibility to end human trafficking (Alexandre, Sha, Pollock, Baier & Johnston 2014, 2015).
5. Although CIRI originally included a variable for women's social rights, this variable was discontinued in 2005.
6. Data are also available for 2007 and 2014, but I have opted to go with the 2009 data because more countries are covered for 2009 than 2007 and because of the limited availability of other variables for 2014.
7. Richards and Haglund (2015) have recently developed a dataset on the strength of domestic laws prohibiting violence against women. Since the focus of this study is more on practice than on legal protections, I have opted to use the WomanStats data.
8. Because of limited availability of other data, we are only able to include 143 of these countries.
9. For more information about the Global Media Freedom Dataset and how it compares to other conceptualizations and measurements of media freedom, see "The Correlates of Media Freedom: An Introduction of the Global Media Freedom Dataset" (Whitten-Woodring and Van Belle 2015).
10. Table 2 provides the results from an ordered logistic regression. The standard interpretation of these coefficients is the expected change in the dependent variable (in the ordered log-odds scale) for a one-unit increase in the independent variable, while all of the other independent variables in the model are held constant. Generally, it is easier to interpret results from this type of analysis by focusing on predicted probabilities of the different levels of the dependent variable.
11. This is an average marginal effect computed using Stata and the SPost13 mchange command (Long and Freese 2014).
12. The Bayesian Information Criterion (BIC) is lower for Model 3, indicating that it is the preferred model. Note that the BIC is even lower for Model 1, but, because Model 1 uses a different set of cases, the BICs are not comparable.

References

ACHEN, Christopher H. (2000) *Why Lagged Dependent Variables Can Suppress the Explanatory Power of Other Independent Variables*. Paper presented at the Annual Meeting of the Political Methodology Society, Los Angeles, California.

ALEXANDRE, Kelly, SHA, Cynthia, POLLOCK, John C., BAIER, Kelsey, and JOHNSON, Jessica. (2014) Cross-national coverage of human trafficking: A community structure approach. *Atlantic Journal of Communication*, 22(3–4), 160–174.

ALEXANDRE, Kelly, SHA, Cynthia, POLLOCK, John C., BAIER, Kelsey, and JOHNSON, Jessica. (2015) Cross-national coverage of human trafficking: A community structure approach. In *Journalism and Human Rights: How Demographics Drive Media Coverage*, John C. Pollock (ed.) (London: Routledge).

AKER, Jenny C., and MBITI, Isaac M. (2010) Mobile phones and economic development in Africa. *Journal of Economic Perspectives*, 24(3), 207–232.

AMNESTY INTERNATIONAL. (2006) *Press Freedom: Journalists in Need of Protection*. [Online]. Available: http://www.amnesty.org/en/news-and-updates/feature-stories/press-freedom-journalists-in-need-of-protection-20060503 [31 October 2015].

MAKING HUMAN RIGHTS NEWS

AMNESTY INTERNATIONAL. (2015) *Ordered Rape of Dalit Sisters Highlights Severe Caste and Gender Discrimination in India.* [Online]. Available: http://blog.amnestyusa.org/asia/ordered-rape-of-dalit-sisters-highlights-severe-caste-and-gender-discrimination-in-india/ [31 October 2015].

ANNAN, Kofi. (2006) *Message of the Secretary-General International Women's Day 8 March 2006.* [Online]. Available: http://www.un.org/events/women/iwd/2006/message.html [31 October 2015].

APODACA, Clair. (2007) The whole world could be watching: Human rights and the media. *The Journal of Human Rights*, 6(2), 147–164.

BASU, Indrani. (2015, September 8) 9 things you need to know about the Khap "rape order" in India. *The Huffington Post* (in Association with the Times of India Group). [Online]. http://www.huffing tonpost.in/2015/09/08/dalit-girls-india_n_8095322.html [9 September 2015].

BENNETT, W. Lance, LAWRENCE, Regina G., and LIVINGSTON, Steven. (2007) *When the Press Fails: Political Power and the News Media from Iraq to Katrina* (Chicago: University of Chicago Press).

BUNCH, Charlotte. (1990) Women's rights as human rights: Toward a re-vision of human rights. *Human Rights Quarterly*, 12(4), 486–498.

CAMP KEITH, Linda. (1999) The United Nations International Covenant on Civil and Political Rights: Does it make a difference in human rights behavior? *Journal of Peace Research*, 36(1), 95–118.

CHOI, Seung-Whan, and JAMES, Patrick. (2006) Media openness, democracy and militarized interstate disputes: An empirical analysis. *British Journal of Political Science*, 37(1), 23–46.

CINGRANELLI, David L., RICHARDS, David L., and CLAY, K. Chad. (2014a) *The Cingranelli-Richards (CIRI) Human Rights Dataset*, Version 2014.04.14. [Online]. Available: http://www.humanrightsdata.com [31 October 2015].

CINGRANELLI, David L., RICHARDS, David L., and CLAY, K. Chad. (2014b) *Cingranelli-Richards (CIRI) Human Rights Data Project Coding Manual* (Manual Version 5.20.14).

COLEMAN, Isobel. (2004) The payoff from women's rights. *Foreign Affairs*, 83(3), 80–95.

DALIT WOMEN FIGHT. (2015) *#dalitwomenfight* (@dalitwomenfight) [Tweet]. [Online]. Available: https://twitter.com/dalitwomenfight/with_replies?lang=en&lang=en [31 October 2015].

ENGLEHART, Neil A. (2009) State capacity, state failure, and human rights. *Journal of Peace Research*, 46(2), 163–180.

ENGLEHART, Neil A., and MILLER, Milissa K. (2014) The CEDAW effect: International law's impact on women's rights. *The Journal of Human Rights*, 13(1), 22–47.

DAVENPORT, Christian, and ARMSTRONG, David A. (2004) Democracy and the violation of human rights: A statistical analysis from 1976 to 1996. *American Journal of Political Science*, 48(3), 538–554.

FEENSTRA, Robert C., INKLAAR, Robert, and TIMMER, Marcel P. (2015) The next generation of the Penn World Table. *American Economic Review*, 105(10), 3150–3182.

GLEDITSCH, Kristian S., and WARD, Michael D. (1997) Double take: A reexamination of democracy and autocracy in modern politics. *The Journal of Conflict Resolution*, 41(3), 361–383.

HAFNER-BURTON, Emilie M., and TSUTSUI, Kiyoteru. (2007) Justice lost! The failure of international human rights law to matter where needed most. *Journal of Peace Research*, 44(4), 407–425.

HATHAWAY, Oona. (2002) Do human rights treaties make a difference. *Yale Law Journal*, 111(8), 1935–2042.

HERTEL, Shareen. (2011) Standing on the shoulders of giants, looking up from the grassroots: An economic rights analysis of Rhoda E. Howard-Hassmann's article, "Universal Women's Rights Since 1970." *Journal of Human Rights*, 10(4), 450–457.

HILL, Daniel W., Jr. (2010) Estimating the effects of human rights treaties on state behavior. *The Journal of Politics*, 72(4), 1161–1174.

HOWARD-HASSMANN, Rhoda E. (2011) Universal women's rights since 1970: The centrality of autonomy and agency. *Journal of Human Rights*, 10(4), 433–449.

HUDSON, Valerie M., BALLIF-SPANVILLE, Bonnie, CAPRIOLI, Mary, and EMMET, Chad F. (2014) *Sex & World Peace* (New York: Columbia University Press).

INGLEHART, Ronald, and NORRIS, Pippa. (2003) *Rising Tide: Gender Equality and Cultural Change Around the World* (Cambridge: Cambridge University Press).

INGLEHART, Ronald, NORRIS, Pippa, and WELZEL, Christian. (2002) Gender equality and democracy. *Comparative Sociology*, 1(2–3), 321–345.

INTERNATIONAL TELECOMMUNICATION UNION (ITU) DATABASE. (2014) *ICT Indicators Database* [Online]. Available: https://www.itu.int/en/ITU-D/Statistics/Pages/stat/default.aspx [31 October 2015].

IRIN. (2005) *In-Depth: Razor's Edge—The Controversy of Female Genital Mutilation* (United Nations Office for the Coordination of Humanitarian Affairs).

KECK, Margaret E., and SIKKINK, Kathryn. (1998) *Activists Beyond Borders: Advocacy Networks in International Politics* (Ithaca, NY: Cornell University Press).

KOVACH, Bill, and ROSENSTIEL, Tom. (2001) *The Elements of Journalism: What Newspeople Should Know and the Public Should Expect* (New York: Random House).

LANDMAN, Todd. (2006) *Studying Human Rights* (London: Routledge).

LONG, J. Scott, and FREESE, Jeremy. (2014) *Regression Models for Categorical Dependent Variables Using Stata*, 3rd ed. (College Station, TX: Stata Press).

MANJOO, Rashida. (2013) A Message by UN Special Rapporteur on Violence against Women, Its Causes and Consequences. Rashida Manjoo Side-Event: Dalit Women: Working Together Towards the Elimination of Multiple and Intersecting Forms of Discrimination and Violence Based on Gender and Caste. [Online]. Available: http://idsn.org/wp-content/uploads/user_folder/pdf/New_files/UN/HRC/UNSRVAW_Message_for_Dalit_women_side_event_-_040613.pdf [31 October 2015].

MAOZ, Zeev, and HENDERSON, Errol A. (2013) The World Religion Dataset, 1945–2010: Logic estimates and trends. *International Interactions*, 39(3), 265–291.

MARSHALL, Monty G. (2013) Major Episodes of Political Violence (MEPV) and Conflict Regions, 1946–2012. Center for Systemic Peace. [Online]. Available: www.systemicpeace.org [31 October 2015].

MARSHALL, Monty G., GURR, Ted R., and JAGGERS, Keith. (2013) *Polity IV Project: Political Regime Characteristics and Transitions, 1800–2012*, Dataset Users' Manual (Center for Systematic Peace).

MARSHALL, Monty G., and JAGGERS, Keith. (2002) *Polity IV Project: Political Regime Characteristics and Transitions, 1800-2002 Dataset Users' Manual Integrated Network for Societal Conflict Research Program*. Center for International Development and Conflict Management, University of Maryland.

MARSHALL, Monty G., JAGGERS, Keith, and GURR, Ted R. (2013) *Polity IV Project* (Center for International Development and Conflict Management at the University of Maryland).

PEW RESEARCH CENTER. (2012) *Forum on Religion and Public Life*. [Online]. Available: www.pewforum.org/data [31 October 2015].

POE, Steven C., and TATE, C. Neal. (1994) Repression of human rights to personal integrity in the 1980s: A global analysis. *American Political Science Review*, 88(4), 853–872.

POE, Steven C., TATE, C. Neal, and KEITH, L. C. (1999) Repression of the human right to personal integrity revisited: A global cross-national study covering the years 1976–1993. *International Studies Quarterly*, 43(2), 291–313.

POLLOCK, John C. (2014) Illuminating human rights: How demographics drive media coverage. *Atlantic Journal of Communication*, 22(3–4), 141–159.

POLLOCK, John C. (2015a). Overview: Illuminating human rights: How demographics drive media coverage. In *Journalism and Human Rights: How Demographics Drive Media Coverage*, John C. Pollock (ed.) (London: Routledge).

POLLOCK, John C. (2015b). *Journalism and Human Rights: How Demographics Drive Media Coverage* (London: Routledge).

RAI, Sandeep. (2015, August 19) Khap orders Dalit women raped after brother elopes, SC seeks police reply. *Times of India*. [Online]. Available: http://timesofindia.indiatimes.com/city/meerut/Khap-orders-Dalit-women-raped-after-brother-elopes-SC-seeks-police-reply/articleshow/48547206.cms.

RICHARDS, David L., and HAGLUND, Jillienne. (2015) *Violence Against Women and the Law* (New York: Routledge).

TRIENDREGEOGON, A. (1982) Female circumcision in Upper Volta. In *Traditional Practices Affecting the Health of Women and Children*, Technical Publication No. 2, Vol. 2, T. Baasher, R. H.

Bannerman, H. Rushwan, and I. Sharaf (eds.) (Alexandria, Egypt: World Health Organization, Regional Office for the Eastern Mediterranean).

TSUI, Lokman. (2010) *A Journalism of Hospitality, Communication* (Philadelphia: University of Pennsylvania).

UNITED NATIONS. (2009) *The Convention on the Elimination of All Forms of Discrimination against Women.* [Online]. Available: http://www.un.org/womenwatch/daw/cedaw/cedaw.htm [31 October 2015].

UNITED NATIONS CHILDREN'S FUND (UNICEF). (2013) *Female Genital Mutilation/Cutting: A Statistical Overview and Exploration of the Dynamics of Change* (New York: UNICEF).

WHITTEN-WOODRING, Jenifer. (2009) Watchdog or lapdog?: Media freedom, regime type and government respect for human rights. *International Studies Quarterly*, 53, 595–625.

WHITTEN-WOODRING, Jenifer, and VAN BELLE, D. A. (2014) *Historical Guide to World Media Freedom: A Country-by-Country Analysis* (Los Angeles: CQ Press).

WHITTEN-WOODRING, Jenifer, and VAN BELLE, D. A. (2015) The correlates of media freedom: An introduction of the Global Media Freedom Dataset. *Political Science Research and Methods.* Advance online publication. http://dx.doi.org/10.1017/psrm.2015.68

WOMANSTATS PROJECT. (2015) *WomanStats Codebook.* [Online]. Available: http://www.woman stats.org/new/codebook.

WOMANSTATS PROJECT DATABASE. (2015) [Online]. Available: http://www.womanstats.org.

Beyond naming and shaming: New modalities of information politics in human rights

Joel R. Pruce and Alexandra Cosima Budabin

University of Dayton

ABSTRACT

How and why does information become currency in human rights advocacy? Human rights organizations (HROs) produce media content in an increasingly diverse manner today across multiple platforms, for divergent purposes, and for distinct audiences. Advocacy practices are no longer confined to fact-based reporting aimed at exposing abuse. The sheer magnitude of resources expended in communication evidences the early stages of a shift in which HROs widen their broadcast and target mass audiences. However, human rights scholarship has not adequately addressed this new trend, which has the capacity to radically alter the advocacy landscape. Moving beyond the traditionally narrow focus on "naming and shaming," we contend that a critical, detailed approach to understanding the strategic use of information will reveal a more complete image of how HROs build influence through their communications strategies. Expanding upon Keck and Sikkink's concept of "information politics," we develop a theoretical framework that distinguishes a set of practices we call *media advocacy*. Three unique modalities of media advocacy (juridical, revelatory, and activating) capture a robust portrait of information politics in twenty-first century human rights advocacy. Our innovative tools disclose specific operational and pragmatic implications for HROs, as well as help structure future research in this area.

Introduction

In 2012, Invisible Children launched KONY2012, a campaign designed to make Lord's Resistance Army commander Joseph Kony a household name. With this ambitious objective, the communication strategy centered on a 30-minute film and an action plan consciously executed to maximize mass dissemination and impact by targeting celebrities, politicians, and cultural figures. The film was produced for $140,698 and the campaign cost nearly $3.5 million ("Invisible Children - 2012 Annual Report" 2013: 37). This investment reaped hundreds of millions of YouTube views, nearly four million pledges of support delivered to the United Nations, and $100 million authorized in humanitarian aid for impacted countries and allegedly initiated a US military mission in Central Africa ("Invisible Children - 2012 Annual Report" 2013: 28–31). Finally, from the sale of merchandise, action kits, and outright donations,

MAKING HUMAN RIGHTS NEWS

KONY2012 netted over $12.5 million for Invisible Children—all from the production of a sleek video, clever marketing, and opportune resonance across social media. While financial gain and Internet sensation are potentially two measures of success, the actual impact of the campaign on the security of civilians in the affected regions remains suspect. This snapshot captures one extreme story within the contemporary landscape of human rights advocacy that is increasingly focused on fostering and wielding media clout as a means to an end, as well as an end in itself. The strategic logic that catapulted KONY2012 forecasts a sea change in the practice of human rights advocacy, in which traditional strategies are subverted for the promise of publicity and popularity.

Since the 1970s, human rights organizations (HROs) have been integral in elevating human rights as priorities within international society and, with the end of the Cold War, they experienced a considerable boost in prominence and expanded reach. But HRO communications tools were limited, relying on the discursive power of "naming and shaming" to build political influence through the combinations of public exposure campaigns and elite lobbying efforts. In the past two decades, the communications tools available to human rights organizations have expanded and have grown more sophisticated. Engaging diverse but selective audiences—from college students and journalists to elected officials and philanthropists—demands that organizations manipulate information to serve broader purposes. Beyond "naming and shaming," today's HROs provide critical fact-finding, hold direct consultations with power brokers, operate with daunting balance sheets, amass wide followings and command impressive media attention. Conversations with HRO staff reveal new priorities for mobilization and action. Meanwhile, advances in technology make it possible to cultivate fresh constituencies as the human rights community constructs and enlists an informed, activated, and empowered citizenry. As the number of HROs increases, a rich but competitive field opens where audiences become valuable commodities. Accessing, capturing, and mobilizing public attention requires a more nuanced approach to information politics, the contours of which are only now being explored. Why do HROs mobilize mass audiences and what can we learn about human rights by focusing on this new emphasis in media advocacy?

Even Amnesty International (AI)—the originator of naming and shaming—has outgrown its original formula. Diligent research produces influential reporting that exposes abuse and attributes blame, yet the full scope of AI media scaffolding raised around the research department supports its core work but also branches out in new directions: social media, photography, music, film, celebrities, contests, and merchandise. Each of these examples bears an ambiguous relationship to the human rights mission of advancing norms and holding perpetrators accountable, of which the naming and shaming method has always been the cornerstone. The puzzle remains: What function does mobilizing a wider public play in human rights advocacy? How does mass mobilization support or deviate from the core human rights agenda?

While commentary from observers and thinkpieces from pundits provide immediate reactions to changes in the human rights universe, scholars arrive fashionably late to the party. Until now, literature that studies human rights advocacy fails to parse the shifting ways that HROs use information by commonly lumping every strategy as some variation of "naming and shaming." We maintain that this traditional mode of information politics is only a sliver of the action. Advocacy targets are diverse. Media platforms are evolving. Audiences are fractured. For instance, states, corporations, diplomats, and high school students occupy distinct corners of the market for human rights and demand unique attention for HRO communications personnel. From the research side, if we intend to meaningfully assess the social practice of human rights (Pruce 2015a), scholars must furnish new tools that better study the work of today's HROs.

The task of this article is to document the expanded scope of HRO communication strategies and explore the logics informing what we call the *practice of media advocacy*. We aim to deepen our understanding of "information politics" by unpacking three modalities for communication strategies that identify the following features: social relations among actors, packaging of information for specific audiences and purposes, and assumptions that guide HRO decision-making in this area. To underscore the implications of this shift for the social practice of human rights, we pay special attention to the changing role of the victim or stakeholder, charting the changing nature of "witness" across these logics. We sketch out the architecture of the *practice of media advocacy*: how information is collected and deployed, against whom, by whom, on whose behalf, to what effect, at what cost. This continuum of activity marks a fundamental transformation in the way HROs operate and is linked to broad political, technological, and social trends in the landscape of advocacy. We critically assess this shift by demonstrating how recent uses of information have a weaker relationship to directly impacting political disputes or threats to human dignity. Overall, we show how communication strategies serve multiple purposes beyond achieving accountability from perpetrators.

This research makes significant contributions to our understanding of HROs. First, we revisit the concept of "information politics" and describe *how* information has come to be assembled and deployed by HROs in the past decade. Since Keck and Sikkink (1998), there has been little research that systematically explores the evolution of communications strategies in light of the shifting nature of human rights advocacy and the expansive and constitutive roles that information plays in HRO operations. Recent work from Alison Brysk (2013) is one notable exception and perhaps signals a new direction. Second, this article contributes to our understanding of the function of information in transnational advocacy by exploring *why* communications take the form they do. This includes explaining why HROs design campaigns that might have only an auxiliary relationship to their core objectives, for instance, using films, celebrity endorsement, or viral marketing. Third, we propose theoretical tools for drawing critical insights from this productive diversity in human rights advocacy and lay the path for future research.

Our investigation takes the following form. We anchor our analysis in the study of transnational human rights advocacy: identifying the centrality of information, problematizing the representative status of witness, and tracking the strategic use of media products. Following a survey of the literature, we propose a theoretical framework that distills the main variations in media advocacy based on a broad review of the field and our own observations from research, including interviews with HRO staff members and an analysis of campaign materials. The framework captures heterogeneity in media advocacy practices with three modes of information politics: juridical, revelatory, and activating. Across these modes, we propose hypotheses to prompt and guide future research in this area. We offer concluding thoughts on facilitating future research and the normative implications of the changing communications strategies of HROs.

Studying human rights advocacy

Fifteen years ago, scholars of International Relations (IR) began to focus attention on a set of human rights actors that had risen to prominence particularly in the years following the fall of the Soviet Union. As an outgrowth of the broader study of nonstate actors in global governance, nongovernmental organizations (NGOs) and the networks they comprise attracted attention due to their ascendance in world politics. By studying HROs as actors and advocacy as social practice, constructivist scholars of IR developed their analytical tools with respect to the role and power of norms. These scholars work to test, to validate, and to enrich the core principle of constructivism in IR: Ideas matter in global politics. The assumption was that human rights, formed on the basis of common values to accomplish shared goals, could confront material power and emerge victorious. Commonly cited campaigns promoting international norms include women's suffrage, antislavery, anti-apartheid, antilandmine, and the treatment of war wounded as neutrals (Klotz 1995; Price 1998; Cameron, Tomlin, and Lawson 1998). These campaigns offer empirical evidence of norm emergence and influence; HROs crafted communications strategies that promoted the wider acceptance of a norm among key constituencies and thus shaped policy and effected wider societal change. The framework developed below can be applied to any historical case study in order to determine the origins of contemporary practices.

Emerging from this stream of work, Keck and Sikkink distinguish the workings of transnational advocacy networks (TANs), which have the goal to "change the behavior of states and international organizations" (Keck and Sikkink 1998: 2). As originally conceived, the TAN "boomerang" is a set of linkages sparked by domestic organizations that "bypass their state and directly search out international allies to try to bring pressure on their states from outside" (Keck and Sikkink 1998: 12). These global allies might include international and domestic HRO research and advocacy organizations, local social movements, foundations, media, churches, regional and intergovernmental organizations, and sympathetic governments. In a campaign, the alliances between the domestic organization and international allies are, at a glance, mutually beneficial: "for less powerful third world actors, networks provide access, leverage, and information (and often money) they could not expect to have on their own; for northern groups, they make credible the assertion that they are struggling with, and not only for, their southern partners" (Keck and Sikkink 1998: 12–13). Information is a key form of exchange here: Northern advocates obtain first-rate intelligence while stakeholders in the South gain a platform for sharing their stories and building influence. But we argue that this information becomes more valuable currency as it is framed and packaged for different audiences and purposes.

Underwriting this early period of scholarship on advocacy was the implicit (and at times explicit) belief that network actors were forces for moral good in a world dominated by arbitrary state power (i.e., actors without "real" power banding together to overwhelm elites). Because David-versus-Goliath stories are compelling and generally rare, providing explanation of how these battles are fought and won is both intellectually interesting and instrumentally useful from an activist's standpoint. Over time, however, researchers built on this foundation and began to push in new directions to fill in gaps and add context—layers of texture that problematize the notion of NGOs as do-gooders. Clifford Bob has highlighted which victim groups gain attention (2002a) in the competitive global marketplace for moral movements (2002b). As well, Bob has enlarged the scope of inquiry by focusing on illiberal global advocacy movements, countering the traditional stress on "feel good," liberal HROs (2012). Charli Carpenter has identified the role played by "gatekeeper" network organizations in providing recognition to peripheral movements (2007) and, more recently, has turned her attention to explore why certain movements fail to gain traction (2014). Also, scholars have peered within organizations (Hopgood 2006) to investigate variables such as structure (Wong 2012) and national origin (Stroup 2012; Stroup and Murdie 2012) to provide instructive explanations for why the world of advocacy looks as it does. This body of work also begins to address the social dynamics across actors within networks (Murdie and Davis 2012), revealing power relationships and privileged roles.

Yet, there is a distinct thread in the literature that has begun to strip away the impetus of moral action and of the centrality of ideas altogether by reasserting the rationalist position. Aseem Prakash and Mary Kay Gugerty have pushed scholars to regard HRO activities as pragmatic and instrumental, as actors that adjust their strategies to gain influence on national and international bodies (Prakash and Gugerty 2010: 13). These authors apply the "theory of the firm" to decision-making and propose that HROs are just like corporations in that they exist to lower collective action costs and operate in an environment of resource scarcity. While certainly provocative, reducing the social practice of advocacy to its rationalist essentials seems, to us, to dilute what is interesting and unique about the role of HROs in global politics: groups of individuals organically constituted to collectively articulate a set of norms and work to see their deeply held values realized even and, especially, when antithetical to the material interests of powerful actors. This perspective on HROs as entities with interests configures the landscape of human rights advocacy as a field of contestation for scarce resources of attention, donations, and influence.

Throughout these diverse approaches, methods, and investigations, a consistent refrain sustains the argument that HROs engage in a politics of information as they collect evidence, identify culpable parties, frame their issues, target audiences and broadcast demands. Political and technological trends contextualize and incite shifts in HRO priorities, made visible through communications strategies. We aim to further explore the landscape of human rights advocacy and the contestation implied in such a "politics" by distinguishing communications strategies as modes and interrogating the logics underpinning the various uses of information. Secondarily, we explore the effect of this repurposing of information as currency on the nature of representation, interrogating how the status of the victim or stakeholder changes within these different modes.

Information politics

In their reading of human rights advocacy, Keck and Sikkink's full "typology of tactics" includes information politics, symbolic politics, leverage politics, and accountability politics (Keck and Sikkink 1998: 16–25). Collectively, each phrase relates directly to an HRO's use of information in some form or another: framing, agenda-setting, labeling, categorizing, exposing, researching, reporting, monitoring, explaining, or persuading. Each of these verbs identifies a range of ways in which advocacy groups utilize information and knowledge to their advantage. Whether symbolically, as a lever, or to hold accountable, the political deployment of information remains central to each type. We utilize "information politics" as a catch-all: Each of Keck and Sikkink's types—and those introduced here as well—revolve around information. In our usage, "information politics" subsumes the other categories (symbolic, leverage, accountability) because, in our view, they blur too often to merit distinction.

We aim to expand and deepen the category of "information politics" as an umbrella term that captures the ways in which HROs create, collect, manipulate and implement resources in campaigns and organizational operations. This is precisely the kind of issue that can be addressed when a scholar's gaze turns from the relationship between institutions, or between institutions and states, to examine the social bond forged between HROs and their audiences in the practice of media advocacy. We are especially interested in investigating how and why HROs represent stakeholders and frame human rights claims to facilitate mass mobilization campaigns and the grassroots diffusion of human rights norms through media. Thinking about information politics as a "social practice" in this sense opens new space for conceptualizing and understanding actors, strategies, and the real micro-level work that takes place in the world of human rights advocacy (Pruce 2015b).

Critically, the suffix "politics" conveys a sense of the contestation and power dynamics in the collection and deployment of information. Following Barnett and Duvall's breakdown of forms of power in global governance, advocacy groups flex "productive power" in their ability to shape and control the discursive realm (2005). But HROs are also operating on somewhat illusory grounds; as Wade suggests, advocacy HROs can "derive power from the perception that they supply accurate but suppressed or overlooked information. [...] Not only have such groups become powerful, but they have also, as a category, come to command more trust among the public in industrialized countries than governments, companies and the media" (Wade 2009: 26). We claim that the maintenance of this "perception" of accuracy and the building of this "trust" are hallmarks of HRO advocacy practices that aim to gain legitimation and credibility through their strategic use of information (Gourevitch et al. 2012).

Relevant for our work are the implications of the outsider–insider formation and its consequences for the basic act of representation: groups coming from elsewhere seeking to assist victims or oppressed groups in distant lands. To begin to tease out questions of power dynamics and perception, we must characterize how the nature of *representation* affects messaging and communication. By and large, a domestic group of victims and stakeholders plays a key role in contributing to a network's success by furnishing technical data and witness testimony to support a human rights claim. Representing the claims of one actor by another is a cornerstone of human rights advocacy but is fraught with controversy. We are primarily interested in the mediation of the victim group's claims on their behalf that occurs across distances; "the prefix 're' in the word 'representation' implies an absence, presenting anew that which is no longer present" (Spence and Navarro 2011: 14).

Essentially, the HRO records and researches the claim of a victim group and then "translates" these claims for an outside audience of political actors, allies, mass publics, or media. The transmission of these claims is customarily directed by the transnational HRO in light of external contexts without much input from the domestic group; "for if [NGOs] have their own ideas of what should be done and how it should be done, ordinary human beings who have experienced, say, injustice in their daily lives are denied the opportunity to frame their responses in their own terms" (Chandhoke 2002: 46). We contend that one of the major gaps in the existing literature—especially around TANs and HROs—is that it inadequately addresses the existing unequal relationships constituted and consolidated through networks. Research around NGO gatekeepers begins to approach such issues but does not do so from a perspective interested in representation as such. Here, in thinking about media advocacy, we propose a typology based on the social relationships underlying dynamics across these modes that are revealed under a close examination of HRO communication strategies.

A new generation of media advocacy

Recent decades have seen rapid technological advancements that have shifted the nature of human rights advocacy. Human rights research into the relationship between media and information politics has thus far attempted to describe how HROs choose their casework (Ron et al. 2005), how HROs shape media coverage (Ramos et al. 2007), and how effective they are (Hafner-Burton 2008). Examining press releases and country reports, scholars test hypotheses that correspond to commonly held expectations about advocacy, for instance, that media focuses on the "worst" crises. More recently, Hendrix and Wong focus our attention on the issues of targeting and audience as they inform the strategic choices HROs make (2014). By using quantitative methods and discourse analysis tools, this research is effective in penetrating certain myths about human rights advocacy but remains limited by its own framework (for a critique, see Rodio and Schmitz 2010). We seek to direct attention to the way that contemporary HROs attract media attention and pressure target actors using a mobilized public. This requires looking at the practices and strategies themselves, not only at their output and expression. Important for us is the ability to explore beneath the surface of institutions and their conduct and expose the psychic glue that gives HRO advocacy campaigns meaning.

How HROs negotiate the "telling of the story" to mobilize the public for the purposes of global campaigns and appeals is one area of inquiry. Keck and Sikkink allude that activists communicate with an audience by building associations of meaning with labels and categories. But, information and media are amorphous and contestable subjects that extend beyond stories we tell and filters we apply. While attention has been paid to the discursive processes of framing through speech and written communication (Benford and Snow 2000), we seek to direct attention to the representations of human rights claims through today's media advocacy that relies on photographs, videos, and visual culture broadly construed. From important work by Susan Sontag (1977, 2003), Jonathan Benthall (1993), Susan Moeller (1999), and Lilie Chouliaraki (2006), notions of distant suffering have impacted the literature by focusing on the role visual media plays in shaping the audience's consciousness of global crises, for better or for worse. More recently, Barbie Zelizer (1998, 2010), Sharon Sliwinski (2011), and Joel R. Pruce (2012) remind us how mediated public events relate to action and memory, as well as influence popular conceptions of human rights. The expansion of media platforms and technological tools has inevitably altered and increased the frames available for representing human rights claims.

To capture these seismic shifts in the use of information by human rights HROs, we need new tools. Counting newspaper mentions or analyzing word usage in HRO reporting no longer suffices as analytically meaningful in a fluid and ever-evolving media environment. In order to grasp the power, pressure, and perception of media advocacy, categories must dissect the social constitution of networks and organizations. HROs must be reassessed as entities with interests operating in a competitive field where information becomes currency for garnering attention, for establishing a reputation, and for building influence. Driving logics must be exposed and held up to scrutiny in order for scholars to determine impact and efficacy.

A framework for media advocacy

In an effort to transcend assumption and opinion, we propose the following framework for examining the practice of media advocacy. The framework introduces categories and distinguishes relationships, outlining the manner in which HROs relate to stakeholder groups, mass publics, media outlets, and states. Establishing guidelines with which to describe the use of information by advocacy organizations builds on existing research with analytically sophisticated devices and enables further work in this area around different aspects and actors in human rights work (see, for example, Budabin 2015).

We insist on the centrality of representation as a key variable because human rights advocates must prioritize the autonomy and dignity of the individuals for whom they purport to work. Failure to do so threatens to severely undercut the credibility of human rights organizations and to further perpetuate the historical legacy of paternalism and imperialism of which Western actors in particular are constantly accused. Focusing attention on how questions of representation factor into media advocacy also bears on the construction of solidarity in transnational human rights practice. The human rights community has begun to think more deeply about what it would mean to constitute a global movement of solidaristic engagement—rather than fleeting expressions of charity and one-off gestures. Communication plays a crucial role in projecting the values of advocates to all of their audiences and, we believe, has a direct role in the political impact of advocacy strategies.

That being said, stripping out representation from the framework produces a more broadly applicable taxonomy of information politics with implications for advocacy in sectors apart from human rights: consider environmentalism or the treatment of animals. The way in which information is uniquely packaged for multiple purposes and is driven by distinct strategic rationales remains constant irrespective of the advocate's issue area. Representation continues to matter for human rights but for advocacy around nonanthropocentric subjects it is not obvious that the relationship with the "stakeholder" (Mother Earth or dairy cows, for instance) is as important, although we admit there are important philosophical concepts to explore here. Norms that address environmental protection and animal welfare rely on the stewardship of advocates in a way that the defense of human dignity does not and should not. Despite the fact that the current framework was developed through observation of the practices of human rights organizations, we can extrapolate the consequences and applications of these categories and extend them across advocacy networks.

We make a deliberate choice to omit what may appear to be an unmistakably important aspect of the media programs of contemporary human rights organizations. In addition to the functions associated with executing specific advocacy initiatives, organizations also operate in a fierce environment in which they must contend with public image, persona, and brand. These issues create a presence for the organization within the culture and society in which it is situated—global and local, terrestrial and digital—but bear at best an ancillary relationship to the HRO's traditional mission. Film festivals, gala events, award shows, photo exhibits, and social-media accounts may serve an ancillary role to draw in fundraising dollars or to "raise awareness" of an issue. However, we believe, these pursuits seek to position

HROs in the media sphere in such a way as to magnify their "real" work. An HRO's reputation amplifies its research, demands, and calls for mobilization. Its brand projects an impression of the organization as cool, hip, current, youthful, edgy, serious, elite, cosmopolitan, or caring and these qualities in turn create associations with the audience. Outright publicity and marketing of the organization itself is not included in our taxonomy. This topic will be the subject of future research for the way in which it is ultimately inseparable from information politics but demands its own investigation.

Table 1 schematizes the currency of information constituted by human rights advocacy by examining representation, packaging, and strategic logics. The rows capture three modes or functions of information utilized in media advocacy campaigns. The typology below captures trends in the use of information and media by HROs and lays bare a robust illustration of the constitution of transnational human rights networks.

The examples of each mode stand in as model organizations that traffic in that particular modality more overtly than the others. Although these categories are not mutually exclusive, the examples listed in the final column are included for the way they each represent the mode. Some campaigns contain each mode. Most organizations participate in multiple modes.

We can imagine tactical considerations that suggest sequencing these modes: Perhaps juridical information establishes the foundation for those that come thereafter, while revelatory and activating information utilize distilled versions of the original in their own manifestations. There may be an additional temporal consideration with respect to the stage of the crisis in which we currently find ourselves. If the event has ended, the juridical mode assesses the damage and preserves the record. If circumstances are still fluid, then revelatory and activating modes may be more useful in applying pressure to intervene or for belligerents to cease hostilities. There may also be a distribution of use of information based on the sensational nature of violation; for instance, media advocacy around a mundane crime (like voter suppression or infringement of due process) may take a different form than more graphic abuse like torture or even more dramatic subject matter like sexual violence. Also, we would expect to observe younger organizations relying less on the juridical modality and skipping ahead to shaming and mobilization. On the other hand, a traditional organization like the International Committee of the Red Cross (ICRC) is more likely to remain steadfast in its commitment to juridical advocacy and to keep a safe distance from the spotlight. How an HRO deploys juridical, revelatory, and activating information sends signals about what audiences it intends to reach and what targets it hopes to influence. For instance, dry textual

Table 1. Modalities of information politics in human rights.

	Representation	Packaging	Logic	Examples
Juridical Mode	HRO documents violations on behalf of stakeholder group	Fact-finding; Collecting witness testimony	Information as legitimacy and objectivity	International Committee of the Red Cross
Revelatory Mode	HRO communicates the stakeholders' experiences to media and global public	Bearing witness; Naming and shaming	Information to expose and hold accountable	Médicins sans Frontières
Activating Mode	HRO mobilizes global public to learn and take action	Raising awareness; Storytelling	Information as moral force	Save Darfur Coalition

reporting may be effective for communicating with elected officials, while online videos with flashy editing and dance music are carefully engineered for high school students.

The next section lays out each mode and provides a brief sketch of an ideal-type HRO. The final section that follows wades into the future by considering hypotheses to inform next stages of this research program.

Juridical mode

Filling the chasm between the lofty rhetoric of human rights norms and facts is the modus operandi of human rights organizations. The foundation for waging "information politics" lies in the efforts of human rights HROs to act on behalf of the victim or distant other in need of protection. This representation begins with the documentation of human rights violations through the collection of evidence to assess the nature, scale, and verity of human rights claims. The 1970s and 1980s saw an explosion of onsite investigations by human rights organizations (Thoolen and Verstappen 1986). This practice arises simply from the roots of human rights as legal rights and the traditional role of legal defense to seek redress for criminal abuse. In order to prosecute a case in court, evidence must be solid and beyond reproach, and there must be a clear claim of culpability made against an alleged perpetrator. Because perpetrators will go to tremendous lengths to obscure their abuse, evidence gathering can be complex and require support from forensic scientists, for instance (Claude 2002). When human rights claims are underwritten by factual evidence, HROs (legal and political) can assert themselves as objective interveners.

The collection of information in the "juridical mode" maintains a legal tenor: HROs engage in the practice of "documenting," "fact-finding," "collecting evidence," and "reporting." In this scenario, the "objectivity" of information is nonbiased, neutral, and apolitical. Allegations are made not out of any pursuit of narrow self-interest but in the name of *universal* rights: those rights that reflect values that transcend particularities. For example, in the classic formulation of fact-finding, "In order to inspire corrective efforts by governments, human rights organizations must demonstrate that their factual statements are true and thus constitute a reliable basis for remedial governmental policy. Human rights organizations— as with any finder of fact—must pursue reliability through the use of generally accepted procedures and by establishing a reputation for fairness and impartiality" (Weissbrodt and McCarthy 1981: 5–6). Human rights organizations maintain integrity due to their "appropriate expectations of rigor" (Orentlicher 1990: 106) in research and evidence collection. Scrupulous methods provide defense against charges of impropriety and expose abusers accustomed to hiding in closed societies that lack transparency. Objective facts provide grounding for human rights norms and bring vague language into focus.

The packaging of information in the juridical mode sustains an aura of scientific research and legal practice. HROs that conduct their own investigations publish their findings as "reports," "memorandums," "briefs," and "fact sheets." From these origins in legal evidentiary procedures, organizations evolved to publish routinized country reports and meticulous research on complex crises in progress, from gender-based violence to counterinsurgency. Amnesty International's work particularly in Latin America during the 1970s is often highlighted as ground zero in this regard (see Guest 1990 regarding Amnesty's 1977 report on Argentina's "dirty war" for which it was awarded the Nobel Peace Prize). The professional documentation of violations begins a representation of victim groups that serves the strategic logic of maintaining credibility and integrity for human rights organizations.

The strategic logic of HRO representation of information in the juridical mode hinges on the manner of its collection *as well as* the manner of its use. The majority of HROs engaged in collecting information in the juridical mode move onto revealing their reports and mobilizing the larger public to gain greater influence. However, there remains one prime example focused on collecting and deploying information about human rights without publicly targeting perpetrators or raising mass awareness: the International Committee of the Red Cross (ICRC). Permitted into prisons and other detention centers, the ICRC delivers relief and conducts fact-finding missions. But the information collected is not broadcast; indeed, the ICRC has for over a century strived to maintain a high standard of neutrality and impartiality by refusing to broadcast its findings. The Red Cross is famous (and notorious) for its traits of "discretion and reluctance to publicly confront state wrong-doing" (Forsythe 2005: 14). Instead, the ICRC prefers the avenue of "quiet advocacy," meeting in private with government officials to press human rights claims. Staying in the juridical mode serves ICRC's status as an HRO whose use of information is acclaimed as strictly objective and neutral.

Revelatory mode

Central to the strategic logic of the revelatory mode is the principle that secrecy breeds impunity and exposing abuse is the enemy of its persistence. As Orentlicher explains, the so-called "human rights methodology" rests on this assumption that "human rights professionals believe that no action is more effective in promoting governments to curb human rights violations than aiming the spotlight of public scrutiny on the depredations themselves" (1990: 84). Summed up more simply as "promoting change by reporting facts," this strategy has been the hallmark of HROs (Orentlicher 1990: 84). Here, the HRO represents the interests of the stakeholders by publicizing information about human rights violations; the tactic commonly referred to as "naming and shaming." Perpetrators are held to account as the HROs expose the gap between human rights obligations and the actual policies of abusive regimes, between rhetoric and reality.

The revelatory mode flows directly from the information gathered in the juridical mode to shape a climate of intolerance. HROs "name" the human rights violations and the responsible actors, citing collected evidence and reports. But in this case, information is packaged to gain the maximum effect of "shaming." This includes the use of time-sensitive press releases, news alerts, and bulletins. Shorter than reports, information about human rights violations loses nuance, accentuating victims and perpetrators in a generalized manner.

Amnesty International pioneered "naming and shaming" as an overtly political methodology for manipulating information into actionable demands against perpetrators. By exposing abusers and publicizing their wrongdoings, the organization invites embarrassment on the regime. Amnesty members and supporters participate in letter-writing campaigns aimed at letting both violators and victims that the world is aware *and committed to seeing the problem resolved.* Médicins sans Frontières (MSF, or Doctors without Borders), however, distinguishes its own relationship to information politics manifested in the priority of "bearing witness." Health care professionals that operate with a coherent system of ethics are uniquely positioned to bear witness and attest to crimes due to their neutral stance and humanitarian outlook (Tanguy and Terry 1999). Witnessing is closely tied to humanitarianism and the

Red Cross tradition that predates MSF. Emerging as a foil to the Red Cross, MSF's doctrine of *"témoignage"* is a weaponized version of witnessing.

In this case, witnessing means to observe and speak out, thus, bearing direct connection to advocacy and driving humanitarianism in the direction of human rights. Bearing witness depends on the assumption that being present will act as a deterrent to abuse by virtue of the threat posed by publicity—and any consequences that would follow from that publicity (which is itself another assumption worth unpacking). In this case, MSF professionals translate the claims of the victims as an interlocutor. By utilizing an interlocutor to transport and transmit the information to the outside world, "bearing witness" has come to serve an important function. However, not all interlocutors carry the same reputation as MSF health professionals nor possess the classic background and expertise in development and human rights issues.

The practice of media advocacy in the revelatory mode takes shape when HROs aim to broadcast their information widely and with a normative tone. Audiences for these revealing stories of violence and brutality in detail include journalists, experts, and laypeople. Platforms for broadcasting the information about human rights violations might run from e-mail alerts to press conferences to publication of a country report. As intended audiences shift, so do expectations: The mass public is frequently asked to take action in response to an urgent notice of abuse. Or, at the very least, concerned citizens should share the news broadly, promoting a sphere of public knowledge that, theoretically, becomes an independent moral and political force.

The strategic logic behind the revelatory mode hinges on leveraging this publicity of human rights crimes to raise the costs of violation. With the external attention, actors appear center stage in the global court of public opinion. This "court" is a departure from the juridical mode of media advocacy because it operationalizes information in a distinctly social manner and places one's reputation on trial. The standing threat posed by human rights HROs, to uncover hidden tales of suffering, relies on an assumption that abusive actors fear exposure and therefore restrain their behavior or at least go to greater lengths to evade identification As AI's slogan declares, it is "better to light a candle than curse the darkness."

Activating mode

This final modality of media advocacy scales up representation of human rights claims to global audiences. The driving impetus in the activating mode is the necessity to not only *reach* large numbers of people but also to *mobilize* them to take action. An HRO must communicate its objectives to the public in a way that galvanizes their support and transforms their moral consciousness into tangible action. "Raising awareness" is a generalized charge to spread information of human rights issues to the masses. It is a trope as commonly heard among our idealistic students engaged in campus activism as it is on the tax forms of major human rights organizations as a task justifying six- and seven-figure expenses.

Politically, the field of advocacy has shifted to the perceived need for volume capitalization. We believe this approach is a generational response popularized by hindsight thinking following the Rwandan genocide of 1994. In the aftermath, the late US Senator Paul Simon provided a poignant quote subsequently published in Samantha Power's opus, *"A Problem from Hell": America in the Age of Genocide*: "If every member of the House and Senate had received one hundred letters from people back home saying we have to do something about

Rwanda, when the crisis was first developing, then I think the response would have been different" (2007: 377). The human rights community learned a central lesson from the failure in Rwanda and from Power's reporting in this influential book (Hamilton 2011; Budabin 2012). Political leaders could not hide behind the excuse that they did not know about the genocide; they could not blame information deficit. Instead they blamed lack of collective will, which is best motivated from below. In order to do so, we believe that HROs have pivoted toward raising awareness and mobilizing a mass public as a central objective in their work.

The audience for the activating mode is imagined as less knowledgeable, globally constructed, and with limited time resources. Rather than the literate audience of the revelatory mode, the public does not possess intimate knowledge of human rights norms, country context, and legal obligations. For this reason, activating media advocacy revolves around emotional pleas wrapped in clever catch phrases. Graphic imagery of suffering reels in the audience, while the campaigns demand very little in terms of action. These messages rely on base connections and weak ties. Narratives are constructed without history in order to retain the attention of the audience before their eyes gloss over with unfamiliar and complex details. The trouble is that human rights crises are inherently composed of unfamiliar and complex details.

Supporters are not activists in the traditional sense, but merely a list of names and e-mail addresses that the HRO can reference in order to validate its own relevance. Central to the activating mode is "you": the engaged activist attuned to global issues and hopeful about the future. In order to cultivate hordes of "you's," the rationale driving this strategy rests on the correlation between the consciousness of the public on an issue and the way in which this consciousness exerts moral force on decision makers to act.

Storytelling, as a variety of content produced through the practice of media advocacy, relies on "the transnational moral and empathetic discourse of solidarity that underlies the modern-day practice of mass-mobilized human rights activism" (Gregory 2006: 195). In order to capitalize on the potential for empathy and solidarity among the audience, HROs must craft a message of what is going on and why the public should care enough to act. In certain circumstances, the story can be succinct, especially in a discrete case of a political prisoner. However, the more complex the circumstances are, the more complicated it is to communicate a narrative to a lay audience, as in a civil war. HRO storytelling must paint a picture of the causes of the crisis, categorize the actors involved and propose a resolution that requires citizen engagement. Historical context and geopolitical implications certainly add a robust dimension to any story and a degree of legitimacy but are often avoided so as not to present a convoluted narrative.

As an example, when the specter of genocide was raised regarding conflict in Darfur, Sudan, in 2004, groups in the United States quickly coalesced into a social movement called the Save Darfur Coalition. At its formation, Save Darfur decided to pursue a strategy of mass mobilization to build pressure on US political actors, as well as the United Nations, influenced by Power's mantra and a related argument about political will: "[T]he battle to stop genocide has thus been repeatedly lost in the realm of domestic politics" (2002: xviii). Save Darfur amassed over a million members and initiated campaigns that called for an ambitious scale of mobilization. For example, "Million Voices for Darfur" delivered postcards to President George W. Bush in April 2006. Save Darfur also launched a number of million dollar advertising campaigns that spread its message through newspaper, television, billboards, lawn signs, and green wristbands.

Indeed, the ultimate impact of the tens of millions of dollars spent by the Save Darfur Coalition fostering a mass response to the Darfur conflict is open to debate (Just 2008).[1] In this case, mobilization on a wider scale also resulted in a simplification of the conflict (Mamdani 2010), relied on US activists and celebrities rather than witnesses and stakeholders (Budabin 2014) and pursued misguided policy asks (Lanz 2009). The experience of the Save Darfur Coalition signals the viability of an activating mode for raising money and driving awareness but presents obstacles toward accomplishing goals. Indeed, activating strategies risk elevating publicity as a substitute for political action.

Taken together, juridical, revelatory, and activating modes constitute a robust portrait of information politics in twenty-first-century human rights advocacy. They each deserve articulation and investigation in order for scholars to approximate having a working knowledge of the communication strategies of HROs.

Five hypotheses for studying media advocacy

We propose the following hypotheses that emerge from the framework to inform future research, and encourage readers to discover useful ways to apply the framework well beyond this list:

1. *Advances in information and communications technology shape the practice of media advocacy.*

In the early 1990s, Human Rights Watch press releases went out over fax machine, in black ink on white paper, and today Human Rights Watch is likely to publicize its reports over Instagram and Twitter. With the advent of mobile and social digital networks, information is increasingly packaged for visual consumption. As well, there is heightened sense of personalization of communication strategies, given the capabilities for data mining in information technologies. Are these penetrating media platforms useful? How has technological capacity changed media advocacy strategies? How do shifts in technology permit outreach with new and different audiences and demographics?

2. *Media advocacy is currently undergoing a period of transition that is best understood in historical context.*

Our inclination is that the example set by #KONY2012 may have a deep influence on the field and may signal a diminished reliance on traditional juridical information in favor of activating media content. But only a more precise conceptualization of human rights history can prepare us to understand current events. If the ICRC and AI carry the torch of a previous generation, how have their uses of media changed and to what effect? Furthermore, do younger organizations like Invisible Children signal a marked departure or are they old wine in new, viral bottles? Historicizing media advocacy demands making connections between primordial glimmers from the Cold War era, for instance, with practices we observe today.

3. *The commodification of the audience negatively affects the potential for human rights movement building.*

As HROs compete for viewers, readers, and supporters, the audience is transformed into a commodity. Commodification suggests placing a value on individuals for their ability to serve the interests of the organization. How does this impact sustainability of the human rights movement? Is there a trade-off between short-term support and attention and long-term solidarity? The desire to produce resonant and compelling media content may provide a spark for a campaign but fails to engage the audience on more profound issues of injustice and power. Furthermore, does the pursuit of an audience compel HROs to cut corners and dumb-down narratives—and if so, what is the political impact?

4. *Stakeholder groups (victims/survivors) are marginalized and exploited in the process of informational packaging and HRO translation of their voices for a global audience.*

Taking representation seriously requires scholars to expose the relationship between the pictures of refugees and the claims and policy asks that HROs make in their names. Transnational NGOs remain headquartered in the West and North, despite their best efforts to shift the center. As well, most HRO leadership does not look or sound like the populations they purport to represent. What happens when stakeholder groups become marginalized or even exploited for the sake of a campaign? What are the ethical constraints that govern representation of stakeholders by powerful, global organizations?

5. *"Raising awareness," for all the pomp surrounding this lofty goal, is a weak substitute for direct action and little more than an optical tactic to leverage in elite lobbying efforts.*

In the parlance of our times, raising awareness refers to the mass mobilization of private citizens for the purpose of bringing grassroots pressure against elected officials. As an outgrowth of Samantha Power's book, HROs presume that if the public can be made aware of a certain situation and feel outrage or grief for the suffering of others, then public policy can shift in favor of human rights protection. For this purpose, advocacy organizations have directed a significant degree of their resources toward raising awareness of human rights issues as broadly as possible so as to embolden themselves to represent the domestic victim/oppressed group. But does this strategy actually work in politics? Linked to issues of commodification, do large "aware" audiences merely provide the appearance of a mass movement, when one does not actually exist? If so, does this matter?

Pursuing these and other research questions demands specific empirical studies that utilize multidisciplinary methods of inquiry to explore images and video, as well as text and testimony. Our objective in building theory is to set the stage for future research that can deploy the framework and contribute critical case studies to deepen our understanding of the social practice of media advocacy for human rights.

Conclusion

Promoting human rights causes through media has become an increasingly visible part of the human rights landscape. We intend for this framework to create space for investigating crucial dimensions in advocacy studies that have thus far eluded inquiry. We believe this new direction in scholarship on human rights advocacy is appropriate because it penetrates beneath the institutional level and examines the ideational sphere in which important human rights work takes place. In this arena, ordinary laypeople come into contact with international human rights norms and cultural shifts in human rights consciousness can occur. The exploration above unpacks common assumptions both in the study and practice of human rights advocacy and points toward potential new avenues of research. Many presumed truths about the power of raising awareness, for instance, demand investigation. Furthermore, exploring the instantiation of these categories and modes in particular media platforms will be necessary.

KONY2012 may indeed be the future of human rights advocacy. The public resonance and social penetration of the campaign is beyond doubt, even if its political impact and sustainability are questionable. We have proposed a set of tools with which future research on the impact and efficacy of media advocacy can be undertaken. At the crux of the design sits a desire to understand the impacts of this social practice on prevailing notions of cosmopolitanism, distant suffering, and human dignity. At the very least, we strive to pose provocative questions and to stimulate some second-guessing among scholars and practitioners alike.

Note

1. It bears mentioning that Invisible Children's KONY2012 campaign received similar critiques in the aftermath of its own media blitz: Was the information presented accurate? Did the campaign have the support of Ugandans? Why were the "white saviors" the heroes of the video, instead of highlighting local efforts? Were the funds raised being effectively spent? Why focus on a military response? Both Save Darfur and KONY2012 demonstrate the potential penetration of human rights advocacy into the mainstream but also exhibit the pitfalls of mass mobilization. For discussion of these critiques and others, see Edmonson (2012), Gregory (2012), Herman (2014) Kagumire (2012), Mackey (2012), and de Waal (2012).

References

BARNETT, Michael, and DUVALL, Raymond. (2005) Power in global governance. In *Power in Global Governance*, Michael Barnett and Raymond Duvall (eds.) (Cambridge: Cambridge University Press).

BENFORD, Robert, and SNOW, David. (2000) Framing processes and social movements: An overview and assessment. *Annual Review of Sociology*, 26(1), 611–639.

BENTHALL, Jonathan. (1993) *Disasters, Relief and the Media* (London: I. B. Tauris).

BOB, Clifford. (2002a) Globalization and the social construction of human rights campaigns. In *Globalization and Human Rights*, Alison Brysk (ed.) (Berkeley, CA: University of California Press).

BOB, Clifford. (2002b) Merchants of morality. *Foreign Policy*, 129, 36–45. [Online]. Available: http://www.foreignpolicy.com/articles/2002/03/01/merchants_of_morality [23 March 2013].

BOB, Clifford. (2012) *The Global Right Wing and the Clash of World Politics* (Cambridge: Cambridge University Press).

BRYSK, Alison. (2013) *Speaking Rights to Power: Constructing Political Will* (New York: Oxford University Press).

BUDABIN, Alexandra C. (2012) Citizens' army for Darfur: The impact of a social movement on international conflict resolution. Unpublished manuscript, New School for Social Research.

BUDABIN, Alexandra C. (2015) Documentarian, witness, and organizer: Exploring celebrity roles in human rights media advocacy. In *The Social Practice of Human Rights*, Joel R. Pruce (ed.) (New York: Palgrave Macmillan).

CAMERON, Maxwell, TOMLIN, Brian, and LAWSON, Robert (eds.). (1998) *To Walk Without Fear: The Global Movement to Ban Landmines* (Oxford: Oxford University Press).

CARPENTER, Charli. (2007) Setting the advocacy agenda: Theorizing issue emergence and nonemergence in Transnational Advocacy Networks. *International Studies Quarterly*, 51(1), 99–120.

CARPENTER, Charli. (2014) *"Lost" Causes: Agenda-Setting and Agenda-Vetting in Global Issue Networks* (Ithaca, NY: Cornell University Press).

CHANDHOKE, Neera. (2002) The limits of global civil society. In *Global Civil Society 2002*, Marlies Glasius, Mary Kaldor, and Helmut Anheier (eds.) (Oxford: Oxford University Press).

CHOULIARAKI, Lilie. (2006) *The Spectatorship of Suffering* (London: Sage).

CLAUDE, Richard Pierre. (2002) *Science in the Service of Human Rights* (Philadelphia: University of Pennsylvania Press).

DE WAAL, Alex. (2012) Don't elevate Kony. *World Peace Foundation Reinventing Peace Blog*. [Online]. Available: http://sites.tufts.edu/reinventingpeace/2012/03/10/dont-elevate-kony/ [30 June 2015].

EDMONSON, Laura. (2012) Uganda is too sexy: Reflections on Kony 2012. *TDR/The Drama Review*, 56(3), 10–17.

FORSYTHE, David. (2005) *The Humanitarians: The International Committee of the Red Cross* (New York: Cambridge University Press).

GOUREVITCH, Peter, LAKE, David, and STEIN, Janice Gross. (2012) *The Credibility of Transnational NGOs: When Virtue Is Not Enough* (New York: Cambridge University Press).

GREGORY, Sam. (2006) Transnational storytelling: Human rights, WITNESS, and video advocacy. *American Anthropologist*, 108(1), 195–204.

GREGORY, Sam. (2012) Kony 2012 through a prism of video advocacy practices and trends. *Journal of Human Rights Practice*, 4(3), 463–468.

GUEST, Iain. (1990) *Behind the Disappearances: Argentina's Dirty War Against Human Rights and the United Nations* (Philadelphia: University of Pennsylvania Press).

HAFNER-BURTON, Emilie. (2008) Sticks and stones: Naming and shaming the human rights enforcement problem. *International Organization*, 62(4), 689–716.

HAMILTON, Rebecca. (2011) *Fighting for Darfur: Public Action and the Struggle to Stop Genocide* (New York: Palgrave Macmillan).

HENDRIX, Cullen, and WONG, Wendy. (2014) Knowing your audience: How the structure of international relations and organizational choices affect Amnesty International's advocacy. *The Review of International Organizations*, 9(1), 29–58.

HERMAN, Johanna. (2014) Hashtags and human rights: Activism in the age of twitter. *Carnegie Ethics Online*. [Online]. Available: http://www.carnegiecouncil.org/publications/ethics_online/0099 [15 December 2015].

HOPGOOD, Stephen. (2006) *Keepers of the Flame: Understanding Amnesty International* (Ithaca, NY: Cornell University Press).

INVISIBLE CHILDREN. (2013) 2012 Annual Report. [Online]. Available: http://files.invisiblechildren.com/annualreport2012/index.html [9 March 2016].

JUST, Richard. (2008) The truth will not set you free. *The New Republic*, 27, 36–47. [Online]. Available: http://www.newrepublic.com/article/the-truth-will-not-set-you-free-0# [12 August 2013].

KAGUMIRE, Rosebell. (2012) *Kony2012: My response to Invisible Children's campaign*. [Online]. Available: http://rosebellkagumire.com/2012/03/08/kony2012-my-response-to-invisible-childrens-campaign [15 December 2015].

KECK, Margaret, and SIKKINK, Kathryn. (1998) *Activists Beyond Borders: Advocacy Networks in International Politics* (Ithaca, NY: Cornell University Press).

KLOTZ, Audie. (1995) *Norms in International Relations: The Struggle against Apartheid* (Ithaca, NY: Cornell University Press).

LANZ, David. (2009) Save Darfur: A movement and its discontents. *African Affairs*, 108(433), 669–677.

MACKEY, Robert. (2012) African critics of Kony campaign see a "white man's burden" for the Facebook generation. *The New York Times News Blog*. [Online]. Available: http://thelede.blogs.nytimes.com/2012/03/09/african-critics-of-kony-campaign-hear-echoes-of-the-white-mans-burden [15 December 2015].

MAMDANI, Mahmood. (2010) *Saviors and Survivors: Darfur, Politics, and the War on Terror* (New York: Doubleday).

MOELLER, Susan. (1999) *Compassion Fatigue: How the Media Sell Disease, Famine, War and Death* (New York: Routledge).

MURDIE, Amanda, and DAVIS, David. (2012) Looking in the mirror: Comparing INGO networks across issue areas. *The Review of International Organizations*, 7(2), 177–202.

ORENTLICHER, Diane. (1990) Bearing witness: The art and science of human rights fact-finding. *Harvard Human Rights Journal*, 3, 83–135.

POWER, Samantha. (2002) *"A Problem From Hell": America and the Age of Genocide* (New York: Basic Books).

POWER, Samantha. (2007) *"A Problem from Hell": America and the Age of Genocide* (New York: Harper Perennial).

PRAKASH, Aseem, and GUGERTY, Mary Kay. (2010) Advocacy organizations and collective action: An introduction. *Advocacy Organizations and Collective Action*, Aseem Prakash and Mary Kay Gugerty (eds.) (Cambridge: Cambridge University Press).

PRICE, Richard. (1998) Reversing the gun sights: Transnational civil society targets land mines. *International Organization*, 52(3), 613–644.

PRUCE, Joel R. (2012) The spectacle of suffering and humanitarian intervention in Somalia. In *Media, Mobilization, and Human Rights: Mediating Suffering*, Tristan Borer (ed.) (London: Zed Books).

PRUCE, Joel R. (2015a) The practice turn in human rights research. In *The Social Practice of Human Rights*, Joel R. Pruce (ed.) (New York: Palgrave Macmillan).

PRUCE, Joel R. (2015b) *The Social Practice of Human Rights* (New York: Palgrave Macmillan).

RAMOS, Howard, RON, James, and THOMS, Oskar N.T. (2007) Shaping the Northern media's human rights coverage, 1986–2000. *Journal of Peace Research*, 44(4), 385–406.

RODIO, Emily, and SCHMITZ, Hans Peter. (2010) Beyond norms and interests: Understanding the evolution of transnational human rights activism. *International Journal of Human Rights*, 14(3), 442–459.

RON, James, RAMOS, Howard, and RODGERS, Kathleen. (2005) Transnational information politics: NGO human rights reporting, 1986–2000. *International Studies Quarterly*, 49, 557–587.

SLIWINSKI, Sharon. (2011) *Human Rights in Camera* (Chicago: University Of Chicago Press).

SONTAG, Susan. (1977) *On Photography* (New York: Farrar, Straus and Giroux).

SONTAG, Susan. (2003) *Regarding the Pain of Others* (New York: Farrar, Straus and Giroux).

SPENCE, Louise, and NAVARRO, Vinicius. (2011) *Crafting Truth* (New Brunswick, NJ: Rutgers University Press).

STROUP, Sarah. (2012) *Borders Among Activists: International NGOs in the United States, Britain, and France* (Ithaca, NY: Cornell University Press).

STROUP, Sarah, and MURDIE, Amanda. (2012) There's no place like home: Explaining international NGO advocacy. *The Review of International Organizations*, 7(4), 425–448.

TANGUY, Joelle, and TERRY, Fiona. (1999). Humanitarian responsibility and committed action: Response to "Principles, politics, and humanitarian action." *Ethics & International Affairs*, 13(1), 29–34.

THOOLEN, Hans, and VERSTAPPEN, Berth. (1986). *Human Rights Missions: A Study of the Fact-Finding Practice of Non-Governmental Organizations* (Boston: Martinus Nijhoff Publishers).

WADE, Robert. (2009) Accountability gone wrong: The World Bank, NGOs, and the US government in a fight over China. *New Political Economy*, 14(1), 25–48.

WEISSBRODT, David, and MCCARTHY, James. (1981) Fact-finding by international nongovernmental human rights organizations. *Virginia Journal of International Law*, 22(1), 1–89.

WONG, Wendy. (2012) *Internal Affairs: How the Structure of NGOs Transforms Human Rights* (Ithaca, NY: Cornell University Press).

ZELIZER, Barbie. (1998) *Remembering to Forget: Holocaust Memory through the Camera's Eye* (Chicago: University of Chicago Press).

ZELIZER, Barbie. (2010) *About to Die: How News Images Move the Public* (New York: Oxford University Press).

Index